11/09

book smart

Your Essential Reading List
for Becoming a Literary Genius
in 365 Days

jane mallison

McGraw Hill

New York Chicago San Francisco Lisbon London Madrid Mexico City
Milan New Delhi San Juan Seoul Singapore Sydney Toronto

Library of Congress Cataloging-in-Publication Data

Mallison, Jane.
      Book smart : your essential reading list for becoming a literary genius in 365 days / by Jane Mallison.
            p.   cm.
      ISBN 0-07-148271-7 (alk. paper)
      1. Best books.   2. Literature—History and criticism.   3. Books and reading.   I. Title.

  Z1035.A1M326   2007
  011'.73—dc22   2007011397

1 2 3 4 5 6 7 8 9 0   DOC/DOC   0 9 8 7

ISBN 978-0-07-148271-4
MHID   0-07-148271-7

McGraw-Hill books are available at special quantity discounts to use as premiums and sales promotions, or for use in corporate training programs. For more information, please write to the Director of Special Sales, Professional Publishing, McGraw-Hill, Two Penn Plaza, New York, NY 10121-2298. Or contact your local bookstore.

This book is printed on acid-free paper.

Contents

iii

AUGUST
Lighten Up:
Smiles at the Human Condition 169

SEPTEMBER
Back in the Day:
Some Great Eighteenth-Century Works 193

The Glittering Prizes:
Winners of Major Awards

Preface

There are worse crimes than burning books. One of them is not reading them.
—Joseph Brodsky

THE GREAT Italian poet Petrarch confessed in a letter to a relative that he had an insatiable desire (*una inexplebilis cupiditas*) for books. He expanded on his longing with the statement that "Books delight us profoundly, they speak to us, they give us good counsel, they enter into an intimate companionship with us."

Petrarch, of course, was writing in the mid-fourteenth century and had no access to printed books, much less to films, video games, reality television, or netsurfing. And yet his words resound strikingly today to all who find that reading and books continue to exercise an indefinable witchery. The news of the death of the book—or, indeed, the death of the author—is greatly exaggerated. Love of reading lives on in the hearts of many of us, all who are proud to brand ourselves as bibliophiles, benign bibliomaniacs, or even nonrecovering biblioholics. (I take this last term from Tom Raabe's delightful 1991 book *Biblioholism: The Literary Addiction.*) Eschew the term *bookworm* and replace it with the more exotic *Corrodentia*, a toothy order of insects that devours books.

Finding a Good Book

A secondary trait of committed readers is the pleasure we get in passing on the joy we have got from a book. (I like the phrase of Barbara Fister of the Alaska Library Association, who says that the practice of devouring what others have read or are reading makes reading "a contact sport.") I enjoy passing on titles of books to friends, and people often remain in my memories because they introduced me to a certain author. (Thanks, David Lipscomb, for Robertson Davies, and thanks, Tom Van Essen, for Kate Atkinson!)

Beyond recommendations, what are other ways of finding a good book? I have vivid memories of a chancy procedure. At sixteen, I often went to my public library in Kingsport, Tennessee, with my best friend, Margaret Gruver. There we took turns being led, eyes shut, to a shelf where we chose a book. I discovered Ayn Rand's *The Fountainhead* that way, but I also consumed a lot of junk. If you're over sixteen, don't try it. Thomas Wolfe, "the gargantuan writer with gargantuan appetites," in the fine phrase of Richard Marius, took on yet another system. He seriously aspired to read all the books in Harvard's Widener Library. (Take a look at the interesting *Widener: Biography of a Library* by Matthew Battles.) Life is just not long enough for this method of book selection, be it Dewey decimal or Library of Congress. Even Petrarch, whose personal library of several hundred books was large for its day, sorted out a select group that he labeled "*libri mei peculiares*"—his special friends, the ones he wanted to turn to most often.

Yes, we must all seek varying ways to trawl the ever-rolling sea of books to net those books that will bring us the most benefit or pleasure and spare us the "wilderment and despair" that Thomas Wolfe eventually experienced as he faced the shelves of serried volumes. Those suggestions from personal acquaintances are wonderful as are recommendations from librarians or book dealers: I have a friend who swears by a Canadian bookseller who, once he learned that John much admires the mysteries of Ian Rankin, was able to put him on to several other authors he enjoys.

Sometimes, though, we exhaust the immediate resources of friends, even those who, like Gertrude Stein, find reading "synonymous with living" and in-the-flesh professionals. Bestseller lists have both their uses and their limitations, and listings of the "top ten" of books of various sorts can, of course, be found online: I easily discovered categories as specialized as "banned books" or "submarine thrillers," but list fatigue sets in quickly when you peruse a mere catalogue of names.

This book is designed to offer you the names of some 120 "good reads" as well as quite a few extra suggestions slipped in here and there.

It also presents a vestige of a system to help you read more and read to greater effect. There is much to be said for serendipity, reading as fancy takes you, picking up whatever comes to hand. There is also considerable weight on the other side of the argument. Robert Burton, the great seventeenth-century author of *The Anatomy of Melancholy*, had this to say: "I have read many books but to little purpose, for want of good method; I have confusedly tumbled over divers authors in our libraries with small profit for want of art, order, memory, judgment." Burton is of course overly modest (great writers ultimately put everything to use), but a little system as you confront "divers authors" can help.

The Joys of Being Well-Read

As a well-read person, I certainly feel satisfaction when I recognize a literary allusion in a newspaper article or when I can identify an older author's influence on an emerging writer. And how satisfying it is to see myself as a part of the wondrous continuum of lovers of books through the centuries—Brother Petrarch, Sister Stein. Still, all these things seem as external as P. J. O'Rourke's charmingly cynical statement "Always read something that will make you look good if you die in the middle of it."

The condition of "being well-read" seems too static, a sealed-off definition. Passionate turners of pages can never feel "been there, done that." We need to know where our next book is coming from. Having read and continuing to read—we need them both.

The joys of reading—let me count the ways. One joy of reading: the stimulation of our own thinking. Ralph Waldo Emerson's utterance "Books are for nothing but to inspire" is pithy as is his assertion in a different essay that some books take rank in our lives with parents and lovers. Franz Kafka stuns us with his statement about our need for books that wake us up "with a blow on the head," books that strike "like an axe at the frozen sea within us."

A second joy, the vicarious gaining of experience, is voiced by Ernest Hemingway in his article for *Esquire* magazine entitled "An Old Newsman Writes: A Letter from Cuba." "All good books are alike in that they are truer than if they had really happened and after you are finished reading one you will feel that all that happened to you and afterwards it all belongs to you." How else can I hang out with bullfighters? Be a teenager on a raft going down the Mississippi? Marry the owner of Pemberley—or dream I went back to Manderley?

C. S. Lewis puts well a third joy in books: "We read to know that we are not alone." The right book is always out there whether we seek consolation, distraction, amusement, or verification of our thoughts and feelings in ways we ne'er so well expressed, such as Vivian Gornick's description of the claims of romantic love being "injected like dye into the nervous system of my emotions."

How to Use This Book

Book Smart is organized by the months of the year. Here's the basic plan for using it as your companion for a year of reading. January is an ideal starting point, but you can dive in at the month of your choice. Set yourself the goal of reading one book each month. You may have limited time to read on many days, but even a fifteen-minute stint can keep you involved with your book. (I also recommend interstitial reading—reading you can sneak in between the more substantive actions of the day, reading between the cracks.) Scan the write-up of each of the recommended books (they vary greatly in their scope and depth), and choose the one you find most appealing. At the end of a calendar year, your brain will be twelve books richer. If you can read more than one book per month, so much the better! The plan works for solitary readers, for two friends who make a plan to read together, or for a larger group such as a book club. (I long to believe there's one wild completist out there who will set out to use the book for ten years.)

Alternatively, for those who prefer always to color outside the lines, ignore the monthly setup and customize the write-ups of these 120 books to suit your fancy. A few possibilities follow.

▪ Launch yourself on a plan to select your twelve books alphabetically by author's last name (Chinua Achebe on the June list will be your starting point and A. B. Yehoshua from that same list your Ultima Thule; the midpoint falls between two very different books: Charlotte Lennox's *The Female Quixote* and David Levering Lewis's biography of W. E. B. Du Bois.)

- Choose chronology, starting with Homer's *Iliad* from the November list and ending with Claire Messud's 2006 novel from the October list.

- Try going from the alpha to the omega of estimated seriousness or challenge (start, say, with James Thurber from the August list and aim toward Thomas Mann—just one possibility—on the March list).

- Take the horizontal approach of picking your favorite category and reading 100 percent of the books in that grouping; you'll be able to read 20 percent of a second category as well in the span of a year.

- Start with Virginia Woolf's classic nonfiction book *A Room of One's Own* (in the April listing) and take on eleven other female writers in various categories.

- Follow in the steps of Ralph Waldo Emerson and write "Whim" on your lintel-post by choosing your favorite means of chance. You could cast the I Ching or devise your variant on the *sortes virgilianae*. Just as people used to open, randomly, Virgil's *Aeneid* (see January), touch one line, and interpret it in light of their lives, so you might flip this book open anywhere and slap your finger on the write-up of a book you'll then read that month. (Since all books described here are guaranteed to be books worth reading, you won't experience a quagmire of so-so books, as I did back there in the Kingsport library.)

The Book Smart 120

Other than being worthy objects of your attention, what else characterizes these books? Two ground rules: (1) The Bible and Shakespeare are "givens," so they don't appear, and (2) with one exception, no writer is represented by more than one book. (Homer, the rule-proving exception, appears twice, but he may have been two different people, if he existed at all.) The great majority are novels, books that bring to mind Robert Coles's fine phrase "the call of stories." These novels range from the cradle of the genre, seventeenth-century Spain (*Don Quixote* on the January list) and eighteenth-century England (four books on the September list) on up to 2006. There are four plays, scattered among four lists. Many of the January classical choices are poetry, and Milton (May), Juvenal (August), and Whitman (December) join them. Ninety percent of February is biography (Julian Barnes's book being a novel about biography), and other nonfiction books appear sporadically, like pop-ups (Thoreau in March, Woolf in April, Capote in May, Sedaris in August, Boswell and Thrale in September, Edmund Wilson in November, and Lewis Thomas, lone scientist, in December).

The problem of dinosaur dimensions: (1) the interesting categories of organization that were unconceived or unused (an all-Venice grouping lies on the floor) and (2) the excellent authors that are unrepresented. I identify with the operatic Don Giovanni, who notes that being faithful to one woman entails being unfaithful to all the rest. When I survey my own list, I shout phrases like "No Philip Roth?!" and I hear you, reader, saying, "I can't believe _____ isn't here!" (Supply your favorite outrage of omission.) See the introduction to the April list to explain the missing Jane Austen and George Eliot, and know that many splendid authors are omitted not for want of worth but for lack of room.

But I must conclude. I've just been given a copy of Liam Callanan's fresh-from-the-press novel *All Saints*. (The author's a man, the narrator's a woman—a phenomenon I haven't experienced since Norman Rush's *Mating*.) Can't wait to start it.

It's out there waiting for me, and for you—the old magic of books.

Acknowledgments

ALL THAT remains is the pleasant job of thanks. Grace Freedson and Karen Young are professional book women *extraordinaires*. Andrea Pasinetti, a young man once my student, now my friend, opened my eyes to an author new to me and contributed to the entry on that author, José Rizal. He also provided the epigraph for the introduction. Tom Sullivan, my teaching colleague, suggested good ideas for the June listing and supplied its title. I am blessed with more bookishly delightful friends than I can list, but I'm pleased to indite here a sextet of "reading women" in six different states of the union, with whom I've talked about books for more than twenty years: Katherine Sproles Barr, Mary Bevilacqua, Marilyn Bonner, Barbara Morrison, Marilyn Wulliger, and Louise Zak. I owe most to Kenneth Silverman, book smart, street-smart man. More learned than most, he still knows how to look up in perfect silence at the stars.

Because They Are There:
Towering Works to Read in Translation

Beowulf
  Anonymous (translated by Seamus Heaney)

Don Quixote
  Miguel de Cervantes (translated by Edith Grossman)

The Canterbury Tales
  Geoffrey Chaucer (translated by Nevill Coghill)

Inferno
  Dante Alighieri (translated by Robert and Jean Hollander)

The Odyssey
  Homer (translated by Robert Fitzgerald)

The Metamorphosis
  Franz Kafka (translated by Stanley Corngold)

The Tale of Genji
  Murasaki Shikibu (translated by Royall Tyler)

Tales from Ovid (Metamorphoses)
  Ovid (translated by Ted Hughes)

Oedipus Rex
  Sophocles (translated by Dudley Fitts and Robert Fitzgerald)

The Aeneid
  Virgil (translated by Robert Fagles)

> *"Classic"—a book people praise and don't read.*
> —Mark Twain

IT'S JANUARY, month of fresh starts, and a good time to tackle one of those major classics you've always meant to read. This list of works in translation offers you a choice of four books from the classical era (two Greek and two Roman), two works from England (one originally in Anglo-Saxon, the other in Middle English), two from Romance languages (one originally Italian, one Spanish), one from Germany, and one from Japan.

The oldest of these is Homer's epic poem the *Odyssey*, probably composed in the eighth or seventh century BCE, but in Fitzgerald's twentieth-century translation, a story of adventure, trickery, and romance focused on a hero much seasoned in the ways of the world. A couple of centuries later Sophocles brought forth his play *Oedipus Rex*, a kind of detective story involving both tragedy and bravery. The works originally in Latin, Virgil's *Aeneid* and selections from Ovid's *Metamorphoses*, offer a contrast of an epic poem about a man who sacrifices personal happiness so that Rome may come into being with an array of tales about bodies changed into new forms.

The works that came to birth in earlier stages of English appear here in more modern garb. The warrior Beowulf remains as fierce as he was in eleventh-century script, and Chaucer's fourteenth-century travelers to Canterbury retain their timeless verve.

The remaining four selections are vastly different from each other. You can decide whether you're in the mood for the thoughts of an eleventh-century Japanese woman (Lady Mura-saki's *The Tale of Genji*), a fourteenth-century trip through an idiosyncratic version of hell (Dante's *Inferno*), a seventeenth-century romp through the Spanish countryside (Cervantes' *Don Quixote*), or the disturbingly bizarre adventures of the early twentieth-century German character Gregor Samsa, who wakes to find himself transformed into a giant bug (in Kafka's *The Metamorphosis*) .

If Borges is right and heaven is a vast library, perhaps the elect among us will someday be able to read these works in their original languages—without, of course, first memorizing any pesky irregular verbs. Until that day, these translations serve well all those trapped in the Anglophone chamber. Meanwhile, my resolution for the next new year is to start once again (and this time finish) another book that could appear on this list: Marcel Proust's *Swann's Way*, as translated by Lydia Davis.

Beowulf

Anonymous (translated by Seamus Heaney)

O f all the literary works described in this book, *Beowulf*, a poem originally written in Anglo-Saxon, is the third oldest and probably the shortest. Both the original and the Heaney translation clock in at 3,182 lines of poetry. They are wonderful lines, and Heaney's translation, full of what he calls Hibernicisms (words used in Ireland), is especially compelling, as is his preface. Do not, however, be deceived into believing the brevity of the poem makes it an "easy read."

Why is it challenging? The predominant factor is that the poem describes a world for which we have no immediate cultural references. As Heaney points out, first-time readers of the *Odyssey* or the *Iliad* have, at a minimum, heard of Odysseus (possibly by his Roman name Ulysses), of Helen of Troy, or of Achilles and thus are able to get their bearings. But Scyld Scefing? Queen Modthryth? They're not going to be on "Jeopardy"!

Part of the delight of *Beowulf* is this air of strangeness, the feel of entering a pleasingly alien world. (Heaney's translation diminishes the oddness a bit by transforming Scyld Scefing, for example, into Shield Sheafson, who sounds like someone who might have bunked, briefly, with Heath Ledger.) Much about the background of the poem is mysterious, starting with the fact only a single copy of the manuscript survived into modern times and that the author's name is unknown to us. He (and it was doubtless a he) lived, scholars believe, around the end of the first millennium (the tenth century), and it's a pleasing phenomenon that Heaney's translation was undertaken around the end of the second millennium. The author was a Christian, writing about a pre-Christian world; an Englishman, writing about his forebears at a time going back to the mid-seventh century when they were still in southern Sweden and in Denmark.

The basic plotline of the poem, however, is familiar enough to be made into a comic book. Beowulf, a great warrior, must confront three threats to the civilized world: the monster Grendel (in his preface, Heaney charmingly describes Grendel as "a kind of dog-breath in the dark"), the grieving mother of Grendel (sometimes called by the archaic term "Grendel's dam"), and, in his old age, a *wyrm*, Anglo-Saxon for dragon. He defeats them all, but the dragon does not go gently, and the "molten venom" he spews at Beowulf consumes his waning strength. The poem ends with the heroic funeral of Beowulf, a king said to be the "kindest to his people and keenest to win fame."

The world of the poem contains, of course, much more than this action-movie-like synopsis. Descriptions of Anglo-Saxon jewelry, the courtliness of King Hrothgar and Queen Wealhtheow at Heorot, the digressive "saga of Finn" (a poem within a poem sung by the court scop) the sailing over the "swan's road" between Sweden and Denmark, a sword that begins to "wilt into gory icicles/slather and thaw"—details like these and wording like Heaney's are as pleasing as is the vicarious zapping of "that swamp-thing from hell."

Book Smart
Recommended Reading

If you like modern prose borrowings from great literary works, take a look at Michael Crichton's *Eaters of the Dead*, and if you incorrigibly cheer for the underdog, pick up a copy of John Gardner's *Grendel*. When your wanderings are through, you'll come back to Heaney's *Beowulf*.

Don Quixote

Miguel de Cervantes (translated by Edith Grossman)

Although the great Samuel Johnson named it as one of three books he wished were longer, it used to be a truism that everyone read *Don Quixote*, but no one read it twice. Today, alas, many people, familiar with the ubiquitous reproductions of Picasso's version of the tall Don Quixote and his short amigo Sancho Panza and over-dosed with multiple renditions of "To Dream the Impossible Dream," feel they've experienced the book without opening its pages. This book, sometimes called the first modern novel, demands to be read. It is more than four hundred years old; this excellent translation is not yet five. The translator notes that she preserves the archaic spelling of *Quixote* (the modern is *Quijote*) because she wants the English derivative *quixotic* to be apparent. You're always aware it's a seventeenth-century work, but the English is crisply, but never distractingly, modern.

There are many ways to describe this long, two-part novel. Carlos Fuentes says that as a subtitle "The Praise of Folly" would be apt; Terry Castle suggests "Silly Walks." A book that can simultaneously inspire allusions to Erasmus and Monty Python inspires respect, and indeed it recently took first place as "the best work of fiction in the world" in a poll of modern writers conducted by the Nobel Prize Institute.

Okay, we've got these ur-buddies, the poetic beanpole knight on his nag Rocinante and his prosaic squat sidekick on his nameless donkey. What now? It's a literary setup, a joke about genre. The aging don, crazed by excessive reading of books about chivalry, begins to see himself as a hero of epic dimensions and feels compelled to take lance in hand and set out to right the world's wrongs. All will be done for the honor of the fair Dulcinea, a pleasant peasant girl who in the don's addled pate is a rarefied princess. What follows is wry treatment of their on-the-road adventures. Don Quixote, with Sancho's help, frees galley slaves, thwarts a farmer's evil designs, and, in the most famous incident, tilts at windmills perceived to be flailing giants. But all is not success, for, among other misadventures, the duo get run down by a pack of "stout and discourteous" pigs, and Don Quixote's face is bloodily pummeled by a goatherd in this "encyclopedia of cruelty," as Vladimir Nabokov called it.

Along with the adventures and the jokes is a continuing fest of literary techniques: in these 126 chapters romances are parodied, interpolated tales are told, comedy jousts with tragedy (and narrowly wins), poetry and madrigals interlard the prose, and farce nestles snugly beside philosophical wisdom. References to the *Aeneid* and to the Bible abound, including, slyly, "Post tenebras spero lucem" (after the darkness I hope for the light), the motto of the printer of the original edition. Discussions of etymology and theories of translation make appearances, with the latter giving us the stunning comparison of translation to the reverse side of a tapestry. Indeed, Cervantes feigns that this work is a translation—from a manuscript by an Arab nobleman, a Muslim named Cide Hamete Benengeli. (Such a reference poignantly evokes the legal expulsion of the Moors from Spain in the years between the publication of Part I in 1605 and Part II in 1615.)

Cervantes, a man with no formal education, fought against the Turks in the battle of Lepanto, was captured by Barbary pirates, served as a slave in Algiers, and did time in debtors' prison. He died on April 23, 1616, the same day as one of his few literary equals—William Shakespeare.

The Canterbury Tales

Geoffrey Chaucer (translated by Nevill Coghill)

"Here is God's plenty," said seventeenth-century John Dryden of his fourteenth-century fellow poet. This long poem is written in English, but English of a six hundred-year-old vintage. Your school days may have given you a brush with the opening, "Whan that Aprille with his shoures soote / The droughte of Marche hath perced to the rote . . . ." If you have patience and linguistic leanings, you may want to take on the original Middle English (you'll be rewarded with fascinating details about changes in the language), but most folks nowadays go for the Modern English, and Coghill's readable version retains Chaucer's format of (mostly) rhyming couplets.

The fictional premise: twenty-nine men and women join a character named "Geoffrey Chaucer" at the Tabard Inn in Southwark, just across the Thames River from London (today a part of London, Southwark was, just some two hundred years after Chaucer, the site of Shakespeare's Globe Theatre). The coming of April has made travel not only possible but pleasurable, and the pilgrims are undertaking a trip to the shrine of "the holy blissful martyr" Thomas à Becket, some sixty miles northeast at Canterbury Cathedral. Fourteenth-century travelers faced a horseback trip of some three days' duration, and these pilgrims decide to lighten the journey by the telling of tales. Chaucer completed stories for twenty-three of them.

First, though, Chaucer, consummate artist with words, gives us thumbnail sketches of each sojourner. Ecclesiastical characters such as a monk, a friar, a parson, a prioress, and three nuns, a summoner to the ecclesiastical courts, and a pardoner (it is hinted that he and the summoner are "a couple") jostle against such secular sorts as a knight and his son, a businessman, a sailor, an excellent cloth maker (she's the only non-nun female on the trip), a lawyer, a doctor, and a plowman. In short, rather like a modern-day jury pool, we have a cross section of the era. Chaucer's sketches vary in tone from straightforward to sly, and the combination weaves a panorama as expressively varied as the visual effect of the Bayeux Tapestry, that remarkable embroidered account of the 1066 Norman invasion of England, the event that ultimately engendered Chaucer's (and our) language with its flexible amalgam of Germanic Anglo-Saxon (think *sheep, cow,* and *chicken*) and French (think *mutton, beef,* and *poultry*).

As for the generous potpourri of tales, read them straight through as Chaucer arranged them, or pick and choose as your fancy dictates. If you're in a meditative mode, you can go straight to the Parson's prose sermon on the Seven Deadly Sins, but you're more likely, first, to take a taste of the Knight's tale of the rivalry of Palamon and Arcite for the love of Emily, or the Nun's Priest's unexpectedly hilarious animal fable, where Chanticleer, a Cato-quoting rooster, possessed of "azure toes with nails of lily white" gets advice from Pertelote, the most comely of his harem of hens, about curing bad dreams by taking a laxative. Hollywood has yet to plunder the saucy Reeve's Tale, where the deep dark of unelectrified night produces a lot of bed-swapping, accidental and otherwise, or the scabrous Miller's Tale, which features flatulence and a few seconds of accidental oral sex. (Decency forbids me to mention the role of a red-hot farm implement.) One wonders how the nuns in the group reacted. My favorite is the story and the self-revelatory prologue of the Wife of Bath. Along with other evergreen insights on gender relations, this woman who "knew the oldest dances of love" anticipates Freud's famous question of "What do women want?"—and answers it.

Inferno

Dante Alighieri (translated by Robert and Jean Hollander)

man is lost in the dark woods, surrounded by threatening
beasts. Prompted by love, a beautiful woman sends a wizard
to guide him on an intriguing but arduous journey. He'll meet
up with people he used to know as well as plenty of strangers. He'll
see some scary sights but eventually gain some wisdom. Whatever else
this fourteenth-century Italian poem may be, it is a fascinating *story*.
So carry to your reading of Dante the advice Samuel Johnson gave to
new readers of Shakespeare: as you approach the great writer, ignore all
critical materials and plunge right in. Ignore for now those names you
don't know, those allusions you don't get, and let the delight of novelty
bear you along. Once you become a confirmed *Dantista*, you can start
filling in the gaps in your knowledge, a liberal education in itself.

Inferno is the first of three parts of a work Dante called the *Com-
media*, a work that has a happy ending. A later scholar, perhaps seeking to prevent misreading of this serious work, supplied the qualifying
adjective always used today—*Divine*. Dante's vision of a hellish afterlife
is, of course, rooted in Catholic theology, but readers of other faiths
(and those of no religious belief) will find the poem compelling on a
psychological as well as an aesthetic basis. Dante's imaginative inven-
tion is the *contrapasso*, a sense of poetic justice, a punishment that fits
the crime. For example, thieves, those who do not distinguish between
"yours" and "mine," perpetually lose their own human shapes, con-
tinually "stealing" the form of a reptile only to morph back again.

Like any poem, it's better in its native tongue—though the Holland-
ers do an outstanding job of translation. T. S. Eliot is said to have taught
himself Italian through immersion in the bilingual Temple Classics

edition. The opening is famous in its Italian—"Nel mezzo del cammin di nostra vita/Mi ritrovai per una selva oscura/Che la via diritta era smarrita"—and in English—"In the middle of our life's way, I found myself in a dark wood, for the straight way was lost." The fiction of the poem is that it is not fiction, as Hollander says elsewhere, and the main character is Dante himself, purporting to tell us of a real trip he took through hell. He knows readers can learn from his experience, so he'll force himself to recount it. The author Dante, who had earlier written only in Latin, wanted everyone, even women, to be able to comprehend this poem, so he startled his readership by writing in the vernacular, Italian.

Dante's design for his hell is famous and often parodied: nine concentric circles, tapering as the sins become more execrable. We go from the "good neighborhood" of hell where live virtuous people with the plain bad luck of not knowing about Christ to the circle of sexual sin. Watch out for Ulysses farther down, and then get your handkerchiefs ready for the penultimate canto. There one sinner perpetually gnaws the brain of another and tells his history: "If you do not weep at that, at what are you accustomed to weep?" Dante queries.

Dante and his guide Virgil crawl over the shaggy, three-headed body of Satan himself, frozen in ice at the bottom of hell, and emerge from this blind world, happy once again to see the stars. The first part, *Inferno*, has ended, but you may want to "re-up," as Dante and Virgil continue on a second journey up the Mountain of Purgatory, and then, in the third part, as Dante is guided by the beautiful Beatrice into the heart of Paradise itself.

The Odyssey

Homer (translated by Robert Fitzgerald)

For more than 2,500 years people have thought this a great story. First listeners knew that fact, and later readers learned it as well.

Before Homer—if there was a Homer—assembled this version of the tale, the cycle of stories was already known. Indeed, the singer of this tale early on instructs the Muse to take up the story at whatever place she pleases. You can do the same. The opening line announces that this poem will be the story of a man who is *polytropos*—literally, "many-turning." The word can be translated as all the following: clever, resourceful, versatile, shrewd, ingenious, never at a loss. Perhaps the best modern English equivalent is "James Bond–like."

Like a modern-day rock star, Odysseus delays his appearance until Book 5, letting his just-grown son Telemachus "open for him." If you want in your initial reading to skip or postpone Books 1 through 4, the so-called Telemachy, where the son, helped by the goddess Athena, travels around interviewing people who might have news of the where-abouts of his missing father, go straight to Book 5 and meet Mr. Polytropos himself. For years now Odysseus has been kept on the island of the immortal and beautiful Calypso, who's deeply in love with him. Not a bad life, you say, but as his years there add up to seven, he itches to get back to his island kingdom of Ithaca. He's been away for a total of twenty years: the ten years fighting in the Trojan War, three years on the seas, and now the septet of Calypso years. Whatever the attractions of life with Calypso—the not small perk of immortality is one of her offers—he now longs for home and for Penelope, the wife he left behind.

With mortal and immortal help, Odysseus arrives at the Disneyland-esque island of Phaeacia. His account of his wanderings to the royal court there fills Books 7 through 12, with the wonderful tales of such people and places as the Cyclops, Circe, the Sirens, Scylla and Charybdis, the island of the god of the winds, and the underworld. Most of the remaining books of this twenty-four-book epic tell of Odysseus's homecoming—his disguise as a beggar, his reunion with his son, his defeat of the gluttonous suitors for Penelope's hand who have squatted in his great hall, and finally, gloriously, his reunion with Penelope.

Homer's handling of the psychology of Penelope, the way in which she wilily tests this wiliest of men, is magnificent. (Indeed, the poet's keenness of observation of Penelope and also of the young princess Nausicaa back on Phaeacia has prompted some to speculate that the author of this poem might have been a woman.) No matter what sex its author, Book 23 is a paean to the married love of true minds, to the love of a man and a woman no longer young. It justifies the words about marriage that the naked Odysseus offers to the nubile princess Nausicaa for her future: "And may the gods accomplish your desire: a home, a husband, and harmonious converse with him—the best thing in the world being a strong house held in serenity where man and wife agree."

Book Smart
Recommended Reading

Reading the *Odyssey* prepares you for much else in Western literature. Start with Constantine Cavafy's beautiful poem "Ithaka" and move on to Canto 26 of Dante's *Inferno* for a look at the Greek adventurer as a false counselor imprisoned in a tongue of fire. Take a look at Caribbean poet Derek Walcott's *Omeros*, and by all means read Margaret Atwood's recent short book *The Penelopiad*. All that done, plan the day when you'll take on a twentieth-century Odysseus in Dublin—James Joyce's *Ulysses*.

The Metamorphosis

Franz Kafka (translated by Stanley Corngold)

The first sentence comes as a clash of cymbals: "When Gregor Samsa woke up one morning from unsettling dreams, he found himself changed in his bed into a monstrous vermin." No preface, no buildup, no explanation—just wham, this startling and bare declaration. How different from Ovid's *Metamorphoses*, where the transformation comes at the end! Now some readers are thinking, "I thought he turned into a cockroach." The original German phrase for Gregor's transformation is *ungeheuren Ungeziefer*. Even the Teutonically challenged sense the harsh power of that repeated initial "unguh, unguh"; it's fascinating to learn further, from an essay by this translator, that the second word derives from an old word for "the unclean animal not suitable for sacrifice." Cockroach, vermin, dung beetle—whatever it was, it was bad, a creature repellent to man and to God. (Kafka was Jewish, but the Samsa family seems to be Christian.)

An expected reaction to such an awakening might be sheer horror, a Munch-like scream. Gregor, however, worries that he may not be able to get to work on time. Once an army lieutenant who commanded respect, he now is a traveling salesman, the sole support of his parents, who owe money to his employer, and his younger sister; and although the story was written in 1912 (Kafka was twenty-nine, with only eleven more years to live), Gregor's concerns feel startlingly contemporary: he daydreams about telling off his sadistic boss, worries about calling in sick, frets about his health insurance.

Things proceed badly. His mother can't look at him, his father shoves him back into his room, the maid resigns. At first his sixteen-year-old sister is compassionate, bringing him foods his new coleopteran body might enjoy, but she comes to resent and denounce him. His father throws apples at him, one imbedding itself in his back and festering. Only the cleaning woman regards him with something like affectionate equanimity: "Come over here for a minute, you old dung beetle." It is she who eventually finds his desiccated body and tosses it out.

The family undergoes its own transformation: the senescent father, again a wage-earner, holds himself newly erect; the mother looks forward to the new apartment they'll take; and the sister blossoms into adulthood. It's spring, and the sun is warm.

Kafka, whom Vladimir Nabokov terms "the greatest German writer of our time," instructed his friend Max Brod to burn all of his works after his death. All readers thank Brod for ignoring such a charge. This novella, about forty pages in a standard edition, has generated reams of criticism. Pick your favorite brand—Marxist, Freudian, New Criticism, Feminist—it's got all these and more. Or, better still, form your own untutored response to this unforgettable tale (I know what *I* think it means) that Elias Canetti has called "one of the few great, perfect poetic works of this century." When Kafka read it to a circle of friends in his native Prague, we're told that they—and he—laughed.

 Book Smart
Recommended Reading

Kafka's short stories, particularly the harrowing "In the Penal Colony," are wonderful, as are his novels *The Trial* and *The Castle*. If you want another tale of a strange human metamorphosis, seek out Philip Roth's *The Breast*, where the main character becomes, yes, a giant mammary gland.

The Tale of Genji

Murasaki Shikibu (translated by Royall Tyler)

In 1010, a half-century before William the Conqueror invaded England, an author far away from any knowledge of that event was nearing completion of a novel now regarded as a landmark of world literature. It was long, almost twice as thick—in modern terms—as *War and Peace* would be. It soon became wildly popular. The country? Japan. The author? Remarkably, a woman—now sometimes called "Lady Murasaki," more fully Murasaki Shikibu. Like her female characters, however, she had no real name of her own: "Shikibu" refers to one of the titles held by her father, and "Murasaki," literally a flower used for purple dye, was the name of her chief female character that transferred itself to her even during her lifetime. Some nine hundred years later when Arthur Waley produced the first volume of his translation, Anglophones swelled the crowd of readers, and Murasaki made the pages of *Vogue* in a review of qualified admiration by Virginia Woolf.

The prospect of reading *The Tale of Genji* can daunt. Its length alone makes it a work for people with time or with the patience for a protracted read or with both. (Give yourself provisional license to close your reading with Genji's death; the last third may be by Murasaki's daughter.) The world it depicts is half a globe and more than a millennium away. It's worth the effort, however. This 2001 version gives you clear modern English and provides a helpful introduction, delightful drawings, a detailed chronology, references for the nearly eight hundred poems, a glossary that tells, for example, of the prescribed position for the elbows of court ritualists, and a separate guide to the myriad costumes.

The linear thread of Genji's life forms the boldest pattern in this variegated tale, but the shuttlings of the many women in the narrative add attractive slubs. The opening words—"In a certain reign (whose can it have been?)"—herald the telling of a tale of the past, about a century earlier than the author's life. The child that will become known as Genji is born to the emperor, though not by his consort. The boy is astonishingly beautiful in appearance and, as the years go by, in personality. But, sometimes egotistical or sulky, he's no Mr. Darcy, and though the novel frequently evokes Buddhist principles of striving for absence of desire, his world teems with rivalry and plotting. Women are no exception, for as "borrowed wombs," they are deeply involved in the advancement of their offspring.

Genji's mother dies when he is three. Genji will spend much of his life seeking his patrimony and her image. Although he makes multiple marriages that befit his high rank (including a disastrous match with the daughter of his half-brother), it's Murasaki, an orphaned young girl resembling his mother, who most obsesses him (in this culture romantic love is not deemed an ideal). When a typhoon permits Genji's son by another woman a forbidden glimpse of Murasaki, he instantly links her with a "lovely mountain cherry tree in perfect bloom." (In this world it was taboo for a woman of status to be seen by men outside her family, but thrilling examples of *kaimami*—accidental or clandestine viewing—do occur.) When Murasaki becomes ill, she piously arranges for the making of a thousand copies of the important *Lotus Sutra* and dies, causing Genji to retire from the world.

In this era, educated Japanese men did their serious writing in the prestigious Chinese language; Japanese was considered private, for women. This woman took her disdained domestic tongue, built a lasting masterpiece, and gave herself a name.

Tales from Ovid (Metamorphoses)

(Translated by Ted Hughes)

This book is a step away from a literal translation of some of Ovid's *Metamorphoses*, but if so, it's only a baby step. Ted Hughes has taken twenty-four of Ovid's more than two hundred shape-shiftings and transformed them into powerful free verse poems. At least once Hughes retains Ovid's flowing transition from one metamorphosis to the next, but for the most part the poems are freestanding.

Ovid's collection of hexameter poems was written in the period from 2 to 8 CE during the reign of Augustus. Since Ovid's wife was a cousin of Livia, the wife of Augustus, he may, in the words of Ovid translator David R. Slavitt, have been "on the B list for palace parties." At any rate he was close enough to this man of power to offend him (possibly through his knowledge of the antics of Augustus's prominently promiscuous granddaughter Julia) and get himself exiled to Tomis (in modern-day Romania), where he pined for nine years and died. Augustus also banned Ovid's books from Rome's public libraries. As with banned books today, this act made Ovid even more popular, and private copies of his newly polished *Metamorphoses* were greatly prized. In the medieval period Ovid was heavily allegorized and moralized, and Shakespeare, along with other uses, pinched the story of Pyramus and Thisbe, whose feuding parents build a wall between their neighboring houses, for the plot of *Romeo and Juliet*. A few years later he turned that sad story about lovers whose spouting blood transforms the berries on the mulberry tree from white to purple into a hilarious play-in-a-play in *A Midsummer Night's Dream*.

In his brief but piercing introduction Hughes notes that Ovid dealt with "catastrophic extremes of passion that border on the grotesque," passion that might "mutate" or "combust." Some of his chosen tales have the power to shock even today, such as the story of Myrrha, whose erotic passion for her father Cinyras consumes her. After her despairing frustration (and equally despairing guilt) drives her to attempt suicide, her sympathetic old nurse collaborates to allow her to overcome the frustration (but not the guilt). Nights were very dark back then, and the nurse connives a "bed trick" that allows Myrrha, during her mother's nine-day absence for a religious festival, eight nights of bliss in the marriage bed of her parents. On the last night the father puts a lamp to the head of his new bedmate and, consumed by *his* guilt, takes out after her, sword in hand. Myrrha, pregnant with her half-brother/son, flees, begging the gods for an existence between life and death. They oblige by turning her into a tree, forever oozing "warm drops from her rind." And that, children, is how myrrh came into the world.

The sequel is the enthralling tale of the birth of Myrrha's child, Adonis. Helped by the celestial midwife Lucina, the baby splits the bark of his mother, possibly the only child ever to be born of a bush. (A boar gouge to the groin will undo the adult Adonis, but only after a passionate affair with Venus, who sees to it that he posthumously becomes a flower.)

Book Smart
Recommended Reading

After this fine introduction to Ovid, you may want to look at the full *Metamorphoses*, possibly in the 2003 translation by Charles Martin. Then go to *After Ovid: New Metamorphoses*, edited by Michael Hofmann and James Lasdun, for delightful spins on the original by poets such as Seamus Heaney and Charles Simic. And immerse yourself in a fictional version of Ovid's world just before his exile in Jane Alison's wonderful novel *The Love-Artist*.

Oedipus Rex

Sophocles (translated by Dudley Fitts and Robert Fitzgerald)

In 1834 poet and critic Samuel Taylor Coleridge described this play as one of three works of literature with perfect plots; in 1900 Freud plucked out the name Oedipus for his theory of a son's unconscious sexual longing for his mother; in 1974 lyrics to a song in the film *That's Entertainment* jauntily croon of "Oedipus Rex, where a chap kills his father and starts a lot of bother." These allusions to a Greek tragedy of circa 425 BCE suggest the wildly varying ways in which *Oedipus Rex* continues to inform Western culture.

Everyone knows the plot: a man unwittingly kills his father and marries his mother. He "came to his father's bed wet with his father's blood," in Sophocles' terrible line. Yes, the plot is perfect. A beneficent king becomes quickly transformed into the most despised of creatures, a man aware that he has violated the stringent taboos of patricide and incest, becoming an exile from a land he ruled. Modern courts might find this man not guilty, for neither the paternal murder nor the incestuous mating was intentional. The verdicts of the world of myth are harsher, yet even modern citizens might helplessly shrink from the four children "sown in the womb of her who bore him."

If Oedipus's crimes were part of a modern thriller, they would be filed under "cold case," for the play takes place some fifteen years later. King Oedipus is a metaphorical detective whose persistence of inquiry and skill at questioning result in the discovery of the criminal—himself. (Agatha Christie adopts this plot in her sly *Who Killed Roger Ackroyd?*) The viewer of Sophocles' play hears lines smoking with dramatic irony and watches spellbound as witnesses are called, details are unveiled, and two and two inexorably start adding up to four. The language of the play reinforces this sense of figuring out, adding up, calculating, for Sophocles' contemporaries gloried in man's intelligence and noted that "man is the measure of all things." Like a good Athenian responding to a threat, the dishonored Oedipus takes action, punishing himself vigorously—and gorily. He stabs out his eyes, the blinding instrument at hand the brooch that had fastened the robe of Jocasta. He has found her body hanging from a "cruel cord."

But this play offers more than brilliant plotting. Centuries could be spent—*have* been spent—attempting to dissect the character of Oedipus and the accompanying meaning of the play. One interpretation: a man who becomes too aware of his own excellence deserves a reminder that the gods are in control. A spectrum away, an equally valid reading: events in life are random, and cruel coincidences can occur, but attempts to find meaning are futile. Like all great works of art, this play yields up no absolute secret but presents itself, prismlike, mirrorlike, to the questing viewer.

 Book Smart
Recommended Reading

Move on to Sophocles' sequel, *Oedipus at Colonus*, a tragedy with something close to a happy ending, and consider a look at Aristotle's *Poetics*. Written a generation later, it uses *Oedipus Rex* as the quintessential example of a tragedy. Or cut straight to an unlikely successor, Thomas Pynchon's *The Crying of Lot 49*, featuring Mrs. Oedipa Maas. Follow up your reading with the visually striking Pasolini film *Edipo Re* (Italian with English subtitles). All this continuing attention to *Oedipus Rex*? Not bad for a play whose debut performance at the Festival of Dionysus took second prize.

The Aeneid

Virgil (translated by Robert Fagles)

This Latin poem about events leading to the founding of Rome is more than two thousand years old, but Fagles's translation of 2006 gives us the best of the old world and the new. His notes and the superb introduction by Bernard Knox offer guidance without drowning us in scholarship.

Virgil designed the first six of his twelve books to pay homage to Homer's *Odyssey* and the latter six an equivalent tribute to the *Iliad*. The *Aeneid's* opening phrase, "Wars and a man I sing" sums up, in reverse order, that plan. If you know either of those Homeric works, you'll detect an extra layer of meaning in many scenes, but don't get the idea that Virgil is "copying" Homer.

If the age and fame of this work are intimidating, make your first plan the reading of the very accessible Books I, II, and IV. The poem begins excitingly, even frighteningly, with the epic hero Aeneas in an unheroic position: he's in danger of drowning in a storm and is equally at sea figuratively thinking longingly of an honorable death in battle. Aeneas has fled his homeland following the Greek triumph in the Trojan War. A vision in a dream has given him a vague mission to found a new nation, but right now, with his ship breaking up and his men drowning, a high sense of destiny seems remote. This flailing leader reaches shore in Carthage where Dido, founder of the city and a strong female ruler, offers him refuge. Your mini epic now offers you two enthralling plots: (1) a detailed flashback to the Greeks' victory over the Trojans, thanks to their successful stratagem of the Trojan horse, a ploy that makes the gullible Trojans complicit in the sacking of their city and (2) Aeneas's conflict between his sense of duty and a passionate love affair with Queen Dido, who believes they have been mystically married. A reminding push from the gods and Aeneas—man or chess piece?—sets sail again. The heartbroken Dido mounts her own funeral pyre to choose—like the real-life Cleopatra who also became erotically involved with a Roman—an active death by suicide, stabbing herself with Aeneas's sword before immolation. Dido's character remains immortal in Hector Berlioz's opera *Les Troyens*.

If you're ready for more, venture to stage two and read three more books: Book VI, the famous descent into the underworld; the very different Book VII, where Aeneas finds himself in Italy, facing not only battle with indigenous people but an emotional struggle with the hyper-emotional Amata, his future mother-in-law; and the fascinating Book VIII, which tours the spot that will become Rome. To become a full Virgilian, fill in with the remaining books at your leisure.

All readers must look ahead to the end of the poem where Aeneas kills Turnus, the leading native Italian warrior who is also his rival for the hand of Lavinia. Aeneas has consistently chosen duty over passion, but in the final lines of the poem he succumbs to irrationality, killing a man who has surrendered.

You're now qualified to join the debate over this ambiguous ending: Was Virgil, who knew Augustus well and received patronage from the emperor's friend Maecenas, subtly undermining the war culture of the nascent Empire? Or does a work of art offer to a new era meanings unintended by the author? Whatever Virgil's motives, his acknowledgment of the loss and pain in the world is undeniable, as illustrated by the Virgilian phrase *lacrimae rerum* (there are tears in the nature of things).

Footprints on the Sands of Time:
Some Notable Biographies

Flaubert's Parrot
Julian Barnes

The Path to Power (The Years of Lyndon Johnson, vol. 1)
Robert Caro

Narrative of the Life of Frederick Douglass, an American Slave, Written by Himself
Frederick Douglass

Autobiography
Benjamin Franklin

Last Train to Memphis: The Rise of Elvis Presley
Peter Guralnick

W. E. B. Du Bois: Biography of a Race, 1868–1919
David Levering Lewis

The Peabody Sisters
Megan Marshall

The Five of Hearts: An Intimate Portrait of Henry Adams and His Friends, 1880–1918
Patricia O'Toole

The Life and Times of Cotton Mather
Kenneth Silverman

Eminent Victorians
Lytton Strachey

Books swept me away, one after the other; this way and that; I made endless vows according to their lights, for I believed them.

—Annie Dillard

FEBRUARY, WITH its Presidents' Day celebration of the birthdays of George Washington and Abraham Lincoln and its status as Black History month, is a natural time to think about past lives and about books that preserve the records of those lives for posterity. The godfather of modern biography is James Boswell, who is listed with his eighteenth-century peers in our offerings for September. His biography of Samuel Johnson was published in 1791, just two years before the English publication of the oldest book on this February list, Benjamin Franklin's *Autobiography*. The other autobiography offered here is *Narrative of the Life of Frederick Douglass*, published in 1845. Each of these is the compelling story of the rise of a self-made man—but with one major difference. Franklin, a white man, could employ his intelligence and his work ethic very early in life, whereas Douglass could make no use of his enormous personal assets until he escaped from slavery.

Benjamin Franklin was much influenced by Cotton Mather and, as a young man, sought out a meeting with this older New England minister and polymath. Kenneth Silverman's superb biography *The Life and Times of Cotton Mather*, which won both the Pulitzer Prize for Biography and the Bancroft Prize, removes Mather from the veils of stereotyping and reveals him as a complex and fascinating human being.

Three of the books here are the start of excellent multivolume biographies of fascinating men, each of whom left an indelible mark on the twentieth century: W. E. B. Du Bois, Lyndon Baines Johnson, and Elvis Aron Presley. David Levering Lewis, the Du Bois biographer, gives us a highly readable analysis of the African-American man who lived a remarkable life for ninety-five years (1868–1963). The subtitle of this first volume, *Biography of a Race*, makes clear the fact that the life of Du Bois both reflected and helped shape attitudes toward his race. Robert Caro, currently writing the fourth and final volume of his magisterial work on LBJ, gets us off to an excellent start in this first volume, *The Path to Power*. Presley—"The King"—reigned in a very different world from that of Du Bois or LBJ, but Guralnick's biography is no less serious, no less well written. *Last Train to Memphis* is Volume 1 (of two), the equivalent of the "skinny Elvis" postage stamp of a few years ago.

Three of the listed books are group biographies: Lytton Strachey's groundbreaking *Eminent Victorians* (1918), Patricia O'Toole's intriguing study of the circle of Henry Adams, *The Five of Hearts* (1991), and Megan Marshall's look at a trio of talented siblings, *The Peabody Sisters* (2005).

The odd man out on the list is Julian Barnes's novel *Flaubert's Parrot*. Trust me: this work of fiction will teach you a lot about Flaubert and about the art of biography.

Flaubert's Parrot

Julian Barnes

This novel invades the ranks of nonfiction biographies because of the light it sheds on biography in general as well as on its subject, the nineteenth-century French novelist Gustave Flaubert. Barnes himself describes this subtle work in facetious polysyllables as "an at times attenuated fictional infrastructure to support a factual superstructure." I describe it as one of the most brilliant books I've ever read. However you put it, this parrot flies! The narrator is one Geoffrey Braithwaite, a retired doctor in his sixties, a World War II veteran, a widower. He's touring France, the beaches of Normandy where comrades died and Rouen, Flaubert country. Braithwaite has become obsessed with the life and writings of Flaubert, best known for *Madame Bovary*, whose title heroine commits adultery, then suicide.

Readers learn a prodigious amount about Flaubert, none of it told in orthodox womb-to-tomb biographical style. Braithwaite supplies various chronologies of events in Flaubert's life, a bestiary of all the animals mentioned in his letters or novels, nuggets of information about Flaubert's acquaintances, a brilliant chapter narrating events of Flaubert's life from the viewpoint of his mistress Louise Colet, a final exam, and much more, including thoughtful disquisitions on the nature of truth, on the inevitable misleading caused by selection of detail, and the impossibility of really knowing the life of another person, including yourself (especially yourself?). As for Flaubert, we enjoy learning of his delight in the white bearskin in his room, his climbing of the Pyramids—and his plan to drop a Rouen businessman's card there, the postage stamps that bear his image, his deep sense of filial love, and the macabre humor of his ill-dug grave.

And the eponymous parrot? That's the start of the book. In his story "A Simple Heart" Flaubert created an uneducated servant who fancies that the dove, the symbol of the Holy Spirit, might more logically be displaced by the parrot. Would not a talking bird, she reasons, better suggest the Holy Spirit, that entity which can endow men with the gift of tongues? Flaubert supposedly placed on his writing table a stuffed parrot, Loulou, borrowed from a local museum to give the spur of authenticity to his labors. Braithwaite spots "Flaubert's parrot" in a room dedicated to the author in the Hotel-Dieu in Rouen and feels a frisson of authentic connection to the past. Then he visits the remnant of Flaubert's residence, a summerhouse, where he sees on display . . . a second Loulou and senses a considerable dilution of frisson. This redundancy of relics disturbs our pilgrim, Braithwaite, who sets off on The Case of the Stuffed Parrot.

Meanwhile, slowly, gradually, late in this "upside-down novel," as Barnes described it, early on, to Kingsley Amis, we learn a little more about our narrator, more about his wife, more about the ways she resembled Flaubert's most famous character, that wife of a doctor. "Books are where things are explained to you; life is where things aren't," notes Braithwaite and moves on to a bang-up finale on those plural parrots.

Book Smart
Recommended Reading

The author says that he feared the book might interest only "a few Flaubertians" and a small number of "psittacophiles." Not so! For a fine conventional biography, try Frederick Brown's 2006 publication, *Flaubert*. (First priority, of course, is reading *Madame Bovary*; I like Francis Steegmuller's translation.) If you want more Barnes, start with *England, England*, and go on to everything else. More parrot lore? You're on your own.

The Path to Power (The Years of Lyndon Johnson, vol. 1)

Robert Caro

This is the first volume of a set originally planned for two, then three, now four volumes. It covers events from Johnson's 1908 birth until 1941 and his narrow, fluky defeat for the position of U. S. senator from Texas followed hard upon by Pearl Harbor and Johnson's choosing to exchange his Naval Reserve status for active duty. (There are occasional peeks into later years when thematic concerns override strict chronology.)

If you want to know only a little about the ambitious Johnson (LBJ), this is not the work for you. Readers who will like this book may fall into two sometimes overlapping categories: first, those who want to know *a lot* about LBJ, about the road to the presidency, and about the machinations of politics; and second, those who are fascinated by how a biographer can take nuggets of information—some interviews here, a file from the FDR papers there, now a handful of secondary materials, often boxes of papers in the dauntingly large LBJ library in Austin—and arrange these bits into an appealing mosaic of a text, a true "good read." (The notes about sources for each chapter are fascinating in themselves.)

Perhaps all men and women of power have a loathly aspect, but Caro paints Johnson's ruthless, single-minded lunge at power in Day-Glo. We learn of the many ways that the later LBJ sought to reshape the public's conception of his past. His own lies were a simple example of this: describing an extended trip he made to California between high school and college, LBJ convinced many that he had a vagabondage of Steinbeckian dimensions—an ever-diminishing waistline as he stalked the land, washing dishes, picking grapes, etc. The truth: LBJ worked in the law office of a cousin and lived with him. (In college Johnson acquired the openly used nickname "Bull," a halved version of a crude term for a lie.) More complex Johnsonian attempts to control his own past involved attempts to corral hundreds of copies of his college yearbook and excise pages with revealing information. He cheated on his patient, kind, devoted wife, not with just anybody but with Alice Glass, later the companion (and briefly the wife) of his rich friend and staunch supporter, Charles Marsh.

But then there's the LBJ you can't help admiring or maybe identifying with or at least understanding. Since this volume contains the vulnerable years of his tough childhood, there's much to touch the heart. But for me, Chapter 27, "The Sad Irons," is alone worth the price of the book. Here Caro (his work buttressed by the many interviews his wife, Ina Caro, had with elderly women) shows the hardships of getting through a day in LBJ's native area, the Hill Country of Texas. Kerosene lamps, water hauled from a well, no refrigeration, ironing with a six-pound wedge of, yes, iron—all this because there was no electricity. When Johnson pushed to get the Rural Electrification Administration to bring the lights to the Hill Country, why, *then*, said one lifelong resident, people began to name their children for Lyndon Johnson.

Book Smart
Recommended Reading

Caro's first book, a biography of Robert Moses entitled *The Power Broker*, was excellent apprenticeship for dealing with this life of a man of bottomless ambition for "the bludgeon of power." If you finish this first LBJ volume, here's betting you'll be compelled to take on *Means of Ascent, Master of the Senate*, and the fourth volume, still in the making, tentatively entitled *The Presidency*.

Narrative of the Life of Frederick Douglass, an American Slave, Written by Himself

Frederick Douglass

The long title alerts the reader that this is no "as told to" slave narrative. It is a testimony not only to a brave man's aspiration and ingenuity but also to his intellect and mastery of language. Douglass escaped from his Maryland servitude in 1838 and published this book some seven years later. The phrasing "an American slave" remained literally true, with Douglass remaining subject to "slave catchers" and return to his enslaved condition. Speaking to an audience in Cork, Ireland, in the fall of 1845, Douglass noted, "I am here in order to avoid the scent of the blood hounds of America." English admirers the following year overcame Douglass's initial objections to their dealing with slaveholders and raised money to purchase his freedom.

If any book can be said to make you simultaneously want to weep and to cheer, this autobiography is that book. The repeated descriptions of the whipping of slaves, observed by Douglass from childhood, are obvious examples of repellent reading. These accounts of abuse inflicted on human bodies are only more immediately painful than Douglass's accounts of the repeated abuse of slaves' minds and spirits. Douglass keenly perceives that even the masters' allowing slaves drunken dissipation on rare "holidays" was part of a scheme to stamp out the nascent power to reason. All efforts to keep slaves in a beastlike condition were complements to chains and the "cowskin" (Douglass's term for a whip). When the escaped Douglass was asked to speak to an abolitionist group, he initially expressed reluctance, wryly noting that slavery is a "poor school for the intellect and the heart."

Early on, the young Frederick, born to a loving mother who saw him only a few times and a white father, possibly "the master," had a revelation about the "pathway from slavery to freedom." When the wife of a new master, initially kind, had been for some time teaching him to read, her husband intervened, saying that "learning" made a slave discontented and unhappy, "unfit to be a slave." A revelation!—"what he [the slave owner] most dreaded, I most desired." The boy's clandestine stratagems to improve his reading skills and to acquire the ability to write is inspirational, as is his moving description—"We loved each other"—of teaching reading to as many as forty men and women of all ages, all "ardently desiring to learn."

Even the crudest telling of Douglass's experiences would be affecting, but his skill with words carves his content to a sharp point. His lengthy longing address to the sails of ships, which he could see in Chesapeake Bay ("You are loosed from your moorings, and are free; I am fast in my chains, and am a slave") is matched in emotional power by his description of the "wild" or "apparently incoherent" singing by slaves.

The fictional *Uncle Tom's Cabin*, which appeared seven years later, contains melodramatic scenes of slaves escaping from a pursuing master. Douglass's true tale affects by anticlimax. Protecting the chances of other potential fugitives, he outlines his escape to New York sparely. We learn of the existence of Anna Murray—free woman, domestic worker, intended wife—who hastens north to join him, and we sense his pride in a legal transaction by his printing of their marriage certificate. Then it's on to New Bedford, Massachusetts, where the man who variously bore the last name Bailey or Stanley or Johnson acquires for his new life the name on this enduring book—Frederick Douglass.

Autobiography

Benjamin Franklin

D. H. Lawrence disliked him and referred to him as that "snuff-colored Doctor Franklin." Norman Rockwell painted him reading to bewigged French women in décolleté, three nuzzling against him as a fourth kneels adoringly at his feet. He invented a musical instrument, the glass armonica, for which Mozart and Beethoven wrote pieces, and he consciously developed his arm muscles through swimming. Who is this Benjamin Franklin, the printer who rolled his supplies through the Philadelphia streets in a wheelbarrow and who became one of the wealthiest men in the northern colonies? His autobiography will make everything clear to us, right? Wrong. It's both fascinating and murky, enlightening and misleading.

If we want to know more about his work in helping to draft the Declaration of Independence and the Constitution, there's nothing for us here, for the book breaks off with his activities of 1760. (Possibly he meant to finish this work he usually referred to his "memoirs" but died before he accomplished the job.) Then there's the question of how accurately he recalls events of his youth: he writes the three main sections at ages sixty-five, seventy-eight, and eighty-two (there's a fragmentary fourth section written at eighty-four, in the year of his death). Beyond the question of memory, we can also wonder how much he is deliberately shaping a certain image of himself for posterity. Scholar Robert F. Sayre calls the first three sections "three separate explorations in self-discovery and self-advertisement." Where does the man end and the mask begin? As we read the introductory letter of 1771 to his (illegitimate) son William, we may imagine a father eager to instruct a young man flailing about to find his path in life. Thus, we learn with surprise that William is not only around forty years old at the time but is the "royal governor" of New Jersey! (The two men became permanently estranged during the Revolution when the son remained loyal to England.)

Why should we read this work today? One reason is the fun of getting a firsthand impression of the Franklin anecdotes that have entered into national mythology. Teenaged Ben, newly arrived in Philadelphia, purchases "three great puffy rolls" and walks down the street, eating one roll and holding each of the remaining pair under an arm. A second and more compelling reason is to understand the lessons this "archetypal Man on the Way Up," in the words of one Franklin editor, teaches about how to become a self-made man. His elaborately detailed instructions, replete with graphic schedules, in going from rags to riches inspired later works such as the books in the Horatio Alger series. It also serves as a model for pages in *The Great Gatsby*: young James Gatz not only aims at general health, wealth, and wisdom but studies electricity and "needed inventions," dead giveaways that Franklin is prominently on Fitzgerald's mind.

How wonderful that this man who loved his ten years in London and reveled in his eight years in Paris has gained the image for posterity of being "the first American" and helped to create an American national identity.

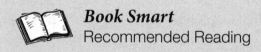

Book Smart
Recommended Reading

To learn more about this intriguing man of many masks, read Walter Isaacson's general biography *Benjamin Franklin* and Gordon S. Wood's *The Americanization of Benjamin Franklin*, a fascinating study that shows how this man who once longed to fit into aristocratic European society achieved that goal by playing the simple American sans wig and, though not himself a Quaker, wearing clothes befitting the phrase "the plain people." The *Autobiography* is where you begin.

Last Train to Memphis:
The Rise of Elvis Presley

Peter Guralnick

n Greek tragedy the audience often knows something a character doesn't know ("Oedipus," you want to shout, "stop asking all those questions!") Similarly, your awareness of how the life of this yearning young man is going to come out is occasionally joyful but more often heartbreaking. This volume, published in 1994, covers the life of Elvis Presley from his 1935 birth in Tupelo, Mississippi, to the 1958 press conference he—now a medal-wearing marksman for the U.S. Army—held before he sailed for Germany with around 1,359 other men.

The words *magisterial* and *Elvis* don't flow together easily, but it's no exaggeration to say Guralnick has written a serious book, one that can interest both Elvis devotees and nonfans. The writer has elsewhere stated that his aim as a biographer is to disappear into the world he's creating, and he's completely achieved that aim; I was startled to learn he was born and bred in Boston because he brings the South so vividly to life, occasionally making unobtrusive use of small Southern touches of language such as noting that Elvis's mother "bragged on him" or that someone "carried" Elvis to such and such a club (rather than the more mainstream "took").

You'll find here the Elvis stories you already know, such as the moment in the Sun recording studios when, after several hours of intensive listening and recording, Sam Phillips heard Elvis's impromptu singing of Arthur Crudup's "That's All Right, Mama" and *knew* this was it. But Guralnick's telling of familiar anecdotes is antitabloid in style. He never caricatures but always finds the human in the young Elvis, beautifully capturing his winning late-adolescent mix of confidence and need. He uses firsthand accounts whenever possible (the impressive notes and acknowledgments are worth a glance), and he occasionally lets you know, say, that a tale is "semiapocryphal." Or he reports on unverifiable details with a sentence such as "he played the record seven times in a row, eleven times, seven times . . . it really doesn't matter" (reporting the first spinning by deejay Dewey Phillips in his WHBQ studio in the Gayoso Hotel in Memphis).

And every reader will find fresh events from Elvis's life. Except for those who saw the September 9, 1956, "Ed Sullivan Show," who knew that it was actually hosted by Charles Laughton? (Sullivan was recuperating from a car accident.) Who knew Laughton's response to the screaming of the studio audience after two verses of "Hound Dog" was a sardonic "Music hath charms to soothe the savage breast"?

Guralnick balances his portrayal of "the King" in the spotlight with vivid vignettes of minor players. (His sketching of Dewey Phillips, a white man fully accepted in the 1950s by the world of Beale Street, made me long for a full biography of that man.) Likewise, he gives us Presley within the landscape of his era, his locale, his economic class.

 Book Smart
Recommended Reading

You'll want to follow up with the subsequent volume, *Careless Love: The Unmaking of Elvis Presley,* which came out in 1999. When you finish both Guralnick volumes on Presley, don't go for another Presley book—it will disappoint. Head for *Dream Boogie,* Guralnick's treatment of Sam Cooke.

W. E. B. Du Bois: Biography of a Race, 1868–1919

David Levering Lewis

This, the biographer estimated, was a five-year project. Volume 1, treated here, came out eight years later. Another seven years elapsed before the public saw *W. E. B. Du Bois: The Fight for Equality and the American Century, 1919–1963*. The long gestation brought forth this long and splendid biography of a man whose life was long—ninety-five years—and eventful. Each scholarly volume won the Pulitzer Prize for Biography. Lewis, additionally, received a MacArthur "genius" grant shortly after the publication of Volume 1.

The subtitles of the two volumes suggest the thrust of Lewis's approach. He's looking at Du Bois (pronounced dew-BOYSS) as an unusual and talented person in himself and also as a man whose existence both reflected and affected the status of African Americans. Du Bois, as the author of the influential book *The Souls of Black Folk* (1903), formulated the concept of a dual identity—both Negro and American. It's widely quoted now, but Du Bois pioneered in identifying the phenomenon and writing about this "two-ness." (Here too he first used the term "the talented tenth," defining it later as the "exceptional men" of the race who filter culture downward.) Lewis describes the effect of the book's fourteen essays as being "like fireworks going off in a cemetery." His twenty-page analysis gives great help to any reader's appreciation of the book's "transcendent intellectual passion and numinous prose." (Lewis's own prose is graceful, but his choice of words such as *spheroidal, apotheosis, clangorous*, and *immiseration* defines his targeted audience as the well educated.)

In this volume, we first learn of Du Bois's early years in Great Barrington, Massachusetts, and his higher education: Fisk College in Tennessee, his first exposure to the South, Harvard College (he transferred there as a junior), and Harvard University, where he was the first African American to receive a Ph.D. His groundbreaking achievements continued as he worked in the new field of sociology, founding the department at Atlanta University. Lewis gives meticulous details of Du Bois's ideological clash with Booker T. Washington and his work in helping to found the NAACP and editing its magazine *The Crisis*.

If Lewis devotes much more attention to his subject's public life than his private life, the same was true of Du Bois himself, and his biographer attempts no cover-up of his subject's culpability as husband and father. On the shoulders of his daughter fell every high expectation of this father who had lost a two-year-old son. In 1914 thirteen-year-old Yolande was shipped off to Bedales, the first coeducational English boarding school, where she—and her mother who stayed behind in London—had two miserable and lonely years. Lewis unsparingly concludes, "There were only insignificant parts available to Nina and Yolande in the drama starring W. E. B. Du Bois."

The first volume closes with the terrible "Red Summer" of 1919. After seventy-eight lynchings in 1918, and with servicemen of color returning home, a wave of violent racial unrest erupted. Du Bois knew there could be no turning back from the struggle for racial equality. Although he did not live to see the fruit of the 1960s campaign for civil rights, he managed a symbolic and theatrical exit. Lewis opens his volume wonderfully with the news of the end of Du Bois's life. August 28, 1963. A crowd of 250,000 people at the Reflecting Pool in Washington, D.C. Shortly before Martin Luther King Jr. soared into one of the most memorable speeches of the millennium, "I have a dream," Roy Wilkins announced the death (midnight, Ghana) of W. E. B. Du Bois.

The Peabody Sisters

Megan Marshall

Megan Marshall's preface describes her book as "the story of three intertwined lives of sisters who both welcomed their group identity and resented it as they strove for independent self-fulfillment." The lives of the Peabody sisters—Elizabeth (1804–1894), Mary (1806–1887), and Sophia (1809–1871)—involve virtually the entire nineteenth century, but except for a brief epilogue, Marshall truncates the story in 1843.

Why should we want to read about these Peabody sisters, who lived out the years covered by the book mostly in Boston and Salem? They interest us, first, in the generic way that we are intrigued by the three Brontë sisters, all authors, whose shorter lives were contemporary, and by fictional sisters such as the Bennet quintet in Jane Austen's *Pride and Prejudice*. We enjoy speculations such as these: Do talented siblings inspire or inhibit one another? Does birth order matter? How much does parental example count?

But Elizabeth, Mary, and Sophia also come to interest us in themselves, their own lively particularities. Who were they? Here's the easy answer: Mary married Horace Mann, the educational reformer. Sophia was the wife of Nathaniel Hawthorne, the novelist. Elizabeth, who remained single, deserves acclaim as the founder of kindergartens in the United States. But, like most easy answers, these sentences conceal as much as they reveal. This biography mostly concerns the sisters in the thirty-five years before these encapsulated truths emerged, the years that Elizabeth and Mary taught in school after school. They helped the family budget, yes, but they also cared deeply about pedagogy and the individual student. These were the years that Sophia, a talented artist, was a "bed case," excused from family responsibilities by mysterious pains (think of Alice James) that vanished after marriage (think of Elizabeth Barrett).

The biography begins with the life of Eliza Palmer (later Peabody) who became the mother of the talented triad of sisters (and—another story—of a later trio of brothers, mostly slackers or wastrels). Readers make their acquaintance with an atmosphere of Boston-area women who see themselves as "practical idealists," a theme that runs through the next generation.

We enjoy the wealth of social history—the mercury poisoning caused by the calomel given to teething babies, the innovative educational techniques in schools for girls, life on a Cuban coffee plantation. And we delight in intellectual history as the sisters interact with William Ellery Channing, Ralph Waldo Emerson, Margaret Fuller, Washington Allston, and Bronson Alcott. And—call me trivial if you wish—I passionately enjoyed the minutiae of Elizabeth's unorthodox friendship with sorrowing widower Horace Mann and her brief engagement to Nathaniel Hawthorne, whom she deemed "handsomer than Lord Byron," before each man carried a sister off in marriage. The epilogue tells us that Mary became a published writer after marriage and children, that Sophia, after motherhood, never painted again, that surviving brother Nat refused to let his daughters learn anything beyond basic skills. We're left pondering this complex nexus of life, art, and gender roles and feeling far from sated by the 452 pages of text, the fruit of almost twenty years of authorial labor.

Book Smart
Recommended Reading

For other interesting family biographies of nineteenth-century American writers, take a look at *The Emerson Brothers: A Fraternal Biography in Letters*, edited by Ronald A. Bosco and Joel Myerson, and *The Jameses: A Family Narrative* by R. W. B. Lewis. For information on the talented writing trio of English sisters, read Lucasta Miller's *The Brontë Myth*.

The Five of Hearts: An Intimate Portrait of Henry Adams and His Friends, 1880–1918

Patricia O'Toole

Two married couples and a bachelor who live in a world of privilege and achievement see their friendship as so bonding that they give it a name, the five of hearts, sometimes displaying outward and visible signs such as enameled pins and stationery with a playing card emblem or carving the image of that card into a boulder in the Rockies. This is one description of the relationship among Henry and Clover Adams, John and Clara Hay, and Clarence King.

Among the males, Henry Adams was the grandson and great-grandson of United States presidents and was himself a successful if often anonymous author. John Hay was secretary to Abraham Lincoln and secretary of state to Theodore Roosevelt. Clarence King, geologist, mine owner, art collector, became the first head of the United States Geological Survey. The women, in accord with their times, lived more private lives, but both came from backgrounds of wealth. Clover, who presided over legendary teas in Washington, taught herself to be a perceptive amateur photographer.

Those of us who idealize friendship, those ties that are chosen rather than imposed, want this to be a much happier book. O'Toole, a talented writer, is by no means setting out to write a mass pathography, a book that stresses the negatives of human lives. Indeed, she ends her narrative by praising the *efforts* of the five to close the "greatest breach in nature," the gap between one mind and another. She is, however, also a skilled researcher and must use what is shown by the relevant documents. Here are some of those facts. Clover Adams—highly intelligent, childless, and nonreligious—and Clara Hay—placid mother of four and conventionally pious—had no affinity with each other. Clover Adams killed herself in 1885 by ingesting potassium cyanide, a chemical she used in her photography. John Hay had a long affair with Anna "Nannie" Lodge, wife of Henry Cabot Lodge. Henry Adams began deepening his worshipful stance toward Lizzie Cameron, wife of a senator from Pennsylvania, even before his wife's death (the alliance remained chaste). Clarence King concealed from his fellow heartlets all his life his bond with Ada Copeland, an African-American nursemaid twenty years his junior who came to be mother of his five children. He exercised a more profound deceit on Copeland herself, telling her he was a railway porter named James Todd and even playing the groom in a license-less religious wedding ceremony with her.

One reviewer amends O'Toole with the news that the average height of the quintet was five feet three, and another in that vein trivializes the book as "dishy." Not so. The word *intimate* in the book's subtitle is accurate in denoting its emphasis, but a book much set in Washington will perforce deal with elections, political appointments, and the nation's growing taste for empire.

The characters aren't particularly lovable, but they're fascinating. You enjoy hearing the central figure of Adams, always a public figure of great dignity even in age, classify himself (to Hay) as "an unnecessary palaeozoic reptile." Similarly, those who know the Saint-Gaudens statue Adams commissioned for his wife's grave are delighted to learn of (and see pictured) a lesser-known work by this famous sculptor. Done at Hay's commission, this bronze medallion displays a caricature of Henry Adams—part angel, part porcupine. Perhaps this hybrid creature is a more apt image than the valentinesque playing card for the affiliation of these five.

The Life and Times of Cotton Mather

Kenneth Silverman

"**V**illain to history" and "national gargoyle"—these are two of Silverman's pungent phrases for Mather's image. It's true that unless you're a follower of the Cotton Mather band in Austin, Texas, you probably scowl reflexively when you hear the name. If you know only the stereotypes of Mather or his excesses, this book will change you. It gives readers no horned demon, and certainly no haloed saint—but a life-sized portrait of a complex human being. Although by profession a theologian, Mather was also interested in telescopes and microscopes and became the target of an assassination attempt because of his support for smallpox vaccination. As a theologian, Mather held a position on religious toleration, contends Silverman, close to that of Thomas Jefferson.

Silverman calls Mather "the first unmistakably American figure in the nation's history." If energy is an American quality, Mather qualifies. In his sixty-five earthly years, he wrote around four hundred works, kept a voluminous diary for more than thirty years, and corresponded copiously—all this while being minister at Boston's Old North Church, composing and delivering lengthy sermons and prayers (one of the latter said to have lasted an hour). He found time for incidental tasks such as persuading a member of the Church of England to give money to found "an Academy for Dissenters," now better known as Yale University in honor of that donor, Elihu Yale. In private life, he married three times, and if anything can humanize Mather, it's the account of his third marriage, to the temperamental ("perhaps psychopathic") Lydia Lee George, a wealthy and worldly widow. She once left him in the middle of the night in what Mather called a "horrid rage," not returning for a week or so, seemingly only after Mather had news of the death of a son by shipwreck. (Of Mather's fifteen children, only two outlived him.)

But what about the Salem witch trials? The negative image of Mather inscribes his name indelibly on this dark chapter in colonial history almost as if he had personally rounded up alleged malefactors and all but hoisted the noose himself. The facts, again, are more complex, for he attended none of the trials, and his feelings were somewhat "ambidexter." But his book *Wonders of the Invisible World*, after considerable waffling, gave his support, his first public dissent from the position of his father, Increase. Cotton Mather deeply believed in the deeds of spectral beings, whether malign or benign. In 1693 he neatly recorded the fact of a visit in his study from an angel who wore "a splendid tiara."

Silverman further liberates Mather from the House of Horrors with the depiction of his childhood. Not only was his father a brilliant and highly esteemed minister, so were both grandfathers. If those with rich heritages face high demands, Mather entered the world with a weight of expectations on his shoulders. We are not surprised to learn that the young Cotton, born to spellbind, had a stammer. (Silverman perceptively uses Mather's stuttering as a kind of metaphor for his often divided perspectives, what he terms "Matherese.")

Elsewhere, Silverman describes a biography as being "a simile, a resemblance, a composite police sketch." The reader is more likely to judge this biography as something closer to a John Singleton Copley. Thomas Carlyle described a well-written life as being "almost as rare as a well-spent one"; if readers continue to disagree about the merits of Mather's life, they won't disagree about his biography.

Eminent Victorians

Lytton Strachey

I f you know the annual *New Yorker* cover drawing of Eustace Til-
ley—a top-hatted, ascot-necked gent peering at a butterfly, somewhat jadedly, through his monocle—then you've got the tone of
this book. Lytton Strachey, member of the tony Bloomsbury coterie in
London, set out to undo the Victorian tradition in biography: suety
"life and letters" volumes attempting to place the subject in his or her
most heroic light. Strachey wanted his biographies to be pithy and art-
ful, producing four sketches in this volume that range, roughly, from
twenty-five to one hundred pages. Just as he aimed at overturning the
immediately preceding style, he didn't mind overturning the images
of the four Victorians he depicts in his 1918 volume. (As you say the
first word of the title, you must slightly curl your lip to show they don't
deserve to be deemed "eminent.")

Andy Warhol's observation on the brevity of fame must be retro-
active, for the first question from most twenty-first-century readers is
"Who *are* these people?" Of Strachey's four subjects—Cardinal Manning, Florence Nightingale, Thomas Arnold, and General Gordon—
most contemporary readers would probably have name recognition only
of Nightingale. So some of Strachey's point has evaporated; what's the
fun in poking a needle in a balloon that's already deflated? Brief definitions are in order. Cardinal Manning became Archbishop of Westminster, the leader of Roman Catholics in England. Dr. Arnold was head
of the Rugby School in England (and father of poet Matthew Arnold).
General Gordon led English troops in spots as far-flung as Sebastopol,
China, and the Sudan, dying at Khartoum after a ten-month siege by

Muslim troops led by the messianic Mahdi. Strachey has Church, Public School, and Empire in his sights.

Of Strachey's four puncturing portraits, Nightingale comes off most handsomely. He makes no attempt to debunk her heroic reform of hospital care, her revolutionary concepts such as the efficacy of fresh air in hospital rooms. What Strachey does attempt is to transform her image of Victorian "angel in the hospital" into that of a privileged young woman who became a steely-eyed, iron-fisted, hard-driving reformer. I had already thought, "What a CEO she'd make!" before I read Queen Victoria's verdict: "What a *head*! I wish we had her at the War Office!" (Victoria, nonetheless, bestowed on her a brooch, designed by the Prince Consort, bearing the demure motto, "Blessed are the merciful.")

Manning comes off as a schemer: he's shocked—shocked!—that some Christians believe the creed they mouth; Arnold gets painted as slightly silly in his stress on "Christian" and "English" values in his school; and Gordon is unfairly portrayed as a hypocritical drunkard with an "open Bible and open bottle of whiskey" before him in his tent. As Strachey says elsewhere, "Discretion is not the better part of biography."

Book Smart
Recommended Reading

Strachey may have changed to some degree the course of biography, but the whirligig of time brings in its revenges. In 1967 and 1968 Michael Holroyd brought out a hefty (and excellent) two-volume biography of Strachey. (There's a 1995 reworking in one volume.) Its revelations of Strachey's many same-sex affairs and ribald witticisms shocked readers of its generation much as Strachey's arch volume had shocked *his* contemporaries. If you like the Romans, try *Lives of the Caesars* by Strachey's first-century role model, Suetonius.

The Good Life:
Young Men on a Quest

Go Tell It on the Mountain
James Baldwin

Great Expectations
Charles Dickens

An American Tragedy
Theodore Dreiser

Invisible Man
Ralph Ellison

The Great Gatsby
F. Scott Fitzgerald

Cold Mountain
Charles Frazier

Jude the Obscure
Thomas Hardy

The Assistant
Bernard Malamud

The Magic Mountain
Thomas Mann

Walden
Henry David Thoreau

Gray matter acting on reading matter is a matter of passion too.

—Craig Raine

IMAGINE TEN young men sitting in a room together, each sizing up the others as congenial partners for conversation. (Nine are the protagonists of novels, the other a person who really existed.) If this attempt at speed relating works, here's an account of how the conversational clusters might develop.

Four of these young men—Pip, Jude, Clyde, and Jay—will be drawn together to talk about their quests for raising their social status. They come, respectively, from the worlds of Charles Dickens's *Great Expectations*, Thomas Hardy's *Jude the Obscure*, Theodore Dreiser's *An American Tragedy*, and F. Scott Fitzgerald's *The Great Gatsby*. Pip and Jude are able to detail the challenge of attempting to move up in life on the widely spaced rungs of the social ladder of nineteenth-century England. Clyde and Jay must try to decide if the scene in the United States in the 1920s offered a much easier climb. All will be able to participate in a *cherchez la femme* discussion and retail their experiences with Estella or Sue or Sondra or Daisy while Biddy or Arabella or Roberta or what-*was*-her-name back home faded away. At the end of the evening only one young man has a lasting smile on his face, for compared to the other three, he flourished, though not, of course, in the way he had planned.

The unnamed young narrator of Ralph Ellison's *Invisible Man* almost fell in with that group, for he certainly hoped for a life above the poverty line. Similarly, he made a preliminary feint toward plucking the sleeve of John Grimes of James Baldwin's *Go Tell It on the Mountain* since they were the two

African Americans in the room. But eventually Ellison's anonymous young man joined up with Henry David Thoreau and with Hans Castorp of Thomas Mann's *The Magic Mountain* for a loftier and more abstract discussion of a quest for meaning in life. Their comparisons of life after a move from the South to Harlem, of life alone in a cabin on a pond outside Concord, Massachusetts, and life in a tuberculosis sanitarium above the German clouds offer infinite possibilities.

Baldwin's John Grimes, a little sad at missing a chance to discuss his native Harlem with the anonymous chap, falls into a surprisingly congenial discussion with Brooklyn-based Frank Alpine of Bernard Malamud's *The Assistant*. Both of them have known bitter experiences, but they're only slightly startled to find themselves talking about religion. Many of the pages of John's life dealt with his attempt to feel worthy of a conversion experience in his family's Pentecostal church, while Catholic-born Frank feels himself drawn to aspects of Judaism.

Circling the room is W. P. Inman, deserting Confederate soldier from Charles Frazier's *Cold Mountain*. Since his driving quest is to get back home, he longs to escape to another room and talk to Odysseus. But I'd like to set him up for a conversation with my favorite octogenarian on a quest—Robert MacIver of Peter Pouncey's touching book (with an intermittent war scene): *Rules for Old Men Waiting*.

Go Tell It on the Mountain

James Baldwin

The title comes from what used to be called a Negro spiritual ("Go tell it on the mountain that Jesus Christ is born!") It's a fine name for the book, as is "In My Father's House," a title Baldwin considered while writing the novel. The working title, which on one level alludes to the biblical line "In my father's house are many mansions," allows a single phrase to capture two major themes of the novel—the central character's troubled relationship with fathers of both the earthly and the heavenly varieties. Some think Baldwin gave the nod to "Go Tell It on the Mountain" in honor of the improbable village, Loèche les Bains in the Swiss Alps, where he wrote most of the book.

In this "alabaster landscape," (Baldwin's phrase) the first "Neger" ever to be seen by many of the local residents tapped out on his typewriter this powerful tale of three generations of African Americans against the 1935 background of Harlem and the earliest years of the twentieth century in the South. Lucien Happersburger, his friend and lover whose family owned a house in the little town, persuaded Baldwin to come, accompanied by no more than his Remington and his Bessie Smith records. Just as Edith Wharton sat in the rue de Rivoli in Paris to write tellingly of snowbound New Hampshire villagers in *Ethan Frome*, so here did Baldwin use his geographical distance from his setting as a catalyst to invoking it brilliantly.

Always present, of course, in Baldwin's head was his knowledge of his own past, and this is a novel based on his own life. Like Baldwin himself, the main character John Grimes struggles with his sense of alienation from most of his family, his distance from community (chiefly the Pentecostal church) and familial expectations. The first line of the book heralds the conflict: "Everyone had always said that John would be a preacher when he grew up, just like his father."

The structure of the novel makes John's struggle with his sense of difference and his struggle with the question of "being saved" the alpha and omega of the book (Baldwin treads innovatively in the steps of such as St. Augustine and Jonathan Edwards and other authors of conversion narratives). Between these two is a stunning three-part section called "The Prayers of the Saints," where the reader gets inside the thoughts and the memories of John's apostate aunt, his wrathful father, and his sensitive mother, whose memories of Richard, her first and tragic love, are, for me, the most poignant part of the book.

Ready yourself for this book by reading the title essay of Baldwin's *Notes of a Native Son*; the themes are all there. Then enjoy immersing yourself in Baldwin's prose. Whatever Baldwin's feelings as an adult about the ecclesiastical heritage of his boyhood, he gained a rich life-long legacy from his years with the tone and cadences of the King James translation of the Bible. The two aspects of this novel—hardscrabble lives in country and city and beautiful language—complement each other wonderfully. I like Langston Hughes's description: "a low down tale in a velvet bag."

Great Expectations

Charles Dickens

In Chapter 8 of this novel the young first-person narrator notes in his childish fancy how happy his Uncle Pumblechook, owner of a seed shop, must be to have "so many little drawers in his shop." Next, young Pip peeps inside the drawers and sees flower seeds and bulbs in "tied-up brown paper packets" and wonders if those seeds and bulbs ever wanted "to break out of those jails, and bloom." What a wonderfully unconscious expression of his own state! An intelligent, perceptive, and sensitive child, the orphaned Pip is being reared by a begrudging older sister and her affectionate but meek husband Joe, a blacksmith and illiterate. The three live in the class-bound world of early nineteenth-century England. Yes, Pip is in a bag, the bag is tied, and the drawer is closed. Pip will need the skills of a Houdini to burst his prison bonds.

Pip's seminal observation comes, surprisingly enough, *before* he has his initial brush with the world of the wealthy. Pumblechook soon leads him to the looming house of the eccentric Miss Havisham, who lives with her adopted daughter, Estella, a haughty child around Pip's age. Here he learns the pangs of *ressentiment*, the humiliation of having scorn heaped on his thick boots and yucks cast at his working-class dialect ("He calls the knaves jacks, this boy!" sneers Estella during a card game).

The plot is complex with characters crossing and recrossing paths as they do in fiction and in real-life big cities. I will do nothing to spoil the startling surprise lobbed at first-time readers—and at Pip—in Chapter 39 except to note that Dickens sets the stage with "violent blasts of rain," "rages of wind," and "gloomy accounts . . . from the coast of shipwreck and death."

Rereaders of the novel will continue to savor the rich gallery of characters. The escaped prisoner Magwitch demanding "wittles" (victuals) of a terrified Pip, who joins the ranks of the criminal by stealing food and drink from his sister's pantry. The jilted Miss Havisham living in her wedding gown with a web-covered "bride's cake." The powerful lawyer Mr. Jaggers with a head full of his clients' dark secrets and with hands that demand washing with scented soap after each appointment. Jaggers's assistant Wemmick: stern guardian of "portable property" on the job, loving caretaker of an old father ("the aged P.") at home. O to have Dickens's imagination and genius with detail! His talent is so prodigal that sometimes a character on only a fraction of a page sticks forever in our memory: check out "Trabb's boy," whose burst of parody nails Pip's arrogance with three sneering words: "Don't know ya!"

The book is a *Bildungsroman*, a novel about growing up. We follow Pip from around the age of seven to twenty-three; a final chapter features Pip in his thirties. He moves from humble beginnings into the "great expectations" of the title—a leap into the life of "a gentleman," a young man who need not sully his hands with work but, rather, lives on the interest of a fortune from an unnamed benefactor. The "seed" bursts into bloom, yes, but the hothouse atmosphere of unearned wealth produces its own blight. While the novel has a deep, karmic moral, nowhere in the nearly five hundred pages does the reader feel "preached at."

On the advice of the popular novelist Sir Edward Bulwer-Lytton, who inspected the proofs, Dickens made the ending of the book sunnier. Since most editions also reprint the original, you can decide which is better. A hint at my opinion: who, these days, reads Bulwer-Lytton?

An American Tragedy

Theodore Dreiser

Dreiser got out of town—New York—a few days before *An American Tragedy* was published (December 17, 1925) because he didn't want to face the reviews. (Noted author Sinclair Lewis disliked the novel and had refused to review it.) So he must have been gratified, down in Fort Lauderdale a month later, to learn that the book had already sold seventeen thousand copies. A few days later he made an unprecedented kind of entry in his diary: "local book store man & asst-cashier 1st national bank arrive to congratulate me on book." Being banned, later, in Boston probably helped its continuing commercial success.

H. L. Mencken suggests—as I do not—that readers short on time skip the first of this long book's three sections, the early adolescence of main character Clyde Griffiths. He's twelve when we meet him, disconsolately following his gospel-preaching parents and his siblings around the streets of Kansas City. Young Clyde longs for a life far from the dreary, the run-down. His sister Esta escapes first. She soon returns, desperately, unwed and pregnant. These plot details prefigure later events, and it's significant that Clyde pays no heed to Esta's fate in his headlong striving for a shinier existence. Work as a bellboy provides his first brush with a more riotous way of life, but when a car in which he's a passenger hits and kills a child, he flees Kansas City. This event, too, give us an important hint of what's later termed Clyde's "mental and moral cowardice."

The famous middle section of the book puts Clyde in Lycurgus, New York. A chance encounter with a factory-owning relative has led to Clyde's ascent to supervisor in the collar-stamping department. There he falls passionately for the pretty and sweet Roberta Alden. Work rules forbid social life between manager and employee, but Clyde pressures the smitten Roberta into surreptitious trysts. A few months of forbidden passion gone by, Clyde's good looks catapult him into social life with the gilded youth of Lycurgus and into the arms of the wealthy Sondra Finchley (think of the young, beautiful Elizabeth Taylor, who plays Sondra in the 1951 film *A Place in the Sun*; Montgomery Clift and Shelley Winters complete that superbly cast love triangle in Hollywood's retitled version of Dreiser's novel).

Events move inexorably along. Roberta gets pregnant. Hopes for an abortion prove futile, and Roberta demands marriage in letters that pierce the reader but leave Clyde unmoved. A newspaper account of a rowboat accident inspires Clyde to murder. Dreiser details Clyde's last-minute change of heart, but fate laughs and causes, yes, a boating accident, while a "devilish bird" repeats its eerie cry overheard. Roberta drowns, and Clyde dons his spare straw hat and flits off to a weekend with Sondra and pals.

Part three elaborately limns the trial, conviction, and execution of the sensitive but selfish Clyde. Minor characters such as a self-interested lawyer, a sensitive priest, and an intelligent fellow inmate of death row stand out here, and Clyde's fiercely loving mother makes her reappearance.

Although Dreiser has a flat-footed style, we are moved by the way he stacks solid details to create a credible world. Dreiser, the next-to-last child of a brood of thirteen born to an illiterate mother, may be, as one critic opined, the author of "the worst written great novel in the world," but you'll find it etches its spot in your mind. Dreiser's style may be inept, but the man obviously had a personality that won him interesting friends. How else could his funeral have featured a reading of a poem by one Charlie Chaplin?

Invisible Man

Ralph Ellison

D on't confuse this book with the 1897 volume of a similar title (*The Invisible Man*) by H. G. Wells. Wells's character Griffin became literally invisible. The protagonist of Ellison's uneven but fascinating novel is only metaphorically invisible, but he's also anonymous. Even when he takes on an assumed name at one point, the reader remains ignorant of that new name as well. Let's call him The Narrator. The character, like his creator, is African American. The novel, while addressing issues of racial prejudice and racial identity, transcends limited categorization to become a novel about the difficulty of being an individual. It's not surprising to learn that Oklahoma-born Ralph Waldo Ellison was named for the nineteenth-century New England essayist Ralph Waldo Emerson, for the need for self-reliance (one of Emerson's most important themes) resounds throughout the novel.

The structure of the novel is cyclical. It opens with The Narrator in an underground hideout in Harlem. (Another clear literary ancestor is Dostoyevsky's similarly unnamed hero of *Notes from the Underground* who has rejected the limits of rationalism and terms himself "spiteful" and "unpleasant.") The cave of the comparatively good-natured Narrator has a manhole cover for a mouth, and he lights this space with more than one thousand lightbulbs with power drained off from Monopolated Light & Power. He's not buried, for he assures us he will come forth in the proper season. Like the more traditional ursine inhabitant of a wintry cave, The Narrator sees himself as in hibernation. He *will* come forth, but meanwhile he listens to Louis Armstrong's recording of "What Did I Do to Be So Black and Blue" and reflects on the chain of events that has placed him here.

The Narrator's journey goes from South to North, from innocence to experience, from reliance on the images, the examples, the assumptions of others to a clearer understanding of the need to take charge of his own life. Sprinkled over the plot details of these differing phases of The Narrator's life is a sense of the surreal, a crackling of sly humor, a wild awareness of near-parodic moments.

The Narrator attempts to please, in chronological order, the white trustee visiting his college (which sounds much like Tuskegee Institute in Alabama, where Ellison studied music), the corrupted-by-power black president of the school, the northern trustees—one named Emerson—from whom The Narrator seeks summer work (readers familiar with the erotic images in Walt Whitman's Calamus poems can decode the fact that Emerson's son, who invites The Narrator to the "Club Calamus," is making a pass at him), his employers at the Liberty Paint company, and the white men of "The Brotherhood" (seemingly Communist though never identified as such) who want to exploit his dark skin and his skill at oratory while discouraging him from thinking. He also refuses to come under the spell of "Ras the Destroyer," a violent Black Nationalist who courses through Harlem on horseback—"leaping like Heigho, the goddam Silver!"—dressed as an Ethiopian chieftain.

If you're not ready for the entire book (about 440 pages), read Chapter 1, printed separately in 1947 in the magazine *Horizon*, for a horripilating introduction to Ellison's power with words. Or select the comic-but-serious vignette in Chapter 13, where The Narrator, liberated from the propriety demanded by his image as a college student, exults in the impulsive act of eating a hot buttered sweet potato bought from a Harlem street cart (first, one potato, then two more). He is now free to make to the vendor a wonderful existentialist declaration: "I yam what I am!"

The Great Gatsby

F. Scott Fitzgerald

At the end of the 1920s Fitzgerald, who gave the decade its nickname "the Jazz Age," wrote an essay calling the ten years "the most expensive orgy in history." This novel, written at the halfway mark of the decade when every bottle of champagne was lawless—Prohibition lasted from 1919 to 1933—captures that sense of easy excess. No celebration of hedonism, the novel explores the longings and the fortunes of one American, Jay Gatsby, born James Gatz to "shiftless farm people" in the Midwest. Through a combination of dreams, luck, personality, and an easy nose-thumbing of the law (his business mentor is a fictional counterpart of the man who fixed the 1919 World Series), he acquires a fancy house and car and a now-legendary array of shirts.

The plot is simply told. As a young army officer, Gatsby falls violently in love with Daisy Fay, a young woman of privilege. His passion is reciprocated, but Daisy, whose forte is not patience, marries Tom Buchanan while Gatsby is awaiting return from the Great War. No toad of work squats on Tom's life: his fortune enables him to buy polo ponies and to spend his days in reverie over his prowess as a footballer for Yale. Gatsby, now returned, amasses a pile of new money and begins to nudge fate to reunite him with Daisy. (We first see him, on his verdant lawn, gazing across Long Island Bay to the green light at the end of the Buchanans' dock.) The plan works, but for a tragically short time.

The plot crackles with interest, but the attractions of the novel go deeper. Much lies in the paradox of Gatsby himself—is he truly great or merely "great" in a hyped, show-biz way? On a single page the narrator describes Gatsby with two verdicts: He "represented everything for which I have an unaffected scorn" and he "turned out all right in the end."

Much charm of the novel lies in the way Fitzgerald tells the tale through the filtering eyes of his narrator, Nick Carraway. Nick becomes an agent of fate by being both Gatsby's neighbor and Daisy's distant cousin. Nick has spent less than a year in the East when he sends himself scurrying back to his native Midwest. (Fitzgerald himself grew up in St. Paul, Minnesota, in what he described as "the worst house in the best part of town," a good backdrop for a man who developed a keen sense of subtle social distinctions.) Nick feeds us details about this disillusioning period while also slowly interweaving details of Gatsby's life, including a childhood in which he inscribed Ben Franklin–like ideas for self-improvement on the flyleaf of his copy of *Hopalong Cassidy*, a fictional hero of the wide-open West.

This novel is marked by the poignance of Gatsby's longing—longing for money, for love, for the grace of renewal. A later Fitzgerald statement, "There are no second chances in American life," became famous; at the end of this novel, however, America itself is retrospectively depicted as one such second chance for European culture—"a fresh green breast of the New World." Fitzgerald once contemplated entitling the novel "Under the Red, White, and Blue," and it's true that some see Gatsby as an embodiment of the American dream, perhaps even of this land of deeply flawed idealism and unwarranted optimism.

Life and art join in the words of the last line of the novel, for they are also the words carved onto Fitzgerald's tombstone: "So we beat on, boats against the current, borne back ceaselessly into the past."

Cold Mountain

Charles Frazier

Our word *nostalgia* comes from the Greek root words for "home" and "pain." Inman, the protagonist of this fine novel of 1997, does indeed, like the Greek hero Odysseus, feel a longing pain to get home. The book opens with Inman, a Confederate soldier recently wounded in battle, stepping out the window of his hospital room and taking the first step of his long, unauthorized trip home. Home is Cold Mountain, the settlement of Black Cove in the western reaches of North Carolina. Like Odysseus, Inman will encounter many adventures on his difficult trek home. Unlike Odysseus, Inman will have his steps dogged by the lethal force of the Home Guard, the organization given the power of hunting down Confederate soldiers who choose to make a separate peace with the deadly conflict.

Home, for Inman, is also Ada, his Penelope. Ada is a young woman of gentle birth from Charleston, South Carolina, now attempting to manage the farm she inherited, once a kind of convalescent plaything for her beloved consumptive father, Monroe, but now a means of survival. Unlike the Ithacan queen of the Homeric world who plays little role in the action until near the end of the literary work, Ada, who endures prolonged struggles to keep the home fires lit, gets attention in alternating chapters. Out of almost nowhere will come Ruby, a local daughter of the earth who pulls the head off a troublesome rooster shortly after meeting Ada. (Accompanied with biscuit dumplings, the bird makes a tasty meal later that evening.) Ruby's wise ways concerning the land will constitute a deep education for Ada and will allow both women to endure.

Despite its temporal setting in 1864, this book is no Civil War novel. It's more a tribute to a region of the country that was, at the time, neither North in the sense of celebrating industry and capitalism nor South in the sense of being dependent on slaves for its agricultural existence. Only Tennessee was later to secede than North Carolina. In an interview elsewhere Frazier calls the book an "elegy for that old America"—a paean to a vanished way of life, a rigorous but independent existence of hoeing, digging, planting, nurturing, harvesting; of killing hogs and scraping their skins, making sausage and souse; of gathering eggs, milking cows, currying horses; of scrubbing shirts on a metal washboard; of gathering with kinfolks and neighbors to make music; of collecting rainwater in a barrel for the women's washing of their hair; of the coolness of the springhouse on a hot summer day.

The novel is a testimony to the beauty of spoken English of another era and, ultimately, to Frazier's enormous skill as a writer. The pastoral feel of the ending and the spirit of the 1874 epilogue in which Ada reads Ovid's tale of Baucis and Philemon, a loving and elderly married couple granted metamorphosis into the verdure of nature as two intertwining trees, will give you a bittersweet kind of joy.

Book Smart
Recommended Reading

Robert Morgan's novel *Brave Enemies* sets an earlier American conflict, the Revolutionary War, in these same Carolina mountains. For more good reading about the people of the "northern South," read Harriette Arnow's fine novel *The Dollmaker*; it deals with a mountain family, headed by the matriarch Gertie Nevels, that is abruptly transplanted from rural Kentucky to Detroit during World War II.

Jude the Obscure

Thomas Hardy

Longing—that's the one-word summary of this novel, first published in book form in 1895. Jude Fawley, son of a farming family, is an odd mixture of intelligence, ambition, and likeable naïveté. His first intense yearning is for a university education. He knows his first step must be the learning of Latin and Greek. Despite setbacks, he surmounts the problem of acquiring texts. Next problem: he must commit to "years of plodding" to infuse all these words in his mind, and he leaps to a thought right out of Aeschylus in wishing "that he had never been born."

Despite his childish assumption that some formula of transmutation will cause these languages to glide into his head, he pursues his dream. An early multitasker, he studies Latin while driving a cart for his aunt's bakery. Christminster (a thin disguise of Oxford) remains a visionary hope, something approximating the New Jerusalem in his adolescent mind.

Enter Arabella Donn and Jude's awareness of sexual longing. The arrival of this daughter of Eve is heavily freighted with symbolism. In the first edition she hurls at him "a pig's pizzle"—it's just what you'd guess. Outrage at such realism caused Hardy to euphemize this porcine phallus into "this novel artillery" for later editions. Unaltered, however, are the lines about the "Cochin's egg" she carries in the warmth of her bosom, explaining to Jude that it's "natural for a woman to want to bring live things into the world." They become lovers, and when she feigns pregnancy, Jude honorably marries her. The end of his dreams? No, for the capricious Arabella soon exits, for a time, heading for new conquests in Australia.

Jude renews his longing for knowledge, moving himself to the town of Christminster, where he remains an outsider. Thoughtful letters requesting advice from dons bring silence or the haughty rebuff to remain "in his own sphere." He sets up shop as an all-purpose artisan, and one frustrated night he uses his mason's chalk to inscribe a line from the book of Job on the college gate: "I have understanding as well as you; I am not inferior to you." We identify with him and cheer this mild vandalism.

New variety of longing: could perhaps his cousin Sue Bridehead, attractive and intellectual neurotic, be the perfect woman for him? You and I can guess the answer, but Jude's ears are stopped to our cries of "No, no!" Even their awareness of forebears who married each other and came to tragic end fails to serve its office. Like Jude, Sue has been married, but there are divorces all 'round. Sue then becomes obsessed with the disagreeableness of the "letter" of legal wedlock, noting to Jude that they are a little ahead of their time in seeing legality as a snuffer out of "cordiality and spontaneousness." They leave, unwed, the church where their union might have been legalized. Years go by. Children arrive, two of their own plus a son by Arabella, shipped home from down under. But the darkest fate of all awaits this proto-bohemian family. I'll say only that Jude, pronounced "a 'andsome corpse" at the end, seems the happiest of the lot.

Response by moralistic Victorians was harsh, and Hardy swore off the writing of novels, saying, "A man must be a fool to deliberately stand up to be shot at."

 Book Smart
Recommended Reading

If you enjoy the pessimism of this final Hardy novel, you'll want to read others. Start with *Tess of the d'Urbervilles*, equally gloomy and equally fascinating. Claire Tomalin's recent biography of Hardy is excellent.

The Assistant

Bernard Malamud

Malamud welcomed publicity from the public's embrace of the Robert Redford film of his first novel *The Natural*, partly from his dislike of being classified as a "Jewish American" writer, a pigeonhole he found reductive and limiting. (His enigmatic statement, "Every man is a Jew, though he may not know it," is often quoted.) *The Natural*, a story involving America's national pastime, has no Jewish characters. *The Assistant*, Malamud's second novel, draws material from his own difficult past. Malamud's father was a Russian Jewish immigrant, a grocer, as is the character Morris Bober. This simple but profound story with themes of suffering and grace has been compared with a morality play.

Members of the Bober family lead a hard-knock life. Morris labors in their woebegone store. His wife, Ida, shares the work and the poverty. Helen, the surviving child—a promising son, Ephraim, died of an ear infection—has given up college for secretarial work to help the family finances. As sufferers know, things are never so bad that they cannot get worse. Inept robbers cannot accept the meagerness of the day's earnings and bash Morris on the head in hopes of learning the whereabouts of the nonexistent stash.

Frank Alpine, born to an Italian family, brought up orphaned and Catholic, tumbles into the life of the Bobers. Seemingly a bit of good fortune when Morris is injured, Frank insists on working for no pay "for the experience." Down on his luck, he seems grateful for milk and rolls, the occasional sandwich. He surreptitiously sleeps on the cellar floor until he's offered a sofa, then a bed. The reader learns what is kept from the Bobers: Frank was the tall member of the thieving duo, whose faces were half-masked by handkerchiefs. Frank quietly returns his meager profit ($7.50) from the heist. Customers like him, and business picks up. Frank is no saint: he still occasionally slips bills from the till into his pocket, and his attraction to Helen Bober, whose "flowerlike panties and restless bras" he eyes on the clothesline, takes the repellent form of peeping on her shower-bound form through the bathroom window. Her attraction to him is matched by her ambivalence, as she hopes Nat Pearl, upwardly mobile law student to whom she yielded her virginity, will return into her life.

Reciprocal ethnic prejudice is openly presented: Frank sometimes feels bad that he's working for Jews, and Ida is uncomfortable with a goy in the house. Rehabilitation, redemption come slowly. Frank's hopes for himself are above his performance; he rescues Helen from a threatened rape in a public park only to ignore her affectionate negative as he himself draws her onto the "star-dark field."

There's a moving scene of transformation where, with only a jack-knife, he transforms a crude board into a bird, another into a flower, a tribute for Helen. She throws it in the trash. Still, the reader's heart has slow cause to lift as Frank comes to identify with the worthy model of the hapless but noble Morris, and the language of the book suggests Helen's eventual acceptance of him. In the novel's last paragraph Frank has himself circumcised and becomes a Jew. It's typical of Malamud that in a preface to one edition of the novel, he ecumenically states he hopes that Frank won't give up reading St. Francis as he takes on Isaiah.

The Magic Mountain

Thomas Mann (translated by John E. Woods)

Mann started this work in 1913, conceiving of it as a short project, a complementary pendant to *Death in Venice*, but the outbreak of the Great War turned his plans and his worldview awry. The "short project" saw completion in 1924, and the Nobel Prize for Literature came to Mann five years later. This richly complex novel draws on concepts from medicine, politics, theology, biology, botany, psychoanalysis, literature, philosophy, and the occult. Mann suggested that after reading these more than seven hundred pages, you should reread for fuller appreciation of his recurring images, but that's possibly a sly joke.

Hans Castorp, our questing if simple protagonist, comes from Hamburg, a patrician orphan about to begin his apprenticeship as an engineer at a steamship company. But first he goes for a visit to his cousin Joachim Ziemssen, a soldier taking the cure for tuberculosis in a sanitarium atop a mountain in Davos. Once Hans enters this sealed-off world *bei uns hier oben*—"of us up here"—he's in another country, a realm with its own rules, its own sense of time. It suits him. With the barest medical encouragement, he metamorphoses from visitor to patient, acquiring his fur-lined sleeping sack and latching on to the residents' custom of taking their temperature several times a day and exchanging results with their peers. He carries his chest x-ray in his pocket, the better to display it. The three weeks elongate into seven years; only when war breaks out does Hans, ashamed of his "phantom safety," make a "wild"—unauthorized—exit.

But before our final glimpse of him, spread-eagled in the mud of battle but struggling to his feet, Hans undergoes the education in life, death, and love on offer in the seductive lassitude of the mountaintop. Instruction in amour comes from Clavdia Chauchat. This Russian "hot cat" slams doors, bites her nails—all part of the book's motif of "eastern" lack of rigor. Her narrow hips, her "Kirghiz" eyes remind Hans of his boyhood passion for his schoolmate, Pribislav Hippe, of the bliss of borrowing his pencil for a few minutes one day. (As did Mann himself, Hans has unresolved same-sex longings and, much later, will ally himself with Clavdia's new lover, Meynheer Peeperkorn.) Hans declares his love to Clavdia. They converse in French, a phenomenon—aided by champagne laced with burgundy—that unties his Teutonic restraints. Speaking French, says Hans, is like speaking in a dream; it's speaking without speaking. When he pitches woo, it's a blend of the sweet—"you are the You of my life"—and the grotesque—"let me kiss your femoral artery." The coy narrator first implies nothing beyond words occurs, but we gradually deduce otherwise.

Further education comes from the lengthy verbal dueling (it later turns literal) of Settembrini, who sometimes speaks for Mann and sometimes parodies a glib humanist, and his antithesis, the Jewish-Communist-Jesuit Naphta, who, frighteningly, defines "terror" as what society really desires. Sometimes Hans learns about himself from himself: Illicitly skiing, he becomes lost in a snowstorm and hallucinates scenes of Arcadian delight and of macabre terror. He resists the lovely, dark, deep urge to lie down quietly, forever, in the snow, a heightened version of the lotus-eating spell of prolonged invalidism.

If novels were sporting events, this novel is the triathlon, but your effort is lavishly rewarded with scenes, characters, and ideas that engrave themselves into your mind. Not for nothing did Mann's children call him "Z" (for *Zauberer*—German for "magician.")

Walden

Henry David Thoreau

ere are the facts. In the spring of 1845 Thoreau began to build a cottage on land owned by his friend and fellow writer Ralph Waldo Emerson at Walden Pond, near Concord, Massachusetts. On Independence Day he moved in. He was able to live mostly on vegetables he himself grew, and he worked occasionally as a handyman to buy the odd bag of Indian meal. He left in September 1847 because he "had several more lives to live." His book *Walden* was published seven years later, in 1854.

Thoreau's name is on almost everyone's lips, *Walden* has become a popular synonym of "living alone with nature," and Thoreau gets name recognition from those who know none of his sentences. Some, I've found, believe he spoke to no other human being during his prolonged stay at Walden Pond, and others think that *Walden* is a kind of "how-to" book about living in the wild.

Although he spent plenty of time in his own good company, one section of *Walden* details the many visitors he had there, at least once twenty-five or thirty simultaneously. Similarly, he's very open about going into town every day or two "to hear some of the gossip" (not only casual conversation but newspapers). He describes this experience, if taken in "homeopathic doses," as being as refreshing as the rustling of leaves or the peeping of frogs. And in February of 1847, with many months remaining as a Walden-dweller, he gave two Lyceum lectures about his life at the lake. No dour hermit here—but a skilled writer who used his journal entries as the raw material for a text he reworked for years.

The scholar Michael West writes perceptively that Thoreau enjoyed playing on the reader's concept of him as a "nature-loving crank," and philosopher Stanley Cavell, who classifies Thoreau, along with Emerson, as "the founder of American thinking," notes that Thoreau typically "uses openness to conceal." Yes, *Walden* is a complicated book, a book that defies tidy taxonomy. Is it philosophy? Essays? A memoir? Nature writing? Mysticism? Social criticism? It's all of these—and none. While any of the nineteen sections can be read separately, only by going from start to finish can you appreciate the organic form of the book, the way Thoreau skillfully sculpts his two-year residence into the seasonal rhythms of a single year.

As you continue to read, you'll become aware of the recurring sets of opposites: civilization/the wild, philosophy/literature, the past/the future, humans/other animals, fantasy or imagination/observation and experience. Maybe you'll marvel, as I did, at how funny some of the book is. I was happy to discover Mark Van Doren's statement that "it was written in bounding spirits with eyes sparkling and tongue in cheek," but that view is darkened by West's assertion that Thoreau, whose family history included early deaths from consumption (he died at forty-five) used joke-making as an attempt to blot out the fact of death. Perhaps that defiance or denial of death underlies the close of the book, but his optimism for the individual and for the United States rings out with beauty: "There is more day to dawn. The sun is but a morning star."

Those lines are worth copying out, but you should memorize the earlier famous passage (section 2, paragraph 13) that begins, "I went to the woods because I wished to live deliberately, to front only the essential facts of life, and see if I could not learn what it had to teach, and not, when I came to die, discover that I had not lived."

Top Girls:
Strong Women, Admirably So and Otherwise

The Handmaid's Tale
Margaret Atwood

Jane Eyre
Charlotte Brontë

Moll Flanders
Daniel Defoe

Medea
Euripides

The Odd Woman
Gail Godwin

Vanity Fair
William Makepeace Thackeray

Anna Karenina
Leo Tolstoy

Kristin Lavransdatter
Sigrid Undset

The House of Mirth
Edith Wharton

A Room of One's Own
Virginia Woolf

> *The only advice, indeed, that one person*
> *can give another about reading*
> *is to take no advice.*
> —Virginia Woolf (from "How Should One Read a Book?")

CARYL CHURCHILL'S play *Top Girls* might well be on this list. It features five female historical characters as varied as Pope Joan, the Victorian traveler Isabella Bird, and Dulle Griet, heroine of a Brueghel painting who charges into hell, clad in an apron as well as more traditional armaments, there to confront devils.

The protagonists of the nine novels featured here have wills as sturdy as those of Churchill's crew. Some channel their energies toward lofty goals, some are intermittently admirable, and at least one amazes us with her power if not her purpose. In this last category is our earliest female character, the eponymous heroine of Euripides fifth-century BCE tragedy *Medea*. She achieves her ends, but we cringe at her means.

At the other end of the spectrum we have no reservations as we cheer on four other female protagonists. Charlotte Brontë's creation Jane Eyre struggles externally with repression in her home and her school, and internally with her unequal romantic attraction to her employer, the smoldering Mr. Rochester. Similarly, Kristin Lavransdatter, a woman of fourteenth-century Norway created by Sigrid Undset, amazes us as she stands up for the right to shape her own life—and she chooses many different shapes for herself in this three-volume work. Jane Clifford, main character of Gail Godwin's *The Odd Woman*, lacks the ferocity of Jane Eyre or Kristin Lavransdatter, but in her quieter way she stands up for principles she holds dear even though that act may deepen her long loneliness. The plucky narrator of Margaret Atwood's futurist novel, *The Handmaid's Tale*, has no real name of her own but is known only as "Offred" (of-Fred), a derivation that speaks volumes.

Likely opinions of four other female protagonists fall in the realm of ambiguity. Our brains know there's reason to criticize each of them, but our hearts cheer them on. This quartet of women all deal with the need for money and/or the respectability of an established social class and with the need for love, although they span three centuries and three countries: Moll Flanders inhabits eighteenth-century England (with a side trip to the colony of Virginia), Becky Sharp of *Vanity Fair* lives in England more than a century later and spends a good bit of time on the Continent. Anna Karenina lives in roughly the same time period but in Russia. And Lily Bart inhabits the newest country, the United States, in the newly arrived twentieth century.

The tenth book is Virginia Woolf's *A Room of One's Own*. A series of essays based on lectures given by Woolf in the late 1920s, this delightful work deals with the question of how women with literary talent may or may not be able to use it.

If you're wondering why Jane Austen and George Eliot are not on this list, know that I regard them as I regard Shakespeare and the Bible: the importance of reading them is too obvious to list! Supplement your reading of Eliot with Cynthia Ozick's *The Puttermesser Papers*.

The Handmaid's Tale

Margaret Atwood

The blurb on my edition of this book describes it as both "funny" and "horrifying." I agree. This combination is much of the charm of this novel that belongs to the category of books such as *Brave New World* and *1984* that we call futurist. Atwood began writing this novel in that ominous year of 1984, although she notes that she had the idea a few years earlier but didn't take it seriously until real life began to make her concept seem less fantastical.

Set in the fairly near future, the book depicts a familiar-looking country now known as Gilead and beset by a totalitarian religious regime so puritanically extreme that Baptists are hunted down as dissidents. (Atwood, a Canadian, leaves us in no doubt that Gilead is the former U.S.A.) It has devised a caste system for women that makes those of other futurist books look comparatively benign. Since environmental pollution has rendered most women infertile, those whose ovaries remain in good working order are named "Handmaids" (the name derives from the biblical story of Rachel and her maid Bilhah, the subject of the first of the novel's three epigraphs). Each is assigned to a "Commander," whose sterile wives have no choice but to collude with the handmaids in a bizarre monthly ritual wherein the handmaid forms a grotesque back-to-belly sandwich with the "Wife" while the Commander attempts to impregnate the former. A handmaid known only as "Offred" ("of Fred," her commander) narrates the tale. Fred's Wife, known as Serena Joy, suggests an amalgam of, say, Phyllis Schlafly (remember her?) and perhaps Tammy Faye Bakker (remember her?).

The Handmaid's lot is not a happy one, nor is the Wife's. And who wants to be an "Aunt" (full-time chaperones for the Handmaids), all cozily given monikers such as Cora or Lydia; you'd expect a Jemima except that you've been told all African Americans have been shipped to Africa. You'd rather be a Martha and do all domestic chores for the wealthy? Or maybe an Econowife, an all-purpose poor man's partner? Don't envy the Jezebels, a kind of high-class call girl who provides the illegal but nonmarital, nonprocreative sex we're not surprised to see provided for the alpha males. And if you're male, be sure you're straight, lest you find yourself hanging on a wall, victim of a Male Salvaging. Heterosexual males who don't toe the party line fare no better: their lusty behavior may lead them to the central and lethal spot in a Particicution.

You're getting the "horrifying" part, right? And how about the "funny"? Maybe the tiny wry smile you formed on reading of the Salvagings or the Particicutions would get even a little wider on reading of the Prayvaganzas or the fact that the stores all have biblically derived names such as All Flesh or Milk and Honey. So, all right, maybe "funny" is a bit of an exaggeration.

You come to care enormously about Offred and admire the way she piles up for herself, like a cairn, a small pile of the consolations of memory (her happy marriage to Luke, her daughter), of rebellion (buttressed by finding a message in Latin etched by the previous inhabitant of her room), of physical desire (a highly dangerous liaison with Nick), and of her taboo delight in the written language, in even such small allotments as the handling of Scrabble tiles during an illicit tryst, where spelling out *larynx* or *valance* or *quince* or *zygote* is described as being "voluptuous."

Plenty of faith, but no hope or charity.

Jane Eyre

Charlotte Brontë

The first edition of this 1847 novel billed itself as an autobiography, edited by Currer Bell. After its success, "Bell" claimed authorship and, in a preface, thanked readers for appreciating this "plain tale with few pretensions." The precise identity of the author and her gender took a little longer to become public knowledge.

"Plain tale" strikes modern ears strangely, for we find this story full of passion, mystic coincidences, even melodrama. The very phrases "Jane Eyre," "Mr. Rochester," and "the madwoman in the attic" resonate with even those unfamiliar with the book. The architecture of the basic plot suggests a Cinderella story: a young woman, barely out of boarding school, accepts a position at Thornfield Hall as governess for Adele, the French ward of one Mr. Rochester, himself not often in residence. Life there, with the company of the housekeeper, Mrs. Fairfax, is blandly pleasant, yet the hairs on the back of the reader's neck prickle to learn that Thornfield Hall has a mysterious third story with two rows of "small black doors all shut, like a corridor in some Bluebeard's castle," where occasionally a "curious cachinnation" (laugh) is to be heard.

Enter Mr. Rochester with his "dark, stern, strange" face and thick-chested masculine bearing. Except for the heft of the four-hundred-page volume we are holding, we expect the barriers of social class, a twenty-year gap in age, and a near-fiancée named Blanche Ingram to prove as flimsy as tissue paper and that happily-ever-after will be right around the corner. The expected union occurs ("Reader, I married him"), but not until Bluebeard's dark doors reveal their secret and our heroine undergoes much adventurous misery.

Yes, it's a "good read"; the preeminent novelist of the day, William Makepeace Thackerary, put aside everything to devote a whole day to the book (and astonished his servant who found him weeping over "some of the love passages"). Similarly, Virginia Woolf (who's not entirely admiring) allows, "The writer has us by the hand, forces us along her road, makes us see what she sees."

The plot enthralls, but Jane's character is even more gripping. The novel begins with her childhood: we meet her in "double retirement," on a window seat, behind closed curtains, looking at pictures of birds in "Lapland, Siberia, Spitzbergen, Nova Zembla, Iceland," suitable companions for a bleak and stormy emotional world with an unloving stepmother and her children. Somehow a spirit of independence allows Jane to endure this household, a boarding school whose rations make Oliver Twist's establishment look sumptuous, the shocking revelations at Thornfield, and a brief self-chosen period of wandering, homeless and hungry. Likewise, this corset of independence braces her sufficiently, late in the novel, to refuse a passionless marriage to the high-minded, handsome St. John Rivers, who seeks her wifely partnership as a missionary in India. With few literary predecessors for her independence, Jane is perhaps the first literary heroine not to be "pretty."

Book Smart
Recommended Reading

Loving *Jane Eyre* can lead you to Brontë's less famous novels (they're good too) and to the saga of the Brontë family: Lyndall Gordon's biography of Charlotte Brontë is especially interesting. And don't neglect Jean Rhys's *Wide Sargasso Sea*, a "prequel" that reminds us of the bracing effect of another point of view.

Moll Flanders

Daniel Defoe

s it autobiography or is it fiction? This may sound like a modern publishing conundrum, but this book came out in 1722. Is a child born of a poor, imprisoned mother doomed at birth? Does a woman have an equal chance in a man's world? These two questions, also very current, come from the life of the title character, whose fictional existence was lived out around 1613 to 1683.

Yes, this novel purported to be a woman's true account of her life (it's unclear when the reading public knew otherwise). The full title doubles as plot summary: "The Fortunes and Misfortunes of the Famous Moll Flanders, Who was Born in Newgate, and during a life of three-score Years, besides her Childhood, was Twelve Years a Whore, five Times a Wife (whereof once to her own Brother), Twelve Years a Thief, Eight Years a Transported Felon in Virginia, at last grew Rich, liv'd Honest, and dy'd a Pentitent. Written from her own Memorandums." To be fair, it was only her half-brother she married.

Was this entertaining work written for its sensationalism, the author's need to make a buck (or a pound)? Indeed, Defoe, a hardworking guy, once declared bankruptcy and was chronically in and out of debt. As he put it, "No man has tasted differing fortunes more/And 13 times I have been rich and poor." He also saw the inside of a prison (the same one Moll later inhabits), as punishment for a politically satirical pamphlet judged as containing "seditious libel." The son of a butcher named James Foe, he adopted the more genteel-sounding "Defoe" in adulthood and left journalism and pamphleteering for novel writing late, at the age of fifty-nine. His first novel, *Robinson Crusoe*, took the bones of a true story (that of the unfortunate sailor Alexander Selkirk) and transformed it into fiction. The fact that it sold well kept Defoe in the fiction game, offering up this supposed autobiography of a city-dwelling, thieving prostitute three years after the success of the story of the desert-island sailor.

But branding Moll Flanders as solely commercial in intent denies its survival and the power of the tale. Defoe has successfully infiltrated the psyche of a double outsider—woman and criminal. Virginia Woolf, no stranger to gender inequities two hundred years later, calls this book "indisputably great" and praised the genius of Defoe for putting in "more gold" than his generation could extract. Defoe makes Moll likeable. You know she's a dishonest rogue, but she's trying to survive in a harshly capitalistic, male society. "The market ran all on the men's side," as she puts it. She has a good heart and, when survival permits it, a generous spirit.

Early in the book, after Moll's first theft, Defoe shows her in breathless flight through a maze of London streets. That's a good metaphor for much of her life. We rejoice to see her end up happily, delighting in a loving trophy husband, whom she presents with such gifts as a silver-hilted sword and a scarlet cloak. When, in the novel's last line, Moll expresses her plans to repent for her wicked, wicked ways, we're glad we were there for the transgressions.

Medea

Euripides (translated by Michael Collier and Georgia Ann Machemer)

s this play, written in Athens in 431 BCE, a timeless tale about the oppression of women? Or is it a stunning piece of theater about a unique, larger-than-life woman? The answer, of course, is both.

Up to a point, the play seems a template of the potential for tragedy in the life of any woman in a culture that qualifies for the description "It's a man's world." In the simplest form of her biography, Medea has devoted every molecule of her being to the service of her husband Jason, the man who earned his status as hero by stealing the Golden Fleece. But like a modern-day male Ph.D., let's say, whose talented wife wrote his dissertation, it's no cliché to say Jason couldn't have done it without her. To win for Jason his literal sheepskin, she has forsaken her homeland, murdered her brother. Without her pharmaceutical skills, the reptilian guardians of the fleece would never have drooped their scaly eyelids. Not to mention the time she sweet-talked the daughters of Jason's enemy Pelias into killing and dismembering him. And now they're married, living in Corinth, parents of two young sons.

What's past is prologue, says Shakespeare. When the curtain rises on this play, whose action occurs in a single day, it's Splitsville. Always looking to ascend the ladder of advantage, Jason has announced his marriage to Creusa, golden daughter of King Creon. Ever so logically, he denies that this is a matter of *lexos*—bed-life—but a prudent plan to better his family's condition. His sons by Medea will gain status by alliance with their father's future royal children and, when you come to think about it, he explains, even the fortunes of Medea, that barbarian woman to whom he tossed off a marriage oath not valid in civilized Greece, will eventually benefit in a kind of trickle-down effect.

Every woman in the audience, at this point, loathes Jason, loathes his smarmy pseudorationality. Medea actively seeks this identification with her as she explains her plight to a chorus of women of Corinth. She cancels out men's claim to superior status because they risk death on the battlefield by noting she'd prefer to join the battle line three times rather than undergo the agony of childbirth once.

When Jason ventures on insult, Medea vows revenge—make that Revenge. Here, Euripides has her doff her Everywoman mask and claim her birthright as the literal granddaughter of the sun. Medea carries out the princess's fiery death by sending the children to her with a beautiful but deadly wedding gift—a robe and tiara crafted to ensure the immolation of the wearer. Next on the vengeance list: devastate Jason by killing their sons. She has a gorgeous speech, in the hearing of the chorus, agonizing over the conflict of her maternal love and the necessity of this decision. Careful listeners note the flaws in this impressive theatricality: in the first speech of the play Medea's old nurse foreshadows this move, noting that Medea hates her children now and feels no joy in seeing them. All that's left is for Medea to feast on Jason's visible ruin and, accompanied by the bloodied bodies of the children, light out for Athens in a *coup de théâtre*. Her mode of transportation? A sky-borne chariot pulled by dragons.

Book Smart
Recommended Reading

For a humorous modern variant on *Medea*, see Meg Wolitzer's *The Wife*.

The Odd Woman

Gail Godwin

J ane Clifford, a teacher at a midwestern university in the early
1970s, is "odd" in the sense of being single, as are the women in
the near-namesake title of George Gissing's 1893 novel *The Odd
Women*. She sometimes wonders if others see her as differently odd,
downright weird. She has a Ph.D. in English with a specialty in George
Eliot, another odd woman. She has a lover, a married man, art professor at another midwestern university, named Gabriel Weeks, whom
she sees when discreet trysts can be arranged. She has a family back
in Asheville, North Carolina: a loving mother, Kitty, a stepfather, Ray,
whose cruelty has haunted her dreams (he once hit her hard enough to
puncture her eardrum), and three half-siblings.

Readers now, thirty-five years later, can see her as oddly caught
between two Zeitgeists. Should she, as did her mother, have regarded
her brains as an impediment to a woman's central pursuit in life, the
establishment of a stable marriage? Why can't she, as her spiritual
daughters now do, throw herself more fully into her academic career
and launch into the writing of articles and books, pursue a tenure track
job? Although she earned her doctorate (there are evocative memories
of her sitting in her library carrel in a near trance, finishing her dissertation all through a snowy winter), the only research she's now pursuing is the impromptu tracking down of facts behind a family legend.
Her great-aunt Cleva eloped with an actor touring in the North Carolina mountains; Jane spends time fantasizing Cleva's rapid bonding
with him as he lured her onto that northbound train. This is not only
a family legend but a cautionary tale, for Act II of Cleva's tale, set some
months later, is a desperate scrawl to her sister: "Can someone please

come? The villain has left me." Cleva dies. Her inevitable baby grows up with a distant relative and is now the ultraordinary Cousin Frances. But Jane, a wonderful amalgam of imagination and intelligence, on a New York trip (a failed rendezvous with Gabriel) actually locates the nonagenarian Hugo Von Vorst, who as a young man had played the melodramatic villain, and, in a wonderful chapter, talks with him.

You come to know Jane better through her interactions with the appealing but maddeningly passive Gabriel and with old classmate Gerda Miller, who after a disastrous "marrying up" attempt, has launched herself into a role as "sexy doll" who "runs a feminist newspaper out of her basement." And you get to know her through Godwin's skillful narrations of her racing thoughts. Would it make this saleswoman happy if I bought this dress? How does my colleague Sonia Marks make her life work so well? If I feed this stray cat, will birds stop coming to my neighbor's bird feeder? If the sometime stalker of my neighborhood, the Enema Bandit, entered my apartment, how might I reason him into leaving?

You get to know more about women's lives of this era through Godwin's kaleidoscopic array: Kitty, Gerda, Sonia, the smiling and placating Marsha, the strong-minded half-sister Emily, the abandoned middle-aged wife Eleanor, Jane's African-American student Portia. But mainly you care about Jane Clifford, trying to find her own "best life," struggling to create, in Jane's words that describe her piano-playing neighbor, "something of abiding shape and beauty."

Vanity Fair

William Makepeace Thackeray

Thackeray's readership instantly understood the title when the novel came out in serial installments in 1847–1848. It alludes to the 1678 allegorical tale *The Pilgrim's Progress* by John Bunyan, whose seventeenth-century Vanity Fair was a place of worldly distractions that might interfere with a soul's progress to the Celestial City (heaven). Thackeray is not concerned with the destiny of souls, but he offers a withering view of this earthly life as a place where men and women, full of self-interest, scramble for pleasure and for applause.

Moving away from the original subtitle "Pen and Pencil Sketches of English Society," Thackeray, with his revised phrase "A Novel Without a Hero," supplies on the title page his own delightful drawing of a down-at-the-heels player, antique blunted sword by his side, leaning on what is presumably his trunk of props (one female puppet has fallen from the enclosure). Wig balanced absurdly atop his head, the showman gazes disconsolately into a cracked mirror. This none-too-stalwart "Manager of the Performance" will be our intermittent guide, showing us "some dreadful combats" as well as "some light comic business." This narrator's role is widely debated; see what you make of his remarks.

The novel offers a panoramic scene of mostly middle-class Londoners, at home and abroad. The organizing principle concerns the lives of two schoolmates, Becky Sharp (note the last name) and Amelia Sedley, just finishing six years at Miss Pinkerton's academy for young ladies. Their studies have been similar, but their backgrounds contrast. Amelia's father is a well-to-do merchant, while Becky is the rough equivalent of a scholarship student; her father is a drawing teacher, and her late mother was not only an opera dancer but French to boot. The contrasting treatment each receives as she leaves the school is the earliest satiric unfolding of the unfairness of the Fair, while Thackeray's description of each young woman's luggage is the first instance of Thackeray's keen eye for realistic nuances of society. Amelia is heading home to bide some genteel months before marriage to Anyone Suitable; Becky will spend a few days at the Sedleys before she makes her narrow bed as a governess. If Amelia and Becky had to be constrained in the costume of an allegorical figure, Amelia would be Sentiment and Becky, perhaps, Spunk. (A parallel American duo is Melanie and Scarlett in *Gone with the Wind*.)

The young women will stay in touch as each threads her way through the quadrille of marriage, maternity, changing financial fortunes, and life without a husband by her side. Readers will get much wry pleasure from the feckless George Osborne, the plump and gullible Jos Sedley, various members of the Crawley family, the steadfast Dobbin, and the venal Lord Steyne and will particularly enjoy deciding what they think of Becky and why.

This novel was Thackeray's first publication under his own name, his first expedition out of the world of hack journalism where he gave himself cutesy disguises such as "Michel Angelo Titmarsh." He knew the sadness of losing a wife to "madness," as his century phrased it, and the responsibility of bringing up their two young daughters on his own. His acquaintance with sadness may contribute to the murky nature of moral dilemmas in the novel. In letters Thackeray referred to donning "the jester's habit" in order to tell the truth and to his hopes for "a dark moral." Near the end of the novel, it is our narrator who queries, "Which of us is happy in this world? Which of us has his desire? Or, having it, is satisfied?"

Anna Karenina

Leo Tolstoy (translated by Richard Pevear and Larissa Volokhonsky)

Tolstoy's contemporary Fyodor Dostoyevsky termed it "a perfection." His brilliant exiled countryman of the twentieth century, Vladimir Nabokov (who lambasted Dostoyevsky), opened his lecture on Tolstoy by calling him "the greatest Russian writer of prose fiction." In an early novel Nabokov had even named a character Dorianna Karenina, for the heroine of "one of the greatest love stories." Oprah Winfrey likes it too.

Although the novel goes on for some fifty pages before we see Anna, wife to Alexey Karenin and mother of eight-year-old Sergey, and continues for fifty pages after she departs, the title gives her the undisputed starring role. Nonetheless, it's important to note the side-by-side plots: Anna's passionate adulterous affair with Count Alexey Vronsky unfolds in irregular alternation with the tale of the bobbling courtship and steadily satisfying marriage of Kitty Shcherbatskaya and Constantin Levin, said to represent many aspects of "Lev" (his Russian name) Tolstoy himself. The author's exquisite structure and style let the discerning reader listen to the two plots speaking to each other. For example, we first hear of Count Vronsky in the context of being a breaker of *Kitty's* heart. She has rejected Levin's marriage proposal because she believes an offer from the more glamorous Count is imminent.

Other subtle ironies abound. We first see Anna in the role of mender of troubled marriages: her brother Stiva Oblonsky, guilty of consorting with the French governess, has summoned Anna from St. Petersburg to help extract forgiveness from his wife, Dolly. It's this household that's directly evoked by the novel's famous opening line: "All happy families resemble one another, but each unhappy family is unhappy in its own way." On the train trip to Moscow, caroming fate seats Anna by Vronsky's mother, who soothes Anna's worries about this first separation from her little boy. On arrival, Countess Vronsky introduces Anna to her son, and Anna notes that each of them has talked much about her son. Before you know it, they're dancing the mazurka together. Thus, as critic George Steiner notes, Anna's tragedy begins, as it will end, on a train platform, with the atmosphere at this initial meeting quickly darkened by news that a train has crushed a railway guard to death.

The novel is suffused with the feelings and the motives of the characters, as Tolstoy engages us in a kind of psychological eavesdropping. You care about the vital and passionate Anna even as you judge her actions immoral or self-destructive. She rejects membership in the multitudinous ranks of married women in St. Petersburg discreetly having affairs, nor can she find herself content to renounce her position in society or, more painful, her son. (She has a dream about being married to both Alexeys.) Her conflicted love becomes overwhelming, even Vronsky cannot absorb it all—his treatment of his fallen horse Frou-Frou, beautiful, delicate, female, is a distressing prefiguring of Anna's future.

Tolstoy began undergoing his deep conversion experience (one that rejected organized Christianity) as he was finishing *Anna Karenina*. His choice of epigraph "Vengeance is mine; I will repay" (from the apostle Paul's letter to the Romans) thus takes on a strong sense of divine retribution.

Book Smart
Recommended Reading

If you find this often tormented, idealistic Russian nobleman intriguing, you'll enjoy going on to A. N. Wilson's *Tolstoy* with its rich details about his complex life and his grimly comic death.

Kristin Lavransdatter

Sigrid Undset (three volumes, translated by Tiina Nunnally)

This delightful novel about three stages of the life of a woman deserves to be better known. It pleases by two opposing forces: the strange and the familiar. The reader is plunged into exotic details of life in fourteenth-century Norway (women give birth while kneeling, warriors cover their fingers with rings of gold and precious stones) while simultaneously following the life path of the title character, which is full of the universals of sexual love, parent-child conflicts, jealousy, motherhood, and spiritual concerns.

Sigrid Undset, daughter of a Danish mother and a Norwegian father, came naturally to her interest in the past, for her father was an archeologist, but his early death robbed her of her chance at university education. Her path up to the double peak of commercially successful authorship and critical acclaim was harsh. At seventeen, she began writing, working at night after completing her day's work as a secretary for a German electrical company in Oslo, a position she held for eleven years. She did not crumble when a publisher who saw an early manuscript instructed her not to attempt any more historical novels: "You have no talent for it." Those of us who cheer for the underdog leap to our feet when we read of her receiving the Nobel Prize for Literature in 1928. Our cheers grow louder when we learn she gave away the money accompanying the award and, later, sold the gold medal itself for the benefit of children in Finland displaced by the Russian invasion. She endured World War II in exile in the United States (Brooklyn), making friends here with both Willa Cather and Marjorie Kinnan Rawlings.

Her heroine, Kristin, daughter of Lavrans and Ragnfrid, has more material advantages in her life but is equally indomitable about what she wants of life. Volume 1, "The Wreath," is a love story. After her betrothal to the kind Simon Darre, Kristen meets Erlend Nikulaussen and whirls into a pact of passion with him. But unlike their models, Tristan and Isolde, they do not pay with death and eventually wrench from Lavrans his consent to Kristin's wearing the heavy bridal crown with Erlend. The sequel, "The Wife," places Kristin as Mistress of Husaby and mother of five, then six, then seven sons (and sister-in-law to Simon). As Erlend becomes involved with a plot to remove the boy king, Magnus, and secure the throne for Haakon, we readers become intrigued by the intricate web of power politics as dictated by kinship alliance (Undset adapts many details from epic Icelandic sagas). The last volume in the trilogy, "The Cross," finds the Black Plague entering Norway and brings more focus to Kristen's increasingly spiritual side and to the role of the church in society of the time. (Undset herself, reared as an agnostic in a heavily Protestant country, converted to Catholicism shortly after finishing this book.)

Undset's American translator, making clear she intends a compliment, calls the book "a real 'soap.'" Any possible hint of melodrama in that remark is balanced by her biographer, who praises her realism, calling her "the Zola of the Middle Ages." Perhaps the greatest testimony of all to Undset's achievement is the fact that a larger-than-life statue of the fictional Kristin stands in the Norwegian valley of Sel and attracts more than ten thousand literary pilgrims each year.

The House of Mirth

Edith Wharton

"Do New York," said Henry James to his friend Edith Wharton, native of that city, after she had written a novel, *The Valley of Decision*—seldom read today—set in eighteenth-century Italy. She took his advice and produced this wonderful novel that came out first, in 1905, in eleven monthly installments of *Scribner's Magazine*. It deftly dissects and skewers Manhattan's upper-crust society of the 1890s, but it is more a poignant character study than a satire. As Edith Newbold Jones, Wharton was born into a wealthy family that prided itself on tracing its lineage back through the centuries, and she married (and later divorced) a man from a prosperous Boston banking family. Thus, she was uniquely positioned to observe gilded lives from an insider's perspective. Her family regarded her writing as a kind of social gaffe and took care not to refer to it.

The main character is the beautiful and intelligent Lily Bart, born neither to toil nor to spin, for like her creator, she belonged to a family accustomed to opulent living. But unlike the author's secure prosperity, the wealth of Lily Bart's family is tenuous. One year after Lily's brilliant debut into society, her father announces to his family that he is "ruined." He dies not long after, and after two years of unhappy making do, so does his wife. Lily, an only child, is taken into the reluctant care of a paternal aunt, Mrs. Peniston. No fortune trails in Lily's wake, and she now lacks the essential figure for a young woman of high expectations—the mother who, whether grossly or subtly, helps to negotiate this most delicate of mergers, the Suitable Marriage.

Lily's greatest assets are her beauty and her grace. By heredity and early imprinting of the luxurious life, she wants a husband who can provide her with life in a sumptuous setting. But unlike Jane Austen's Elizabeth Bennet, who magically finds love with a man of surpassing wealth and high character, Lily has for eleven long years found only princes of modest means or wealthy frogs. The upper-class marriage market allows for no old-timers, and at twenty-nine Lily knows it's time to be grateful to ensnare, say, Percy Gryce, priggish, dull, judgmental, rich as Croesus.

Lily's weakness or strength is her lack of single-mindedness. Although her brain tells her to go for Gryce, her spirit holds back. So she misses her chance, at a posh house party, to sit by Mr. Dull at church in order to chat with Lawrence Selden, with whom she can be her real self, since he, a lawyer of modest means, isn't marriage material. This double vision is with her through the entire book: she allows the wealthy and married Gus Trenor to cover her considerable debt for bridge-table wagers without realizing he and their social circle assume his quid means there will be a "quo."

Wharton depicts many fascinating lives in *The House of Mirth*, but the central consciousness of the book is always Lily: her life spirals downward after a reputation-threatening yachting cruise and the death of her aunt. She comes to live on a street "in the last stages of decline from fashion to commerce." The same phrase might be used of her but that her "untutored fingers" preclude her from earning a wage even as a trimmer of hats.

The heart of fools may be, as the Bible declares, in the house of mirth, but by the end of the novel Lily is no fool. Our admiration of her acquisition of clear-eyed and responsible honesty does only a little to lessen the bitterness of the novel's close.

A Room of One's Own

Virginia Woolf

Woolf's title phrase has become so much a part of the language of women's studies that it's instructive to remember it was first the title of this short book published in 1929. (And it's shocking to remember that only the previous year had the novel *The Well of Loneliness* by the female Radclyffe Hall been tried and found guilty of the charge of obscenity.) Woolf's book was an outgrowth of a magazine article based on lectures she had given the previous year at two women's colleges at Cambridge (coeducation was still far in the future at elite universities in both England and the United States). Asked to talk on the topic of "women and fiction," she made a strong case for a woman's economic independence as a prerequisite for her creativity. Woolf herself was fortunate to have not only money in her own right because of a legacy from her aunt but the additional fortunate circumstances of a rich intellectual legacy from her father, Leslie Stephen, and an extraordinary degree of emotional support from her husband, Leonard Woolf.

The book contains six chapters, all of which take up fascinating aspects of the question of women as writers. She begins with a look at the difference between women's colleges and men's colleges, even within the same university, and uses telling details about food and drink in each as subtle marks of the many ways in which women are discouraged from taking themselves seriously as thinkers. A later section anticipates many articles and books of the late twentieth century in its treatment of what she terms the "androgynous mind"; she follows the nineteenth-century writer Samuel Taylor Coleridge in her belief that the greatest minds are those that shun thinking "like a man" or "like a woman."

Perhaps the most memorable chapter is the third, which introduces the often-quoted observation that "Anon" was "often a woman." In this chapter Woolf raises an intriguing question: what if Shakespeare had been female? She postulates the existence of a sibling for William Shakespeare, a hypothetical sister named Judith, whose abilities and passion to use them equal those of her brilliant brother. But her society's resistant prejudices, its sneers and jeers at the attempts of an upstart female to penetrate the all-male world of the theater, defeat her. The genius Judith comes to illegitimate pregnancy and suicide and—in one of Woolf's many startlingly vivid details—burial at the crossroads near the twentieth-century Elephant and Castle bus stop.

 Book Smart
Recommended Reading

This short nonfiction book makes a good introduction both to writing about women's issues and to Woolf herself. For your next read on the former, try Sandra Gilbert and Susan Gubar's groundbreaking *The Madwoman in the Attic*. For Woolf herself, move on to novels she published just a few years earlier: *Mrs. Dalloway* (1925) and *To the Lighthouse* (1927). If you want to read more about Woolf and her literary circle, perhaps subject to overexposure in recent years, start with the biography by her nephew Quentin Bell (1972) or the more recent treatment by Hermione Lee (1997). Or be the first in your set to read her lighthearted biography of the dog of Elizabeth Barrett Browning, a canine with the memorable name of Flush.

Jury Duty:
Crimes of
Various Sorts

Continental Drift
Russell Banks

The Master and Margarita
Mikhail Bulgakov

In Cold Blood
Truman Capote

Crime and Punishment
Fyodor Dostoyevsky

The Scarlet Letter
Nathaniel Hawthorne

Atonement
Ian McEwan

Paradise Lost
John Milton

Early Autumn
Robert B. Parker

Uncle Tom's Cabin
Harriet Beecher Stowe

The Bonfire of the Vanities
Tom Wolfe

Life, being short, is better spent reading great works than mediocre ones.
—Denis Donoghue

QUICK. THINK of a great book that doesn't have a crime in it. It's harder than you'd think. We humans have been fascinated with transgressions ever since Adam and Eve took a bite of the forbidden fruit. (It was John Milton who made that fruit into an apple, but that's a story in itself.) Literal crimes, violations of the law, offer a wide variety of wonderful reading. Do you go for the thrill of the chase—who dunnit?—with the pleasure of tracking down clues under the guidance of an idiosyncratic detective? (Think of Rex Stout's Nero Wolfe on the rooftop with his orchids, Sue Grafton's Kinsey Milhone tooling around Santa Teresa in her VW. And I must mention my latest discovery of detective Terry Orr in Jim Fusilli's wonderful New York–based books.) Or is your thing the drama of the courtroom—will the culprit be punished?—with wily lawyers in a mano a mano legal struggle? Other crimeophiles dismiss quickly the guilty butler and his debt to society and find themselves enthralled by the reason behind it all: "Why would she *do* something like that? I thought she *loved* him."

Our list for this month offers you some good examples of literal crimes. You can't call yourself well read unless you know at least one of the detectives in a twentieth-century series. Spenser, literate gumshoe extraordinaire, is the protagonist in the Robert B. Parker novels, represented here by *Early Autumn*, one of the finest examples. If you like your crime interwoven with late-twentieth-century urban settings, you'll go for Tom

Wolfe's *Bonfire of the Vanities*, which gives us both the law and the order sides of things. For the locus classicus of the concept of crime and punishment, you'll choose Dostoyevsky's magnificent novel, almost 150 years old and as relevant as yesterday. Or if you want true crime, rather than the true-to-life variety, you'll select Truman Capote's *In Cold Blood*; a new generation knows this nonfiction novel through film, but the book is as awing as ever.

In its larger sense, the concept of crime invades many realms unknown to the heavy tread of the policeman or the pounding gavel of the judge. Hawthorne's *The Scarlet Letter* lets you wrestle not so much with the identity of the criminal as with the nature of the crime: who's really to blame here? Russell Banks's *Continental Drift* deals with the mental agony of a man who knows he's done wrong, while Ian McEwan's *Atonement* focuses on the mental processes of the accuser more than those of the accused. Another two choices—*Uncle Tom's Cabin* and *The Master and Margarita*—offer, respectively, Harriet Beecher Stowe's depiction of the crime of slavery that helped bring about the Civil War and Bulgakov's depiction of supernatural romps through 1930s Moscow with a latter-day Lucifer. And with the mention of that name, we are reminded that all of this transgressing goes right back to the primal crime scene of the Garden of Eden so wonderfully rendered by John Milton in his epic poem *Paradise Lost*.

Continental Drift

Russell Banks

R ussell Banks grew up in a working-class family in New Hampshire and later lived in a Florida trailer park. (After the publication of this novel he's come to know what it's like to be a professor at Princeton and to achieve critical and financial success from his books and films of two of them, *The Sweet Hereafter* and *Affliction*.) The diversity of his background combines well with his enormous talent as he explores what he calls the "interconnections between politics and religion and race." These themes figure intensely in Banks's thirteenth novel, *Cloudsplitter*, an account of fiery abolitionist John Brown, but they are also present in his eighth novel, my personal favorite, published in 1985.

This novel's unusual structure presents two plots in alternating chapters: the tale of Bob DuBois (locally pronounced, we're told, Dooboys), an oil burner repairman in Catamount, New Hampshire, married and the father of two daughters and, later, a son, and the life of Vanise Dorsinville, a young, illiterate woman in Haiti, single mother of a baby. William Faulkner uses this technique of alternating story lines in his novel *Pylon*, and at least one critic called the first pages of this novel "Faulknerian." Arthur Miller comes to mind as well, for Bob might be a latter-day descendent of Willy Loman, another decent man whose tragedy stems from his yearning.

Compared with Vanise's life, Bob's looks prosperous, but the daily measure of his existence is not against that of an impoverished Haitian but against the presence of better-off residents of the United States, the sort of people ubiquitous on television and in advertising. Bob and Vanise have in common that longing, sometimes called "American," for a better life, the belief that lighting out for a new location may allow a new self to flourish. Bob goes to Florida, following the overstated promises of his brother Eddie, full of "strut and brag," while Vanise, who also has a brother in Florida, leaves Haiti for the sake of Claude, her adolescent nephew who accompanies her.

Vanise's tale bores into us through its extremes of hardship (she endures rape—as does Claude—forced labor, betrayal) and through the "otherness" of her devout practice of voodoo. I longed for a back-of-book glossary as I strove to understand exotic terms like *loa* and entities like Legba and the frightening Ghede. (These three are, respectively, a spirit that can go between God and humans, a benign spirit who delivers the messages of God, and the spirit of death.) But I am more powerfully affected by her counterpart, Bob. Perhaps it's his complete ordinariness that so powerfully produces, in Vladimir Nabokov's phrase, "a throb in the throat of the story."

The story lines meet when Bob pilots a boat taking stranded Haitians from the Bahamas to Florida. When the Coast Guard appears, Tyrone, the Jamaican entrepreneur, starts hurling "the cargo" into the sea. Though emotionally scarred, Vanise alone survives. Bob's guilt, his decent determination to find Vanise to give her the money paid him by the dead passengers, leads him to Miami's Little Haiti and to his dark fate.

However gripping the book as a whole, it's the "Invocation" and, even more fully, the epilogue-like "Envoi" that grab me hard. Paraphrase or summary falls short of justice. Go and read.

The Master and Margarita

Mikhail Bulgakov (translated by Diana Burgin and
Katherine Tiernan O'Connor)

Polysemous. That's a fancy literary criticism word for this book;
literally meaning "many seeded," it refers to the fact that there
are four different plotlines that converge late, very late, in the
novel. I prefer a descriptive line given to me by a perceptive young
reader—"This book is a circus of the psyche." Much is occurring, and
sometimes it's a little overwhelming, but you finish the book with a
sense of appreciation for its unending energy, its infinite variety.

Here are the four rings of the mental circus: A satire on life in the
Soviet Union in the Stalinist 1930s, particularly as its restrictions
affected creative thinkers in Moscow (the novel couldn't be published
until long after Bulgakov's death in 1940). The love story of the two
title characters that, strangely, emerges fairly late into the book. A vivid
retelling of Jesus' trial before Pontius Pilate and of the Crucifixion. A
spin-off of Goethe's *Faust*, the source for the epigraph to Part One: ". . .
and so who are you, after all?" "—I am part of the power which forever
wills evil and forever works good." As you go along, you think you're
understanding the interrelations of the four plots, only to have an epilogue replace your exploded theory with yet another way of thinking.
(Written shortly before Bulgakov died, the epilogue was pasted in on
the final page of the manuscript. Scholars wonder if, granted a longer
life, Bulgakov would have retained it.)

Circus is one metaphor for this dazzling book; magic show might
be another. Characters within various parts of the novel and you, dear
reader, have occasions to question whether supernatural events are
occurring or whether you're being superbly manipulated by a magician
skilled in misdirection and illusion (and are not all novelists conjurors

of a sort?). Let's zoom in on the two parts of the plot that call on *inter-textuality*, another chichi literary term, this one describing the way some texts draw on a reader's knowledge of other texts.

The more you already know about the biblical story of Jesus' trial and crucifixion, the more you'll enjoy detecting and appreciating the novel's variations. "The Master" of the title seems to be writing a new tale about the trial and execution of "Yeshua Ha-Notsri," aka Jesus of Nazareth. These interspersed chapters, my personal favorites, are written in a very different style from the rest of the novel. Pilate wears a "white cloak with a blood-red lining." He suffers from terrible headaches. He loves his dog, Banga. Yeshua may be a supernatural being who reads Pilate's mind, or he may be a sensitive and perceptive human being who knows how to interpret body language and nuances of wording.

Similarly, the more you already know about the Faust legend Goethe was following in the nineteenth century, the more you'll enjoy reading about the seemingly diabolic Woland and his companions, one a cat "big as a hog and pitch-black . . . and sporting a mustache like a reckless cavalryman's." In its essence the legend depicts the learned Faust, who contracts to sell his soul to Mephistopheles in exchange for experiences not otherwise available to him, including an orgiastic "Walpurgisnacht." (Mick Jagger is said to long to play Bulgakov's Woland in a film, and doubtless the song "Sympathy for the Devil" is an offshoot of that desire.)

Get the book and plunge in. If you're like me, your head may spin a little, but you'll close the novel with a desire to start it all over again.

In Cold Blood

Truman Capote

No matter how satisfying the on-screen moments of the 2005 film *Capote* or 1967's *In Cold Blood*, the beautiful writing in this book is an experience of a different order.

After reading a newspaper item about the brutal shotgun slaying of the Clutter family in the small western Kansas town of Holcomb, Truman Capote contacted William Shawn, editor of *The New Yorker*, about writing a story on the effect of these brutal, unsolved murders on this small community. Fast-forward to five years later: the two murderers have been caught, tried, and executed, and Capote is the acclaimed author of what many saw as a new subgenre of literature: the nonfiction novel. (Capote's on-site research in Kansas was greatly helped by the assistance of his childhood friend Nelle Lee, soon to become famous in her own right as Harper Lee, author of *To Kill a Mockingbird*.) Capote's brand of New Journalism influenced writers such as Tom Wolfe and Norman Mailer. Capote applies to this true story such literary techniques as flashbacks, detailed interviews, shifts in time, and an omniscient third person point of view.

We shudder with delighted horror to read of the violent deaths of the Clutter family, including Herb Clutter, the community's best-known citizen and a successful rancher, his wife, and the two children living at home. Identifying with these victims is almost a reflexive action.

Less simple, however, is the fact that Capote also compels our sympathy with the killers. Richard Hickok, who frequently described himself with the phrase "I'm a normal," was inspired by a fellow convict's tale of the prosperous Clutter spread to conceive the plan of the robbery, a robbery along with sidekick Perry Smith. Neither man had an easy upbringing, but Capote brings out more fully the pathos of Perry Smith's life. His early abuse and his lack of roots are the tragic but common stuff of criminal histories; Capote gives us much more. We learn that the nomadic Smith carried with him a cardboard box full of the meager souvenirs of his "lonely, mean life"—a scrapbook of magazine pictures of bodybuilders, a soiled pillow from Honolulu, the foot of an Alaskan bear. We are frequently reminded of his short stature (a phenomenon shared by Capote), of his legs injured badly in a motorcycle accident (last mentioned as an appendage to his hanged body, "the same childish feet, tilted, dangling"). Capote makes it hard for us to remember only Smith's villainy when he lets us know how Smith, when first jailed, tames an intruding squirrel, dubbing his new pet "Big Red."

You can certainly get pleasurably caught up in all the collateral details of Capote's personal acquaintance with the criminals, the criticism he later received for not doing more to save them, the guilt he may have felt over secretly longing for the often-delayed execution so that he could complete his book, but in the end what touches you is Capote's alchemy with words. You sense this power from the first paragraph of the book when Capote describes Holcomb's grain elevators as "rising as gracefully as Greek temples." It's not a bad image for Capote himself, a man with a fluttery lisp who lived an openly gay life as early as the Eisenhower years, a man who, many thought, often squandered talent and integrity in exchange for riches, fame, and a party for 540 of his closest friends. You can learn more about all these things in Gerald Clarke's excellent biography *Capote* or Deborah Davis's *Party of the Century*. But when all the glitter has faded, this book will loom up in your memory as gracefully as those Arcadian grain elevators.

Crime and Punishment

Fyodor Dostoyevsky (translated by Richard Pevear and Larissa Volokhonsky)

Why has there been no television series based on the life of Dostoyevsky? The father of this renowned nineteenth-century Russian novelist was murdered by his own serfs when the motherless son was only eighteen. An epileptic, the young Dostoyevsky added to his problems by becoming a gambling addict. Now add in his arrest for the writing of dissident political opinions and his sentence to death by firing squad, which at the last moment was changed to eight years of exile, penal servitude in chains followed by an enforced term in the Russian army. Rather than losing his mind as did one fellow prisoner during the pre-execution ordeal, Dostoyevsky in his Siberian exile experienced a religious conversion and, on release from the military, began writing.

It's a tribute to Dostoyevsky's genius as a writer to note that his novels, perhaps especially *Crime and Punishment*, are equally extreme, dramatic, and enthralling. The panoramic plot fits bulkily into the nutshell of plot summary. Poverty has forced a brilliant student, Rodion Raskolnikov, to withdraw from the university. He spends days in his tiny apartment—a "cupboard," a "kennel," a "coffin"—thinking. These thoughts produce a plan to kill, with an axe, an old pawnbroker. This premeditated murder, which quickly engenders a second but spontaneous twin, occurs early in the novel. The reader spends the hundreds of ensuing pages trying to discern what, precisely, was his motive and what, exactly, is going on his head, in his soul, in the next two weeks. The "crime and punishment" of the title are not depicted as disparate steps but conjoined elements like lightning and thunder.

Will he be caught? Will he confess? (Am I, the reader, hoping he'll escape the claws of the police?) The galloping pace of the pages belies the intense amount of work that Dostoyevsky, we know, put into the novel, experimenting with differing modes of narration before deciding on the unusual blend of know-all narrator and third-person interior monologue.

We are fascinated by this complicated young man, whose name contains the Russian root word for "split," and the contrasting facets of his nature make him an enigma we long to pierce. (For a real-life American parallel of this "fantastic, gloomy case" involving "bookish dreams" and "a heart chafed by theories," you may enjoy learning about the 1924 Leopold-Loeb murder case or reading the fictionalized version in Meyer Levin's novel *Compulsion*.) But beyond this intriguing solipsist lies a vast tapestry of life in the slum section of St. Petersburg: the Marmaladov family—the good-hearted but drunken father; his saintly daughter Sonya, a Magdalene who earns the family's living on the street; Katerina, his self-sacrificing snob of a second wife—Razumikin, the friend who falls in love at first sight with Dunya, the smart and loving sister of Raskolnikov, who astonishes us, at one point, by pulling a revolver out of her purse. This partial catalogue cannot omit Svidrigailov, another split soul, whose presence makes us, by relief, reexamine Raskolnikov's nature, and Porfiry, the police detective whose amiability masks the gleam of his snare-trap mind.

Book Smart
Recommended Reading

Reading this novel is likely to make you a member of the posthumous fan club of Dostoyevsky, for his dual powers of plot construction and character development allow him to create a world and allow us to enter that world. Move on to *Notes from the Underground* and to his last novel, *The Brothers Karamazov*—at 824 pages, not a word too long.

The Scarlet Letter

Nathaniel Hawthorne

Call me superficial, but I must disclose that my attitude toward Hawthorne changed in 1983, when the U.S. Postal Service issued a stamp bearing his visage. "He's so handsome!" I cried and set out to reinvestigate his works. Punitive teaching of this novel scarred me early. This second chance showed me why *The Scarlet Letter* deserves to be called "America's first true psychological novel" and why Malcolm Cowley considered it New England's version of "the essence of Greek tragedy." Close friend Herman Melville gave his fellow author the accolade of being "deep as Dante."

Everyone knows the title. (Perhaps you recall the *New Yorker* cartoon where a smiling young woman with "A" on her bosom is outbeamed by another young woman sporting an "A+.") In its most surface meaning, the letter stands for "adultery," the crime and sin of Hester Prynne, resident of Boston in the mid-1700s. Her husband sent her ahead from England, seemingly not fulfilling his pledge to follow. Hester does not fully repent of her adulterous passion with the Reverend Arthur Dimmesdale: "What we did had a consecration of its own," she says to him. "We felt it so!"

Dimmesdale bears a "reputation of whitest sanctity" (think "whited sepulcher"). His eloquence and English education have not sullied his image as a man who has "kept himself simple and childlike." He has given no public acknowledgment of his liaison with Hester and his paternity of their daughter, Pearl. His secret guilt tortures him, imprinting a simulacrum of a scarlet *A* on his heart.

Add a third leg to this triangle and you've got a great plot. Hester's husband is indeed in Boston. He's now called Roger Chillingworth, a name whose frigid connotation is complemented by his twisted, stooped shoulders. He's diabolically interested not in justice but in revenge. He insinuates himself into Dimmesdale's house and, longing to pluck out his mystery, attempts to invade his heart.

A sketch entitled "The Custom House" precedes the novel itself. In addition to satirical in-jokes about Hawthorne's recent unhappy employment there, it provides a fine introduction. A character purporting to be the author himself happens on a passel of papers in the attic wrapped in a crimson rag partly consumed by "a sacrilegious moth." The cloth reveals itself to be the capital letter A. The narrator briefly places it on his breast and feels a burning sensation. He's hooked. Looking ahead to a figurative moonlit room where Action and Imagination meet, he knows he must use the notes wrapped with this cloth to tell the tale of Hester Prynne.

How appropriate that Hawthorne was born on the Fourth of July! His ancestors were influential members of the early settlement, one a magistrate who banished or fined Quakers, another a judge in the 1692 Salem witchcraft trials. These men were "Hathornes," and we hardly wonder that Nathaniel altered the spelling of his name, as if to set himself slightly apart. Creating literature out of a fairly barren culture, Hawthorne has influenced American writers for more than 150 years. Henry James, who says he wept when Hawthorne died, wrote his biography. More recently, John Updike's fascination with *The Scarlet Letter* has revealed itself in three volumes that update (or parody) its elements.

So check out the original of that postage stamp, a portrait by Charles Osgood in the Library of the Peabody Essex Museum in Hawthorne's hometown of Salem, Massachusetts, and read this book. And stay away from the film version starring Demi Moore. Hester Prynne she ain't.

Atonement

Ian McEwan

Before you come to the "gotcha" ending (the phrase comes from David Wiegand of the *San Francisco Chronicle*) of this book, you've had a fantastic journey over widely varying fictional landscapes: a sultry day in the summer of 1935 in the *luxe* house of the Tallis family in the English countryside, the painful retreat of the British army from Dunkirk in 1940, the life of a probationer nurse in a London military hospital around that time, and a leap to 1999 when members of the Tallis family reunite at their old home, now a hotel.

Much of the book is presented through the eyes of Briony Tallis, thirteen years old in the first segment of the novel. Precociously talented and in love with the stories in her head, Briony assumes that her view of events is The Truth. She's just forsaken her previous literary love, the writing of playlets that she can cast with family members, for the more subtle genre of the novel, a mode that allows fuller play of the author's subjectivity. On this sweltering day she inadvertently witnesses events that disturb her. First, her older sister Cecilia, a recent graduate of Cambridge, strips to her underwear and dives into the pool of a fountain in the presence of Robbie Turner, son of the family's charlady and, thanks in part to financial help from Briony's father, also just come down from Cambridge. He has achieved a first-class degree that outshines Cecilia's third. That evening, Briony sees Robbie "assaulting"—her word—Cecilia in a secluded nook of the family library. Late that night, when her visiting fifteen-year-old cousin, Lola Quincey, is attacked by the lake, Briony has no difficulty giving her testimony—eyewitness from afar—that the rapist was Robbie.

The abundance of mysteries, miscarriages, and mistakes suggests a latter-day *Midsummer Night's Dream*: "Such tricks hath strong imagination." Lola's identical twin brothers vanish but are found hours later by Robbie: the shoulder-riding boy gives Robbie the silhouette of a grotesque giant. A Meissen vase, a precious family heirloom, gets broken. Robbie writes two drafts of a letter to Cecilia and, in a move that out-Freuds Freud, places the soul-relieving obscene version in an envelope that he gives to the terminally curious Briony to deliver to her sister. A houseguest, Paul Marshall, extols his family's product, Amo, a chocolate bar that contains no chocolate. Its name echoes the Latin for "I love" but may appeal to military suppliers with its phonetic doubling of "Pass the ammo."

The war pages, seen through Robbie's eyes, limn a distinctly unmagical landscape; similarly, the scenes in the war hospital where Briony changes bandages and sluices bedpans provide a look at the horrors of war accessible to women.

The one-word title of the book raises unanswerable questions about how we handle our most serious mistakes. Can they ever be redeemed? Ultimately, though, this fascinating novel is about time, memory, and the ways in which writers of fiction are godlike in their creation of a paper world: "Let there be whatever I want there to be."

Book Smart
Recommended Reading

Many of McEwan's other novels intrigue the reader, each in its own special way. Try *Amsterdam* with its wry philosophical outlook and its glimpses at euthanasia. Or go for *Enduring Love* with its focus on "erotomania," obsessive romantic love. Another novel, *Saturday*, treats street crimes, antiwar protests in London, poetry, and brain surgery.

Paradise Lost

John Milton

A talented student, fresh from her first encounter with Milton, tells me that if poems were fruits, *Paradise Lost* would be a pomegranate: challenging to crack open, hard to eat, but ultimately quite tasty. This analogy is insightful, and those of you who know the classical myth about Persephone being abducted by the God of Hell may be able to take the image a step further. This challenging epic dealing with Christian-centered theological concerns is indeed hard to approach. Instead of suggesting a resolute march through all twelve books of blank verse, I recommend, first, a shorter three-step process. Step One: Read Books I and II, Milton's account of the newly fallen angels waking to find themselves in newly created hell. Step Two: Go straight to Books IX and X, Milton's account of the successful temptation of Adam and Eve—the response of our "grand parents" (Milton loves serious puns), and Satan's reception back in hell as he attempts to give his victory speech. Step Three: Read the last five lines of Book XII, the end of the epic.

What will this one-third of the epic give you? A lot. Books I and II will bring you into a world that caused poet William Blake to say that "Milton was of the devil's party without knowing it." Milton, a devout Christian, had been safely dead for 116 years by the time of Blake's statement, but one almost expects the older poet to rise from the grave to exact retribution or at least apology from Blake. Milton's Satan, the barely tarnished fallen Lucifer, is heroic, commanding, admirable. He is cast in the mold of classic heroes like Achilles and Aeneas. He knows how to be in charge, how to hide private griefs while consoling his troops, how, in short, to Look Good.

It's hard not to fall in love with Satan and with some of the lesser devils. Belial, for example—"a fairer person lost not Heaven"—offers a Hamlet-like appreciation of life, even with its sorrows: "For who would lose, though full of pain, this intellectual being / Those thoughts that travel through eternity?" Who can fail to be stirred by the very different sentiment embodied in lines such as "The mind is its own place and in itself / Can make a heaven of hell, a hell of heaven."

When you finish Books I and II, mostly set in the newly built city of Pandemonium (Milton's coinage literally means "all-devils" or, roughly, Devil City), you're ready to go to Book IX. Here, Milton follows the book of Genesis in his account of Eden before the Fall and of the temptation by Satan in the form of a snake, but he has plenty of room to add his own embroidery. He follows the Bible and also seventeenth-century thinking in his account of Eve as happily subservient to Adam, but he departs from the theological orthodoxy that makes sex, even between married couples, a product of the Fall of Man. Milton depicts Adam and Eve blissfully united in sex before Satan ever rears his snakely head. Book X displays the wonderful scene, original with Milton, of Satan, while launching into a gloating victory speech, feeling his arms growing to his sides, and seeing himself and all his followers, against their wills, transformed into snakes, all their former eloquence turned to hisses, to the taste of ashes.

All that remains is to skip to the final lines of the epic, lines both lyrical and heartbreaking. These lines depicting Adam and Eve leaving Eden miraculously marry the mingled sense of exile and discovery, of nostalgia and potential, of looking before and after.

Early Autumn

Robert B. Parker

There are two reasons why I haven't tried to lure Spenser, the detective in this novel and some thirty others, into running away to the South Sea Islands with me. One, he's a fictional character, and two, he's devoted to an annoying girlfriend, Susan Silverman.

Why am I so enamored of Spenser? It's his paradoxical mixture of tough and sensitive. An ex-boxer and policeman turned private eye, Spenser is like Odysseus, the man who is never at a loss. He knows how to deal with thugs (verbal abuse first, violence if necessary) and how to make corn bread. He's verbally sassy and savvy. He can lay down a trail of literary allusions with the best of them. (Parker, role model as well as author, has a Ph.D. in literature with a dissertation on the "violent heroes" of Dashiell Hammett, Raymond Chandler, and Ross Macdonald.)

Early Autumn is the seventh novel (1981) and my favorite in the Spenser series. It shows Spenser in his non-thug-bashing role more fully than most. Sure, he and Hawk, his amoral, African-American sometime sidekick (seen here glugging Taittinger Blanc de Blancs from the bottle), do a smidgen of shooting and toss a bad guy off the Mass. Ave. Bridge into the Charles River, but most of the pages show Spenser as a crucial life coach to Paul Giacomin. Paul is a fifteen-year-old boy, sheltered, fed, and clothed (tackily) by warring parents but a neglected child. Patty Giacomin, his mother, enters on page 2. You could be reading a Chandler novel: the seductive prospective client, dressed in "no-nonsense elegance," enters the gumshoe's office. He ponders her figure, smiles, and mentally reflects, "Time was they started to undress when I smiled, but I guess the smile had lost a step."

On to the crime: Mel Giacomin, Patty's husband, has taken Paul to an undisclosed location. Spenser's job: find the boy and return him to Patty. Piece of cake. Spenser also puts in some bodyguard duty, and by the end of the book *he's* the technical criminal, threatening to blackmail both Ma and Pa Giacomin (sluttiness and insurance fraud, respectively) if they don't get with his plan and enroll Paul in a boarding school.

The bulk of the novel places Spenser and Paul in a property up in Maine (ceded to the annoying Susan in a divorce settlement). He's able to give Paul a crash course in becoming both a male and a human. Weight lifting, running, and hitting a punching bag deftly nailed to a tree are mandatory, and Paul and Spenser begin a summer's work of building a cabin. Spenser quotes Frost and Shakespeare and, inspired by two flirtatious squirrels, Keats's "Ode on a Grecian Urn." Even Susan stops sulking about Spenser's absence and researches appropriate boarding schools for Paul, who's showing signs of a passion for dance, a welcome replacement for his earlier all-purpose shrug. He learns to tolerate the Red Sox games on the radio and how to choose when no option is great. The cabin gets built as early autumn stalks the land, but Paul, with new muscles and confidence, is prepared. And, as Spenser has taught him, "Readiness is all."

I'm always happy at Paul's walk-ons in some of the later novels: Spenser as father figure is more appealing with Paul than with Pearl, "the wonder dog," who makes later child-surrogate appearances. Must have been Susan's idea.

Uncle Tom's Cabin

Harriet Beecher Stowe

While everyone can quote Lincoln's greeting to the author as "the little lady who started this big war," most today neglect the book itself. That's too bad, because reading it is a fascinating experience. You see with double consciousness how it looks now and how it looked in the early 1850s. First published serially—forty weekly installments in the *Washington National Enquirer* in 1851–1852—it roused word-of-mouth enthusiasm. In book format later in 1852, it galvanized its readers to action.

The book's subtitle, "Life among the Lowly," tells us what Stowe was trying to do: to depict realistically the lives of enslaved men, women, and children, to replace the abstract noun *slavery* with human faces and bodies. The novel has two plots: the story of the title character, the Christlike Tom, and the story of the Harris family. At the start of the novel Tom and Eliza Harris are both in bondage to the Shelby family in Kentucky. Within the repellent category of slave-owners, Mr. and Mrs. Shelby and their son George are relatively benign, treating their chattel kindly—unless, of course, financial pressure should compel their sale. Tom, valuable because loyal and highly capable, is to be sold down the river by the rapacious Mr. Haley, who also takes a fanciful whim for the son of Eliza, who's young enough to be capering about the household. The tyrannical owner of George Harris, Eliza's husband, is so insecure a man as to resent excellence even among the enslaved. To humble the ingenious George, he removes him from his hired-out factory work, where he's made a bit of a reputation by inventing a hemp-cleaning machine.

The Harris family plot strand has hair-raising episodes, but the family ends up happily. Not so for Tom. In Louisiana, he is first bought by the relaxed and indulgent Mr. St. Clare. But Mr. St. Clare dies early in an accident, and his selfish widow sells Tom to Simon Legree, who among the hell of slave-owners is ninth-circle. Amid a welter of beatings and brutality, Tom remains steadfast even unto death, the martyred embodiment of the gospel of love, an avatar of the man who died on the cross asking forgiveness for his tormentors. Anyone today, however, who thinks "Uncle Tom" should refer to a person of color who kowtows to the powerful must read Tom's stoic refusal to give Legree the information he wants about Tom's escaped comrades: "I han't got nothing to tell, Mar's," says the knowledgeable Tom, legalistically truthful.

Stowe was the daughter, wife, and sister (and, later, mother) of ministers. The book is a kind of sermon, infused with not only Christian principles but with the language of biblical allusions, quotations, and hymns. She was repelled by the passing of the 1850 Fugitive Slave Law that made even Northerners complicit in slavery. As a Christian, she writes this book in the pamphleteering spirit of a reformer in its deepest sense, one who seeks to reform the human heart. In the final chapter of the book version, she makes a direct appeal to her readers. Stowe's nineteenth-century readers found the book so compelling that, commercially, it ranked second only to the Bible.

James Baldwin, writing from the perspective of a black man in the 1950s, heaps wonderfully phrased scorn on the book. Do read his essay "Everybody's Protest Novel," but balance it by looking at the recent refutation of his claims by Henry Louis Gates and by reminding yourself that a hundred years earlier Frederick Douglass—hardly a lackey—printed a highly laudatory review in his newspaper and continued to champion the novel.

The Bonfire of the Vanities

Tom Wolfe

Maybe you know Tom Wolfe as a progenitor of the New Journalism, who burst on the book scene in 1965 with his collection of essays *The Kandy-Colored Tangerine-Flake Streamline Baby*. Or the man who contributed to the language such pulse-tapping phrases as "good ol' boy," "radical chic," "the right stuff," and "the me decade." Or the writer who wrote the 1989 essay in *Harper's*, "Stalking the Billion-Footed Beast," that got the reading and writing community arguing over realism versus modernism and who then incited a literary feud by calling Norman Mailer, John Updike, and John Irving "the three stooges." Or maybe you just know him as "the writer who wears a white suit."

This 1987 book is more than 650 pages long, and you wish it were longer. Although it's Wolfe's eleventh book, it's his first work of fiction, a novel that transfixes the whirling, scrambling, iridescent pixels of New York in the 1980s and makes them stand still for our inspection. The title alludes to the *falo delle vanita*, the 1497 bonfire into which affluent Florentines, seduced by the fanatical rhetoric of Savonarola, a Dominican abbot, flung their fripperies. Sumptuous garments, wigs, playing cards, lascivious literature, makeup, sexualized portraits of the Madonna—all were grist for the roiling mill of smoke and flames in the piazza. (See Lauro Martines's recent historical account *Fire in the City*, or try George Eliot's *Romola* for an interesting nineteenth-century fictional treatment.)

The backbone of the plot concerns Sherman McCoy of the investment banking firm Pierce & Pierce. We meet him as he puts on his "formidable" British riding mac and wrestles an expensive leash onto his dachshund in order to escape his wife, child, and sumptuous Park Avenue co-op to go out in the rain to call his inamorata, Maria, from a pay phone. The delight is in the details: by their raingear ye shall know them—and McCoy's little girl is named Campbell—perfect! These finely observed and phrased specifics are with us through the novel not only in Sherman McCoy's world of privilege, but in the fourth-floor sublet Maria hides from her husband, in the varied labyrinths of the New York criminal justice system, in the varied racial and ethnic hostilities, in the byways of journalism, and in the manipulative hands of the not-very-religious "Reverend Bacon of Harlem."

These worlds bump up against each other—carom and ricochet—after Sherman attempts to chauffeur Maria, back from a week in Italy, home from the airport. A wrong turn sends these Manhattanites into the alien world of the Bronx: the ramp is obstructed by an obstacle, Sherman gets out to clear the way, two young black men approach, a tire is hurled, hurled back. Maria (like her literary ancestor Daisy Buchanan) takes the wheel, there's a "thok!" Sherman throws himself into the passenger seat, one of the guys is heading toward them—they're outta there! The novel then comprises the chain of events resulting from that "thok!"—the sound of the pavement being hit by Henry Lamb of the Edgar Allan Poe Towers.

The tour de force of the book is the fancy dinner party at the Bavardages; as good as anything in Dickens or Thackeray, it will intrude, disturbingly, into your mind when you enter the "hive" of any faintly similar event. A houseguest of the hosts, a noted English poet dying of AIDS, makes a speech evoking Poe's "The Masque of the Red Death." Not even the decadence leading to Savonarola's conflagration provides so apt a parallel with the society that this gripping novel depicts and indicts.

Expand Your Horizons:
Books with Varied Venues

Things Fall Apart
Chinua Achebe

Heart of Darkness
Joseph Conrad

One Hundred Years of Solitude
Gabriel García Márquez

Snow Country
Yasunari Kawabata

Palace Walk
Naguib Mahfouz

Family Matters
Rohinton Mistry

A House for Mr. Biswas
V. S. Naipaul

My Dream of You
Nuala O'Faolain

Noli Me Tangere
José Rizal

Mr. Mani
A. B. Yehoshua

A book is a version of the world. If you do not like it, ignore it, or offer your own version in return.

—Salman Rushdie

JUNE IS often a time for hitting the road or taking to the air, so it's an appropriate month for traveling of the mental variety as well. If you acquired a globe, covered up England and North America, and threw ten darts, you might hit Egypt, Colombia, Trinidad, Israel, Nigeria, Japan, India, Ireland, and the Philippines. If your globe is old enough, your dart could fall in the Belgian Congo. Each of these countries is a setting for a fascinating novel.

The three novels with African settings vary greatly. The oldest and perhaps most famous is Joseph Conrad's *Heart of Darkness* (1902). The title offers many interpretations, the most shallow being a now outdated reference to Belgian ivory traders entering "the dark continent" of Africa. Chinua Achebe's *Things Fall Apart*, written in 1958 by a native of Nigeria, offers an imaginative indigenous perspective to that disruptive phenomenon of European traders' arrival into a centuries-old culture. *Palace Walk*, set in the city of Cairo in the years 1917 to 1919, gives a closely examined depiction of the effect of changing times on one cosmopolitan family. It was written in 1956 but translated from Arabic into English only in 1990.

The three novels from Asia are Yasunari Kawabata's *Snow Country*, set in Japan, *Family Matters*, set in Rohinton Mistry's native Bombay, and *Noli Me Tangere* by Filipino author José Rizal. The families in Mistry's novel seem familiar to us, affected as they have been by the English presence in India.

Kawabata's novel offers a world with a more exotic feel and a world of great beauty. Rizal's novel, published in Spanish in 1887, was a blistering indictment of the colonial regime and a call for Filipino identity.

The continent of Latin America houses the very different novels by two winners of the Nobel Prize for Literature, Gabriel García Márquez and V. S. Naipaul. Gabriel García Márquez is a native of Colombia, but his fictional village of Macondo in *One Hundred Years of Solitude* defies ordinary calculations of both space and time. In contrast, Naipaul's *A House for Mr. Biswas* is firmly rooted in everyday realities but with the special turns of village life of Indian immigrants in Naipaul's native Trinidad, just off the coast of Venezuela.

The novels from Israel and Ireland both take up a large swathe of time. *Mr. Mani* by A. B. Yehoshua covers many generations of a family starting in modern times and working backward to the early nineteenth century. *My Dream of You*, written in 2002, takes place mostly in Ireland, but the action goes back and forth for a century and a half; the few scenes in England exist chiefly to contrast with both the nineteenth- and the twentieth-century scenes in Ireland.

Perhaps Emily Dickinson wrote the best lines about travel via the pages of a book. When she penned, "This traverse may the poorest take / Without oppress of toll," she knew what she was talking about. A native of Amherst, Massachusetts, she mostly stayed right there, never traveling farther than Washington, D.C., but she is among our most cosmopolitan of writers.

Things Fall Apart

Chinua Achebe

For some years of his life, the name of this Nigerian author was Albert Achebe, a name that today rings oddly on our ears. Discarding the name of Queen Victoria's prince consort during his university years and assuming the African name was a harbinger of Achebe's future success. He may today be the most widely known indigenous African writer: more than eighty million copies of this novel have been printed, and it has been translated into more than fifty languages.

This 1958 novel, mostly set in the time just before the start of colonialism in Nigeria, takes its title from a line in W. B. Yeats's powerful poem "The Second Coming": "Things fall apart; the center cannot hold." The dissolving entity is the culture of the Iho or Igbo people, the world of Okonkwo. Proud and fierce, Okonkwo embodies many of the qualities most highly regarded by his tribe. His physical prowess is great (his defeat of the wrestler Amalinze the Cat spread through the nine villages that make up Umuofia), and he has great determination to command respect through his manner and his achievements.

Readers who want Okonkwo to be entirely admirable by modern standards are headed for disappointment. He has enormous respect for his ancestral spirits, but this familial regard is not showered on all relatives he has personally known. His contempt for his "lazy and improvident" father Unoka is equaled by his disgust with his son Nwoye, whom he sees as "degenerate and effeminate." Further, when tribal elders determine that the boy Ikemefuna, who has been a kind of foster child in his household, must be killed, he insists on joining in the process, over the advice of the elders. He has three wives and beats them all.

Nonetheless, the reader does develop sympathy for this often cruel man during his double estrangement from the world that has been his. When his gun accidentally discharges during a funeral, killing a son of the dead man, Okonkwo is exiled for seven years, during which he lives in his mother's village. He eagerly awaits his return to Umuofia, planning advantageous marriages for his daughters and advancement for two of his sons. But this sub-Saharan embodiment of Rip Van Winkle learns you can't go home again. His tribal culture has been disrupted by the arrival of a Christian missionary and a nearby white district commissioner.

Achebe's highest achievement, perhaps, is refraining from a simplistic sense of the "tribal culture good, white man bad" variety. The Christian missionary routinely rescues from the deep forest twins (generically considered an abomination by the village) who have been set out in pots to die, and shelters the *osu*, the pariahs of Umuofia with their tangled and dirty hair. But just as Okonkwo's inability to adapt to change causes the agony of his own great ruin, so does he seem the embodiment of the passing of a culture, a culture that Achebe makes vivid for us: the sacrosanct great python allowed to slither into dwellings (and beds) at will; the awing *egwugwu*, the nine embodiments of the ancestral spirits (tribe members collude in hiding their awareness that they are ornately costumed peers); the copious palm wine, sometimes drunk from a hollow skull; the bags of cowrie shells used for money; all the complexities of growing yams.

His reading of Joseph Conrad's *Heart of Darkness* is said to have stimulated Achebe to write this book. If Conrad shows the reader exotic shadowy glimpses of horned creatures—The Other—dancing by the firelight, Achebe lets us see the culture from the inside out, to know that the dancers' chalk and charcoal and their smoked raffia skirts cloak individual men.

Heart of Darkness

Joseph Conrad

Meet Charlie Marlow, your first-person narrator for 97 percent of this short novel. He enters the book on page 3 with these striking words about England: "And this also has been one of the dark places of the earth." We are on the "cruising yawl" *The Nellie*, waiting for the turn of the tide on the Thames River. The setting, presumably, is a year early in the twentieth century (the book was published in 1902). Marlow speaks to four men, one of whom is the unnamed narrator of 3 percent of the novel. Our anonymous narrator notes at the outset that Marlow, sitting cross-legged on the boat, has "the pose of a Buddha preaching in European clothes and without a lotus-flower" and, again, the length of the book later, reminds us the tale came from a man "in the pose of a meditating Buddha." This frame for Marlow's tale suggests there's something wise here, something to be learned.

Joseph Conrad himself went to sea at sixteen. By birth a Pole named Teodor Josef Konrad Korzeniowski, he taught himself English and worked his way up to the command of merchant ships in the Far East and on the Congo River. At age thirty-two, this Polish sea captain began writing and to the surprise of many had great critical success. He was welcomed into a circle of literary men in England such as Henry James and Stephen Crane.

Like Conrad, Marlow is a man who's been up the snakelike Congo River into the "Congo Free State" (an absurd name for a possession of Belgium), the heart of what was then called the Dark Continent, only one of the many meanings of the title. Conrad says his aim is to make us *see*. And as we enter the Congo, see we do—a small truck on its back with its wheels in the air, looking like the "carcass of some animal"; a native with filed teeth and ornamental cheek scars; a Russian station-master dressed in motley "as though he had absconded from a troupe of mimes"; a "savage and superb" African woman, "wild-eyed and magnificent"; and finally, at the inmost station, a house surrounded by a fence of shrunken heads.

This is the house of Mr. Kurtz. Marlow has heard about Kurtz from everyone he encounters: an idealistic man who speaks beautifully, a man wildly successful at bringing back ivory. Marlow's anticipation—and ours—of meeting this man grows as his boat travels up the river. The house with its palisade of shrunken heads jars our expectations as will the man himself. What has happened? Has Kurtz "gone native" and thus lost the civilized veneer of restraint that every man needs in order to escape "savagery"? Or is Kurtz himself, as agent of a rapacious capitalistic society, always been a "dark" element, now come into a previously unspoiled place? What does he mean by his final words "The horror! The horror!"? Why does Marlow, who so values the truth, lie to Kurtz's fiancée back in Brussels?

When you read this multilayered, complex book, you'll join the host of readers who energetically debate its meaning. Literary classic? Racist parable? Piercing indictment of materialism? Masterful psychological case study? All of the above?

Book Smart
Recommended Reading

Follow up *Heart of Darkness* with *Things Fall Apart* by Chinua Achebe, writing from the perspective of an African in 1958, and regard the film *Apocalypse Now* as a caricature, not an imitation of Conrad's super-subtle masterpiece.

One Hundred Years of Solitude

Gabriel García Márquez (translated by Gregory Rabassa)

The opening sentence of this book fixes itself in your memory: "Many years later, as he faced the firing squad, Colonel Aureliana Buendía was to remember that distant afternoon when his father took him. . . ." Compelling, yes? Now let's add the last three words: "Many years later, as he faced the firing squad, Colonel Aureliana Buendía was to remember that distant afternoon when his father took him to discover ice." *To discover ice!* We're in another realm. Márquez, author-as-god, is here creating the world of Macondo, which is in some ways lifelike (Márquez says it's based on villages of his childhood in Colombia) and some ways emphatically not.

Some reader is muttering "magical realism." This phrase—which, I'm told, Márquez avoids—was devised and abandoned by a German critic of post-expressionist art; its contrasting words boldly proclaim it an oxymoron, a cohabitation of the fantastic and the real. Shakespeare used the combination more than four hundred years ago with the ghost in *Hamlet*; Homer used it more than fifteen hundred years ago in the *Iliad* when Achilles' horses talk to him. Nonetheless, the phrase has gained a certain cachet when it's used for Latin American literature, and this truly transcultural novel is the most popular example. Not only has this novel made Márquez a multimillionaire; it helped bring him the Nobel Prize for Literature in 1982. (His acceptance speech stressed that the "real" Latin America has always been a source of the "fantastic," citing a Florentine explorer's descriptions of birds without feet, pigs with navels on their backs.)

The novel serenely convinces you of this supercharged alternate cosmos. The world has been made anew, and a band of gypsies led by the large and bearded Melquiades is offering residents of Macondo not beaded trinkets or pots and pans but the latest advances of science and technology. There's a magnet, followed by a telescope and a huge magnifying glass. They greatly please José Arcadio Buendía, patriarch of the family that will populate the novel for six generations. He's an incurable progressive but surely a spiritual cousin of Don Quixote. While his wife and children stoop over the earth to tend bananas and yams and eggplants, José Arcadio takes to his study and emerges one Tuesday in December to announce that "The earth is round, like an orange." He is understood only by Melquiades, that bigger-than-normal, time-transcending character in a hat like a raven displaying its wingspan. Melquiades appears and reappears, once declaring he got bored with death; parchments he inscribes and buries will play a part in the novel's apocalyptic close.

Márquez weaves together varied motifs and metaphors ranging from the Bible and *The Arabian Nights* to Greek myths and Catholic imagery and thus dissolves and blurs many of culture's usual categories. Similarly, he replaces our linear sense of time with a cyclical feel as he repeats family names from generation to generation (the page with the family tree is more than decorative).

But the novel is more than a charming fantasy. One critic calls it "the literary mirror" in which Latin Americans first "recognized themselves and their predicaments." A single chapter has a startling underpinning of historical seriousness, the strike by Colombian banana workers against the United Fruit Company in 1928, the year of Márquez's birth. When capitalist monsters Mr. Herbert and Mr. Brown work their legal sleight of hand and "prove" that workers don't exist, a strike breaks out. A Buendía becomes leader, survivor of mass killing, and sole witness-bearer. This massacre of workers sets in motion a five-year plague of rain, and the ruin of Macondo is imminent.

Snow Country

Yasunari Kawabata (translated by Edward G. Seidensticker)

When you start this novel, prepare to exchange your Western notions of plot development and characterization for the feel of a blend of poetry and painting. The setup is simple if often drawn behind a veil of uncertainty. A Tokyo aesthete, a man of inherited wealth, makes trips in various seasons to the mountainous "snow country" of Japan, which Kawabata elsewhere describes as being "on the reverse side" of his country. This Shimamura, filled with longing and cynicism, stays at a hot springs hotel and comes to know two geisha, Komako and Yoko. The two women know each other: both have been involved with a music teacher who dies early in the novel. Komako he has many interactions with and comes to know something of her life. Yoko he sights a few times, but the purity of her voice draws him.

This novel, which came into English in 1956, was first published in installments from 1934 to 1937, with a final section being added two years after the end of World War II. A part of the book's fascination is the subtle portrayal of the geisha, the mix of sexuality and conversation, the cross of revelation and reticence. We get to know Komako's frequent drunken spells, her playing of the stringed instrument the samisen, her stated dislike of "Tokyo people," her private quarters over a store owned by a family who sleep together in one room. Although Shimamura is the central consciousness of the novel, we get to know him very little: a wife and children are mentioned— but just barely— and fairly late on when he's described as too plump to run alongside Komako, you're startled to learn a specific detail. He's a dilettante, a minor expert on Western ballet. The fact that he's never seen a ballet nor does he long to do so conveys the feel of the book—the fascination of the partly known, of incompleteness. He sees Komako's life as "wasted," but her "straining to live" touches him "like naked skin."

What's most entrancing about the book is the lyric beauty of the small details: skin like a freshly peeled onion or like a seashell (Shimamura often describes skin, reflecting that if man had "a tough, hairy hide like a bear, his world would be different indeed"), snow on the maple leaves, snow like white peonies, Chijimi linen once woven by maidens in the snow country, the "voluptuous" beauty of the Milky Way embracing the earth. Kawabata gives the readers small paintings of the various seasons of Shimamura's stays. In mountain autumns a bee walks a little and collapses with trembling feelers; in summer red dragonflies light calmly on the edge of a pair of spectacles; in winter children tramp down snow in their straw boots and sing "the bird-chasing song."

When Kawabata won the Nobel Prize in Literature in 1968, the first Japanese writer so honored, he began his address with the recitation of a thirteenth-century haiku: "In the spring, cherry blossoms, in the summer the cuckoo / In autumn the moon, and in winter the snow, clear cold." These lines immediately evoke the mood of *Snow Country*; the fact that his Nobel address contains some nine other brief poems confirms the importance of this austere lyricism for Kawabata. He also quotes the phrase "eyes in their last extremity," words from the suicide note of Akutagawa Ryunosuke (d. 1927) that "pull at him," but notes that "suicide is not a form of enlightenment." How sad to learn he took his own life—no note—four years later.

Palace Walk

Naguib Mahfouz (translated by William M.
Hutchins and Olive E. Kenny)

Mahfouz was the first Arabic writer to win the Nobel Prize
for Literature. That honor came to him in 1988, and shortly
afterward none other than Jacqueline Kennedy Onassis
obtained the English language rights to fourteen of his forty novels.
Palace Walk is the first, and most famous, novel in the so-called Cairo
Trilogy. It concerns the lives of a Muslim family living in Cairo in the
earliest years of the twentieth century. British forces, including a number of Australians, all still giving allegiance to the aged Queen Victoria, occupy the city. The household of al-Sayyid Ahmad consists of his
wife, Amina, two sons by her, Fahmy and Kamal, two daughters by her,
Khadija and Aisha, and a son, Yasin, by a first wife whom he divorced.

The doings of this novel reflect the time and the place, particularly
at the end when Fahmy becomes tragically involved in a protest against
British occupation. In other aspects al-Sayyid Ahmad and his family
are unique, and a reader's visit to his house is not like a visit to his neighbor's. The determining difference is al-Sayyid himself. He's a man with
an "ultraconservative bias," a domestic tyrant of the variety found, alas,
in all cultures. Unlike other Muslim patriarchs of his acquaintance, he
forbids his wife to leave the house without him, no matter how opaque
the veils she might don. Amina has completely acquiesced to his rules,
accepting a "type of security based on surrender." She's pleased to catch
an hour or two of sleep before rising at midnight to serve al-Sayyid
when he returns from his nightly carousing that includes lavish help-
ings of wine, women, and song. He is, however, no rent soul who, in
more holy moments, laments his bacchanals. His tipsy jests and his
prayers are equally sincere. If we occasionally admire al-Sayyid for his

joie de vivre, we have stronger reasons to dislike him, as when he rejects a suitor for his daughter's hand for not being fully enough motivated by "a sincere desire to be related to me . . . me . . . me . . . me." And so we rejoice when he receives a tongue-lashing, in front of other men, from a former lover, the singer Jalila. In the setting of Aisha's marriage celebration where she is part of the entertainment, Jalila utters just the right observations: "Why do you pretend to be pious around your family when you're a pool of depravity?" Yasin is amused at this mirroring of his own burgeoning libertinism, but the more intellectual Fahmy is aghast at the paternal feet of clay.

In this novel of family rhythms, plot development is minor. When, during al-Sayyid's absence, Amina releases an "imprisoned" desire to make the short walk to the shrine of al-Husayn, it's a major bit of rising action for the reader as well as a bold move by Amina. (She's punished, first by fate in the form of a street accident, and then by the tyrannical al-Sayyid, who banishes her, for a time, to the home of her old, blind mother, a woman wise enough to have declined al-Sayyid's invitation to live under his roof.)

 Book Smart
Recommended Reading

If you, as I do, like sprawling family narratives rich in psychological insights, such as Thomas Mann's *Buddenbrooks* or John Galsworthy's *The Forsyte Saga*, you'll enjoy your immersion in *Palace Walk* and possibly want to follow the generations into *Palace of Desire* and *Sugar Street*.

Family Matters

Rohinton Mistry

This 2002 novel by a native of Bombay who emigrated to Canada at the age of twenty-three offers a blend of the charms of the strange and of the familiar. For non-Indian readers, the Bombay setting and the details of the life of a Parsi family offer exotic diction—what are purple *brinjals*? what are the duties of *sapats* or of a *dustoorji*?—and unfamiliar political details such as those of an extremist group that wants to ban observances of Valentine's Day. On the other hand, the basic plot of this spacious three-generation family tale is familiar to the very bone. Which of us escapes the problems of caring for aging relatives, the conflicting tugs of needs of family of origin, of spouse, of children, and of self?

Nariman Vakeel is the seventy-nine-year-old protagonist, a widower suffering from Parkinson's disease. At the start of the novel he is living with the children of his wife's first marriage, his stepson Jal and his stepdaughter Coomy, in a large apartment in a building called Chateau Felicity. The irony of the building's name becomes even more apparent when Nariman must move to a building whose name is equally faux sunny—Pleasant Villa. The prissy Coomy keeps Nariman on a restricted regimen. The small rebellion of taking a walk breaks, first, her rules and, then, his ankle. A retired professor of English, Nariman fully understands what it means when Coomy decides it's time for him to move out: he's reliving the plot of *King Lear* he taught so often without imagining himself the tragic hero.

When Nariman moves to Pleasant Villa, he swells the cramped quarters occupied by his one biological child, his daughter Roxanna, her husband, Yezad, and their two young sons, Jehangir and Murad. Space is tight and so are finances. (Nariman's retirement savings were spent some years back in buying this apartment for his daughter and son-in-law.) Proximity makes no one's heart grow fonder, and tensions mount between husband and wife, and even their young sons disregard ethics as they seek boyish ways—ever know a corrupted homework monitor?—to add money to the ever slimmer envelopes where their mother keeps the household funds. The boys' father, sometimes cruel to his incontinent father-in-law, sometimes redeemingly kind, begins to turn to the observances of Zoroastrian practice and to criticize his growing sons for interest in girls whose families practice other faiths.

Mistry does a fine job showing how similar patterns form in varying generations of a family. The elderly Nariman increasingly muses on the love of his young life—one Lucy Braganza, a Christian. After nine years of loving Lucy, he yielded to his parents' pressure to marry within the family faith and wedded the widowed mother of Coomy and Jal. His flashback memories of Lucy, rendered in italic type, are poignant.

You may find occasional spots cloying and may tire of the intestinal details of the care of an invalid, but on the whole it's that kind of comfy family saga you don't want to end but with the spice (in all senses) of life in modern Bombay.

 Book Smart
Recommended Reading

If you like this book, you'll want to read Mistry's earlier novels, *Such a Long Journey* and also *A Fine Balance*, which garnered many prizes. If you're less enthusiastic, you can identify with one Indian critic who states, seemingly without intending praise, that the books reminds her of an "old black and white Hindi movie."

A House for Mr. Biswas

V. S. Naipaul

There's not much plot. If the title didn't almost tell it all, the narrator's Prologue reveals that, yes, Mr. Biswas will succeed in his struggle to get his own house. Everything else—which is quite a lot—is tone, voice, setting, and characterization, especially characterization. So distinguished a critic as Joseph Epstein calls Mr. Biswas "one of the small number of memorably comic characters in contemporary literature."

Naipaul's introduction for a later edition of this 1961 novel tells us this is the book that's closest to his heart. It was the breakthrough novel (it was his fourth) where, in finding his bittersweet subject matter, he simultaneously found his voice, and it is the book most closely tied with his own background as a person of Hindu Indian descent who grew up in Trinidad. While Seepersad Naipaul, the author's father, is not synonymous with the risible Mr. Biswas, he was the inspiration for him.

Mr. Biswas is somewhat like that Al Capp cartoon character of the unpronounceable name who bears a perpetual black cloud over his head. Mr. B. is not only a breech baby, but born with six fingers on one hand, a very bad omen in his culture. A pundit is summoned, and suggestions are offered about minimizing the hex: keep him away from water. The sixth finger soon falls off, but the hex remains. As a child, Mr. Biswas (he has a first name—Mohun—but the narrator calls even the baby by the honorific) is earning a penny for supposedly watching a neighbor's calf. A drowned calf is the first fruit of Mr. Biswas's distractable nature and is prelude to a drowned father, dead in a futile dive into the pond, searching for his unharmed son.

Mr. Biswas is a bit of a drip, a sad sack, the kind of late adolescent who drops an unsigned mash note on a salesgirl's counter, "I love you and want to talk to you," and then, panicking, denies his action and attempts to wiggle away from the marriage the Tulsi family sets in motion. But even his tragicomic wiggling isn't vigorous, and soon there's a baby on the way. (Some want to see the smothering Tulsis as a metaphor for Great Britain's role in colonial Trinidad—as if there were no literal in-laws from hell!)

If Mr. Biswas is nebbishy, he's also aspiring, persistent, and resilient. He reads authors like Samuel Smiles, the quintessential motivational writer, before, as a householder, taking on the *Meditations* of Marcus Aurelius as he lies on his Slumberking bed. What he lacks in talent, he makes up for in labor and luck. In Anand, Mr. Biswas's thriving son (he studies with Miss Logic) at the end of the novel, we see a fictional glimmer of the author. Just as Mr. Biswas sent Anand a book called *Overcoming Our Nerves*, Naipaul himself overcame suicidal depression as a university student and aspired and persisted so ardently that, in 1989, he was knighted in his adopted country of England and, in 2001, won the Nobel Prize for Literature. He's come a long way from his grandfather, who entered Trinidad as an indentured servant.

Book Smart
Recommended Reading

When you finish this novel, try *Between Father and Son*, a moving collection—published in 2002—of the letters exchanged between Naipaul and his father while the younger man was at Oxford on a government scholarship. In the letters from his father, you'll hear echoes of the fictional Biswas.

My Dream of You

Nuala O'Faolain

"We used to stay in bed most of the weekend." This provocative opening sentence with its echo of Marcel Proust introduces us to the world of Kathleen de Burca. This novel not only takes us back and forth between various stages of her past and her present but also intercalates a few chapters from an imagined story of Ireland in 1856, shortly after the Great Hunger there. The memory of Saturdays and Sundays in London, happily bedfast with her lover Hugo, comes from her early twenties. Now she's fifty, more than half-way along life's path, as she notes. Thirty years of living in England (but, as a travel writer, spending more time at exotic locales all over the world) have brought her to one of life's dark forests. Her colleague and closest friend Jimmy, a gay Midwestern American man, has died suddenly of a heart attack, an event that hurtles Kathleen into painful self-examination.

She attacks the professional flank of her life first and resigns the cozily familiar TravelWrite job. An old memory of a transcript of a nineteenth-century Irish court case triggers thoughts of writing a historical novel, despite her unflinching agreement with Henry James that historical fiction is bound to be "humbug." The case, a real one set in Ballygall, Ireland, involves Marianne Talbot, wife of an Anglo-Irish landlord, accused—and convicted—of having adulterous relations with an Irish servant named William Mullan. Identifying with this theme of passion, Kathleen sets out for Ballygall, a return to her home island that she's chosen to avoid for so long. Though Kathleen de Burca—or Nuala O'Faolain—holds no monopoly on wrenching memories of an Irish childhood impoverished in both literal and figurative ways, her recollections of a self-absorbed father, a depressed mother make convincingly heartbreaking reading.

Kathleen's investigations into the Talbot case bring, as research so often does, more complications than clarity. What began as an attempt to launch a new career now offers her new slants on her nonprofessional life. You become so deeply interested in the gallery of Kathleen's family members, friends, colleagues, lovers that you almost resent the intrusion of her chapters on the Talbot case. Most interesting to me is her new friend, the over-seventy Ballygall librarian, Miss Leech (her name possibly deriving from the old meaning of *leech* as "doctor," for she does Kathleen a power of good). But some readers may prefer Seamus ("Shay"), a married man now living in England who conceives a fierce attachment for Kathleen as a partner in lovemaking. O'Faolain is a writer skilled enough to present vivid details of their unions that tremble on the edge of comedy before gracefully toppling over into the realm of being touching.

 Book Smart
Recommended Reading

This first novel by O'Faolain is sandwiched between two successful memoirs: *Are You Somebody?* and *Almost There: The Onward Journey of a Dublin Woman*. It's a tribute to her that you can read them all and not be sated but come away with a deep nod of recognition for a line of poetry quoted often in the novel: "The beauty of this world hath made me sad."

Noli Me Tangere

José Rizal (translated by Harold Augenbraum)

What a swirl of nations goes into the making of this 1887 novel! It is credited with first establishing a sense of national consciousness among the native (Tagalog) population of the Philippine Islands. The author was born to an upper-class Philippine family and was educated in Europe (he was a professional ophthalmologist). He began writing this Spanish-language novel in Madrid, continued it in Paris, and oversaw its publication in Berlin. This latest version (2006) is translated by an American, the director of the National Book Foundation, who describes Rizal as "one of the most fascinating people in the history of literature."

Rizal's title, retained here, is Latin, deriving immediately from the New Testament (John 20:17), a passage that tells of the newly risen Jesus instructing Mary Magdalene not to touch him. But it carries the strong subtextual suggestion of the warnings that social outcasts such as lepers were compelled to offer. Rizal's dedication refers to a malignancy in the body politic that is "like a social cancer." (The book is dedicated "To My Country," a sadly ironic touch for a native population that could not read the Spanish original.) It's a stingray denunciation of both the Spanish colonial rule in the Philippines (except for a brief hiatus, Spain had dominated the indigenous people since 1565) and the powerful clerical element, which he deemed abusive.

Rizal wrote at the risk of censure, imprisonment, exile, and ultimately death. Executed by firing squad in 1896 (allegedly saying to the priest hearing his final confession, "My great pride . . . has brought me here"), he earned almost immediate immortality as "the first Filipino." The word itself was his coinage in this novel, a new term to embrace a motley people, equal parts indio, creole, mestizo, and peninsular. The *Noli*, as the novel is familiarly called, became the cornerstone of his country's nationalist canon. Rizal is credited with devising a new social alchemy, one where race was no longer the ultimate cultural homogenizer, a fact of great interest today in a country such as the United States.

The surface layer of the plot offers a love story: it focuses on Crisostomo ("golden mouth") Ibarra, a wealthy and educated young man romantically drawn to Maria Clara de los Santos. She is the daughter of a married Filipina woman and a priest, Padre Damaso, who regards Ibarra with fearful loathing because of his idealistic hopes to help the natives of the country, efforts he first attempts to put into practice with the building of a school.

Some critics consider the details of the indigenous people romanticized, but everyone agrees that Rizal suggests a strong sense of a culture. Certain small touches—such as a dish called *tinola* made with chicken and squash or a medicine composed of marshmallow syrup and lichen—vivify daily life.

It's satisfying to learn that the American novelist William Dean Howells knew the book and praised it in 1901 as "a great novel" with a sense of "unimpeachable veracity."

Book Smart
Recommended Reading

Take a look at the sequel, *El Filibusterismo* (subversion)— originally published in yet another country—Belgium. For a look at the Philippines under the dictator Ferdinand Marcos, try Jessica Hagedorn's 1990 novel *Dogeaters*.

Mr. Mani

A. B. Yehoshua (translated by Hillel Halkin)

The title is delightfully deceptive, for there are multiple Mr. Manis, ten of them. The first Mr. Mani we meet is chronologically late, a judge living in Jerusalem in 1982, just seven years before the publication of this book in its original modern Hebrew (this English translation appeared three years later). But earlier incarnations of Mr. Mani appear serially—1944 in Crete, 1918 in Palestine, 1899 in Poland, and 1848 in Greece—in a reverse ancestral journey. Time's arrow flies backward, allowing the novel to close in Athens with Avraham Mani, born in 1799 in Salonika.

In addition to its retrogressive time scheme, the novel has another unusual feature: each of the five divisions of the work is constructed as a "conversation," but not a literal dialogue. As if present while a friend talked on the telephone, we readers hear only one of the speakers and must divine the response. Each conversation is preceded by a sketch of the speaker and his or her auditor and followed by a biographical supplement, delightfully rich in its concision as it follows the colloquial half-conversation. Yes, the novel is experimental in its form, and its great achievement is that readers don't get caught up in sorting out the novelty or in admiring the ingenuity of the techniques. Although one scholar, Gershom Shaked, provocatively calls this book an "anti-family anti-saga," the common reader will feel caught up in the fortunes of the members of the Mani family, their convoluted private dramas, their survival despite the pull of dark forces such as exile, incest, and murder, including self-murder. No wonder that Cynthia Ozick praises its "near Biblical feel."

Yehoshua gains great variation in his fractured narrative by giving four of the five speaking roles to people outside the Mani family. The first four speakers are all young people, intrigued observers of "Mani-ness," talking to an older person. The first speaker, Hagar Shiloh, a kibbutz student born in 1962, is the lone female. She tells her mother how she met Judge Mani, the father of her boyfriend Efrayim, and was propelled into dissolving his "suicidal frenzy." When Hagar later gives birth, out of wedlock, to Roni, the youngest "Mr. Mani" in the book, the Judge becomes the father figure that the reluctant Efrayim, off to London for his doctorate, is not. The one Gentile speaker is a Homer-reading Nazi soldier stationed on Crete (where the future Judge Mani is a child), talking to his honorary grandmother, an indomitable German woman.

Yehoshua pulls us not only into the tragic history of this family but also into the profundity of Jewish history and the complexity of Jewish identity. The fifth and final conversation is the most complex as Avraham Mani seeks permission for suicide from his rabbi, mute from a stroke at the start and without life by the end. (Readers interested in weighty theological parallels with the biblical story of Abraham and Isaac should seek out Yehoshua's essay "*Mr. Mani* and the *Akedah*.") He conveys form on his sprawling tale not only through the devices described above but through positioning each of the five conversations at a crossroads of Jewish history: the Lebanon War, the Holocaust, the Balfour Declaration, the third Zionist Congress, the revolutions of 1848.

Yehoshua himself was born in Jerusalem in 1936, the son of a mother from Morocco and a father, like the fictional Avraham Mani, from Salonika. That the senior Yehoshua wrote about the history of Sephardic Jews (those from North Africa and the Middle East) in Jerusalem makes the perfect background for the son's accomplishment in this book.

Stranger in a Strange Land:
Unaccustomed Places, Real and Fancied

Time and Again
Jack Finney

A Passage to India
E. M. Forster

Brave New World
Aldous Huxley

The Ambassadors
Henry James

Linden Hills
Gloria Naylor

Animal Farm
George Orwell

The Golden Compass
Philip Pullman

Frankenstein
Mary Shelley

The Songs of the Kings
Barry Unsworth

The Loved One
Evelyn Waugh

> *To acquire the habit of reading is to construct for yourself a refuge from almost all the miseries of life.*
>
> —W. Somerset Maugham

THE BOOKS for June offered readers possibilities of armchair travel to foreign lands. July's offerings continue the theme of a ship made of paper (the phrase comes from novelist Scott Spencer) and extend it further. Three of the works involve a man or woman traveling in an unfamiliar country. In E. M. Forster's *A Passage to India*, the proper Englishwoman Adela Quested examines India, then a part of the British Empire, as she seeks to confirm her decision to join her fiancé there. Similarly, Lambert Strether, rock-ribbed, small town New Englander, confronts the splendors of Paris uneasily—at first—in Henry James's novel *The Ambassadors*. Hollywood is the setting for our third ill-at-ease traveler: Dennis Barlow, young English poet and main character in *The Loved One*, arrives there for a visit from England and finds life forever changed by his desperate attraction to Aimee Thanatogenos, cosmetologist at a mortuary.

A second trio of books offers us as readers a chance to travel through time: Barry Unsworth's *The Songs of the Kings* immerses us in the strange world of events in the camp of Agamemnon shortly before he sets sail for the war in Troy. Estimated date? Thirteenth century BCE. Aldous Huxley's *Brave New World* takes us the other direction, some six centuries into the future for a world, like Unsworth's, that's vastly different from the twentieth or twenty-first century but is nonetheless scarily recognizable. Jack Finney offers the only character who is a literal time traveler. Si Morley's itinerary is small but complex: he shuttles between Manhattan of the early 1970s and Manhattan of the early 1880s with some disorienting effects on his emotions.

The final quartet of books propels us into a different conception of the world. George Orwell's fable, *Animal Farm*, gives us a locale where pigs talk, sing, and employ propaganda. Philip Pullman's *The Golden Compass* presents a world that contains an England, an Oxford, similar to the country and town we might visit today but with a few striking differences (what animal would hover inseparably around you at all times?). Gloria Naylor in *Linden Hills* sketches out a community of African Americans living in a gated community that's realistic enough but is controlled by one Luther Nedeed, who we must hope could never exist on this earth. And Mary Shelley's classic *Frankenstein* offers a quintessential stranger—a creature brought to life by the brilliant Doctor Victor Frankenstein but doomed to be misunderstood as he wanders the strange land that is now his home. He has much in common with Valentine Michael Smith, a young man returned to earth after an upbringing on Mars by Martians. Smith is the protagonist of Robert Heinlein's *Stranger in a Strange Land* (a title derived from the biblical book of Exodus), a novel worth adding to your list.

Time and Again

Jack Finney

You could call it science fiction and not be totally wrong. But it doesn't have that "sci-fi" feel. (Calling it a mystery or a love story can be equally accurate.) *Time and Again* involves time travel that goes back and forth from 1970 New York City (the publication date of the novel) to New York City of 1882.

It was an exciting time: the Dakota apartment building has just opened on the Upper West Side of Manhattan, and the torch-bearing arm of the Statue of Liberty is on display in the Madison Square Park in hopes of inspiring donations for the base of the statue. Trinity Church is the tallest structure on the island. And the usual urban dangers are present: a major plot development involves a fire that devours the building housing the *New York World*. Police brutality and corruption are rampant. Finney admits to a few liberties with historical facts, but he's used exacting research, including stories from the *New York Times* and from *Frank Leslie's Illustrated Weekly*. Photographs and woodcuts from the era aid the verisimilitude.

Finney establishes the time travel in a way you long to buy into. If, as Einstein postulated, time flows like a river, what if you could get to the shore and walk back a bit? A highly secret government project recruits suitable subjects, such as Si Morley, the main character. They immerse themselves in knowledge of an era, living "as if" for a period of time. Then hypnosis—and, from the reader's standpoint, a little suspension of disbelief—vaults them from play-acting into reality. The choices of times and places to revisit are as varied as Notre Dame Cathedral in Paris of 1415 or Vimy Ridge in the war-torn France of 1918. Si, however, has a powerful memory of a friend's enigmatic family story about New

York City in 1882, and he persuades the project to let him make his attempt at time travel right here on his home territory of Manhattan Island. He hopes to leave 1970 and get back to the era of Boss Tweed.

So Si Morley takes an apartment in the Dakota (a beautiful building most associated today with John Lennon, whose time there was brutally truncated by his 1980 murder, right in front of the building). The Dakota timelessly looks out into Central Park, a verdant spot little changed from its appearance of a century ago. Si dresses in cuffless wool pants with wide suspenders and dutifully tips the delivery boy from Fishborn's Market in coins of the era before storing his meat in the icebox. Si's good imagination allows him to muse about Adelina Patti performing that night at the Opera House or to sing "Hide Thou Me" and "Funiculi Funicula" with guests wearing duds of the 1880s (employees of the project—shhhh). One January night a snowstorm rages, and Si walks into the park where he sees a few heavily muffled folks riding in a sleigh. It could be 1970, of course, or has he made it back?

Finney, also the author of *Invasion of the Body Snatchers*, knows how to tell a tale. Si can't stay uninvolved with 1882. He locks horns with the nefarious Jake Pickering, and he falls deeply in love with Julia Charbonneau, whose great-aunt runs Si's Gramercy Park boarding house. After a little pleasant trans-century commuting (once, bringing Julia with him into 1970), he must decide which century will be his permanent home. Will you agree with his choice?

Book Smart
Recommended Reading

Another compelling time-traveling novel is Edward Bellamy's *Looking Backward*, published in 1888. The main character's journey from 1887 to a utopian 2000 remains forceful.

A Passage to India

E. M. Forster

lthough E. M. Forster lived until 1970, he published his last novel, *A Passage to India*, in 1924 when he was forty-five. His title is inspired by Walt Whitman's transcendent poem "Passage to India," written shortly after the opening of the Suez Canal, in 1869. Like Whitman, Forster deals with the new temporal closeness of India and the West as well as the longing for more metaphoric, metaphysical kinds of closeness. Who is more than qualified to encourage the twain of East and West to meet?—for his earlier novel *Howards End* bore the now-famous, imperative epigraph "Only connect . . ."

Forster began writing this novel in 1913, after his first visit to the Asian subcontinent. He completed it only after his prolonged second stay in 1921–22. No tourist, Forster worked in those years as private secretary to the Maharajah of Dewas, receiving an unusual angle of vision on English-Indian relations. (An Indian looking at a photograph of Forster in native dress praises his seeming naturalness, excepting only that he "retains a certain Englishness about the legs.")

The novel is divided into three sections: "Mosque," "Caves," and "Temple," each roughly representing an emphasis on the Muslim, the English, and the Hindu strands of life in Anglo-India. But Forster knew that nothing stays in marked boxes, "ranged coldly on shelves," and he fills the novel with visual images of arches and aural references to echoes, both suggesting extensions, expansions of views and of sounds.

Similarly, readers eager to identify and label a protagonist in the novel will meet with frustration. Is it Adela Quested, the young Englishwoman come out to India to check out her possible fiancé, an

English civil servant, in his professional habitat? Is it her traveling companion, the mother of civil servant Ronny Heaslop, Mrs. Moore, who later becomes mystically transmogrified by chanting Indians to near-goddess "Esmiss Esmoor"? Or possibly the Muslim physician Dr. Aziz, falsely charged with attempted rape by Adela after an unfortunate incident in a cave? Or Cyril Fielding, teacher in a government school, the one English male portrayed as a decent human being? Or, to use Whitman's phrase, the representative of the "old occult Brahma," Professor Godbole, who most senses the underlying unity of things and notes that worship must include "what Christianity has shirked: the inclusion of merriment."

Like the story line of many gripping novels and plays, this one reaches its climax in a trial, a trial conducted in a stifling Indian courtroom where the Indian judge speaks in "his Oxford voice" and a near-naked servant pulls the cord of his "punkah" to activate a barely helpful fan. Here, in a way typical of the novel's concern with theme, not plot, Forster bestows on the trial little more importance than on that strikingly beautiful "punkah wallah."

Book Smart
Recommended Reading

All Forster's novels are worth your time, as are his essays, particularly "My Wood" (where the author sounds much like Cyril Fielding, who likes to "travel light") and "Two Cheers for Democracy," whose titular restraint reminds us of Forster's theme in his India novel where attempts at union ambiguously achieve only a "half-embrace" or a gesture of "half-kissing."

Brave New World

Aldous Huxley

et's start with the title. If you know that "brave new world" is a phrase from Shakespeare, you're on your way to understanding this novel. In *The Tempest* the young woman Miranda, secluded nearly all of her life on an island with her father as her only human companion, has her first glimpse of humans and exclaims, "O brave [Elizabethan for "beautiful"] new world that has such people in it." Her father Prospero, exiled to the island through nefarious political doings when Miranda was a baby, dourly responds, " 'Tis new to thee."

We're ready for Huxley's novel, a book that falls into the category of "dystopia," a futurist society intended as the opposite of paradise. The title allusion to a phrase in Shakespeare's last play sets us up for a contrast between traditional values and the socially engineered standards of *Brave New World*. The trinity of values worshipped in Huxley's imagined world is "Community. Identity. Stability." And the closest thing to a god is the master of standardization, Henry Ford. The society inculcates these qualities in a number of ways, starting with a honed process of laboratory eugenics (all fetuses live their pre-birth, or in *BNW*-speak, pre-decantation, life in a bottle, each fetus carefully concocted as one of five major gradations of quality: Alpha, Beta, Gamma, Delta, Epsilon. This genetic heritage is buttressed with elaborate conditioning of the young child, involving sleep-teaching ("I'm so glad I'm a Beta. Alphas have to work too hard.") and electric shocks: lower-caste Gammas and Delta toddlers are tempted with colorful books and painfully zapped when they yield. If adults have moments where Nature and Nurture wear thin, there's always soma, a readily available pill to yield bliss on demand.

Two outsiders bring conflict into this society where "Everyone is happy now." Bernard Marx, a Citizen of this Brave New World, is the rare, imperfectly made citizen who questions the water in which he swims. Next, a true outsider, John (soon dubbed John the Savage), whom Bernard brings back from an Indian reservation. Both of these characters help us focus on this question: Is a stable society worth the loss of individuality, of idealism, of committed love, of verbal prowess that makes words "pierce like X-rays"?

Huxley invigorates his satire through two techniques: first, the use of parodies of twentieth-century conventions (denizens of this world of A.F. 632—after Ford—cry "O Ford" or "Fordy," make "the sign of the T" and have a churchlike ritual, a Solidarity Service that culminates in a rhythmic "orgy-porgy" with celebrants either "prone or supine.") His second technique is the satiric inversion of early twentieth-century norms: promiscuous sex is now mandatory—"Everyone belongs to everyone now"—but knowledge of the past is taboo. "Father" is a smutty word, but "mother" is truly obscene.

Just as Huxley saw Shakespeare as a cultural touchstone, so the world of the 1960s made Huxley himself a cultural icon: he appears on the record cover for the Beatles' *Sgt. Pepper's Lonely Hearts Club Band*, and his choice of William Blake's phrase "the doors of perception" for a nonfiction book caused Jim Morrison's group to dub themselves "The Doors." This ever-provocative writer continues to intrigue in the twenty-first century. What, if anything, we must ask, is wrong with vapidly hedonistic happiness?

 Book Smart
Recommended Reading

You'll want to compare the very different futurist vision of *1984* by George Orwell, who may have been Huxley's pupil at Eton. Perhaps *Brave New World*'s biggest in-joke is the fact that the Head of Eton in A. F. 632 is a woman.

The Ambassadors

Henry James

Henry James isn't for everyone. Ford Madox Ford describes his style as that of a hippopotamus picking up a pea. But for the rest of us there's the reminder of Cynthia Ozick (worthy disciple of James) that he's the only American-born writer we're encouraged to think of as "The Master."

This 1903 novel marked James's return to the international theme: naive young America encounters sophisticated old Europe, a theme he'd treated some twenty years earlier. Here we have six months in the life of Lewis Lambert Strether. (A character in *The Ambassadors* notes that Strether's first two names echo those of Louis Lambert, protagonist of a novel by Balzac—the novelist from whom James claimed to have learned much of his craft.) A man of fifty-five, Lambert Strether has arrived in Paris from his Massachusetts town of Woollett. He's come at the behest of the widowed Mrs. Newsome, a character so redoubtable as not to deserve a first name. Her son Chad lingers too long in the "vast, bright Babylon" of Paris, and there's the fear some daughter of France has her unworthy claws in him. Strether, ambiguously tied to the wealthy Mrs. Newsome, has been chosen to reel Chad back in, return him to Woollett.

Let's go to the most famous line from the novel: "Live all you can; it's a mistake not to." It comes in the fifth section of this twelve-part novel. Strether speaks to "little Bilham," a friend of Chad's, in the "bird-haunted" garden of Gloriani, a famous sculptor. Strether feels the beauty and interest of the garden, of Gloriani, and of his guests. He intuitively senses it's too late for even the illusion of freedom in his own life, but he generously hopes to encourage it in a young man. The highly quotable line was given to James by a young friend as part of a real-life assertion made to him by writer William Dean Howells. James wrote it in his notebook and returned to it five years later as the germ of this novel.

Here in Gloriani's garden Strether meets Madame de Vionnet, the Frenchwoman of beauty and variety who keeps company with Chad in what Strether is assured is a "virtuous attachment." Strether initially assumes that Mme de Vionnet, married but living apart from her husband, is wooing Chad as a wealthy American husband for her marriageable daughter.

The second pivotal scene—a marvelous one—comes in the novel's eleventh part. Inspired by memories of a painting, Strether seeks a fragment of "French ruralism," choosing his train almost by lot. He lounges on the hillside by the river, observing a couple in a nearing boat—"they knew how to do it," he thinks, before, with a startle, realizing it is Chad and Mme de Vionnet, attired, in this more formal era, in a way that rules out the concept of a day trip.

Yes, Strether fails at his ambassadorial task and in a complex way. In disillusionment he sees that Chad, though superficially improved by his European experience, "was none the less only Chad." When the shallow Chad is last seen in the novel, he's talking excitedly of the money to be made in the new career of advertising.

 Book Smart
Recommended Reading

If this novel daunts you now, fortify yourself with James's *Washington Square* or *The Aspern Papers*. But do try *The Ambassadors* again: as the critic Anatole Broyard says of James, "To go back to him is also to reread oneself."

Linden Hills

Gloria Naylor

I ntertextuality. That's a fancy critical term about the way reading one text of literature affects your reading of another. *Linden Hills* is a perfect example. This novel by a twentieth-century African-American author offers pleasure and instruction to any reader, including those unacquainted with the poetry of Dante. Readers who do know the writings of that fourteenth-century poet will have the special "aha" pleasure that comes with the making of connections.

Linden Hills is a gated community for upper-middle-class African Americans. It's composed of concentric circles of drives and residences, posher and posher as you go down the hill. At the very bottom lives Luther Nedeed, descendent and namesake of the founder of this prestigious real estate development. An opening account of the history of Linden Hills depicts an early Luther Nedeed, who used profits from his undertaking business to invest in real estate. He developed a prospering community designed to "be a wad of black spit right in the eye of white America." These pages read mostly like an intriguing social history of black entrepreneurship, but an occasional odd sentence such as "Like every Nedeed before him, his seed was only released at the vernal equinox so the child would come during the Sign of the Goat when the winter's light was the weakest" will jar and alert discerning readers.

The next section of the novel is set a few days before Christmas; yes, it's a cold day in frozen-over Linden Hills. Lester Montgomery, who lives with his family on First Circle Drive, is slapping high fives with his buddy Willie, who lives in Putney Wayne, the neighboring community. They form the plan of earning extra money by soliciting odd jobs from the affluent residents of Linden Hills. As they descend from circle to circle, just as Dante and Virgil descended the fourteenth-century circular terrain, we observe their interactions with the residents, among them a gay man who's forsaking his beloved male partner for a traditional marriage in order to bolster his professional ascent (a modern transformation of Dante's circle of punishment for "sodomites"); a wealthy new widower simultaneously burying his wife and renovating his home for her successor; and a professional historian of the community, careful never to interact as he clinically observes the doings of the community. (This Professor Braithwaite seems the moral equivalent of Dante's "neutrals," those condemned to a special spot in the afterlife for refusing to choose sides during life.) Have they lost their souls in pursuit of success?

Interspersed with accounts of Willie and Lester's journey are accounts of the Gothic doings inside the Nedeed domain, an additional plot strand unrelated to the layer of plot that echoes Dante. The head of the household has banished his wife to the basement. Luther, in an Othello-like moment, decides the birth of a light-colored son means "Mrs. Nedeed" has been unfaithful. He locks mother and child below ground with a little food and water in hopes of humbling Mrs. Nedeed, of teaching her a lesson. The educational experience isn't the one Luther had in mind. Willa (her first name surfaces late in the novel, significantly restoring to her an identity unrelated to her marriage) explores artifacts stored in the cellar—a Bible, a cookbook, a photograph album of three earlier "Mrs. Nedeeds"—and gets a crash course in consciousness-raising.

Occasionally, you'll feel Naylor has taken on too much in her juggling of the Dante parallels and these two plots. Mostly, though, you can't stop reading, especially when Christmas Eve brings the plots of the similarly named Willie and Willa together in an apocalyptic moment.

Animal Farm

George Orwell

I f books are jewels, *Animal Farm* is a diamond. What doesn't it do well? It's short and easy to read. It has a deep meaning underneath the surface. And if you're learned enough, you'll be rewarded with yet another layer of meaning sandwiched between the simple and the universal meaning.

The simple plane of the meaning is the story. To a naive onlooker, it might seem a children's book, for most of the characters are animals—sheep, horses, dogs, pigs. Orwell reinforces that simplistic glance by subtitling the book "A Fairy Story." The animals on Manor Farm tire of the brutal treatment they receive at the hands of Farmer Jones, and encouraged by the utopian rhetoric of the boar Old Major, they unite against him and wrangle the control of the farm from him. For a while hard work and cooperation allow them to run the farm together. Then greed begins to writhe its ugly neck, and before you can say "Gordon Gecko," some of the animals are lording it over their fellow animals, lying and violating their communal commandments. Not good reading for children!

Most everyone can see that this is a fable, a story about humans told through creatures of hoof and horn. Like a good fable, it has a clear moral, but rather than spelling it out for us in a terminal sentence, Orwell lets us think for ourselves. If, however, I were charged with formulating such a sentence, I'd filch a line from the English statesman Lord Acton and intone, "Power corrupts, and absolute power corrupts absolutely."

Then there's that fascinating topical or "middle" layer for readers who know (or would like to learn) the rudimentary history of the Russian Revolution. Orwell, a socialist disenchanted by the enormities of the Stalinist regime, poured his jeroboam of bitterness into this brilliant tale. Thus the pig aptly named Napoleon is not only any power-mad leader, he can also be seen as Josef Stalin vying for control with fellow pig Snowball aka Leon Trotsky. By the unhappy close of the book when the porkers hold full sway, we can say, "*Plus ça change, plus c'est la meme chose*" (The more it changes, the more it is the same), for the totalitarian Communist leaders came to equal or surpass the usurped Romanov czars in their indifference to the plight of the average Ivan.

Reading about Benjamin, the cynical donkey whose goal is to fly below the metaphorical radar, and about Boxer, the hard worker whose only flaw is unquestioning loyalty to undeserving authority, you begin to ponder various responses—historical, contemporary, personal—to injustice. We begin to see the Napoleons in our own worlds and to identify more accurately the sophistical ways we may allow ourselves to be manipulated. You're likely to find yourself quoting the brilliant words of the final commandment: "All animals are equal, but some animals are more equal than others."

Book Smart
Recommended Reading

George Orwell was the assumed name of the brilliant Englishman born as Eric Blair. To learn more about his long hatred of class inequality in all its forms, read his essay about his school days, "Such, Such Were the Joys." To learn about his keen awareness of how easy it is to disappoint your own high principles, read his essay "Shooting an Elephant." To get a brilliant nightmare vision of the future, read the novel *1984* (written in 1948) and join the throng longing for the coming of a new Orwell for this new century.

The Golden Compass

Philip Pullman

his is the first volume of a trilogy entitled *His Dark Materials*. This evocative phrase appears in the epigraph for this first book: ten lines from Book II of Milton's *Paradise Lost*, a description of the continuing forces of chaos: "Unless the almighty maker them ordain / His dark materials to create more worlds." The grandeur that is Milton may seem an odd opening note for a book officially classified as reading for young adults, but it is quite apt. (Pullman formally thanks the teacher who first introduced him to *Paradise Lost* in the sequel to this book.) Adolescents are fascinated by questions of good and evil, betrayal and loss, especially when they are contained within a compelling story. Pullman, who sees the gaining of knowledge and the leaving of an easy paradise as positive and views a theocracy as one of the scariest things around, is a quintessential storyteller. Make no mistake: this book can be enjoyed by adults as well as younger readers.

The protagonist of the story is eleven-year-old Lyra Belacqua. She's been living in a scruffy stairway room in Jordan College at Oxford University, located in what Pullman describes as "a universe like ours, but different in many ways." She's been told she's an orphan, daughter of a count and countess who perished in "an aeronautical accident in the North." Lord Asriel, Count Belacqua's brother, checks on her from time to time, but mostly she grows up in an Oxford version of a Huck Finn existence. She's received a piecemeal education from various Jordan scholars who have taught her bits of lore from their current projects. Mostly, she's had the seedtime to scramble across the roofs of Oxford buildings with her pal Roger the kitchen boy (and there to spit plum pits at the heads of unwitting passers-by), to visit the houseboats on the canals lived in by people known as "gyptians," and to soak up scary stories of the Gobblers, rumored to kidnap children for unspeakable projects. Her nails are dirty, her knees scraped.

Her adventures in the book will lead her to the mysterious North, where she'll cross paths with the *panserbjorn*, armored ursine creatures who are distinctly unhuggable. More deeply terrifying to Lyra are some of the humans she encounters in the book, such as the glamorous and sophisticated Mrs. Coulter, whose threat to Lyra is cloaked in kindness.

In addition to Lyra's intelligence and general good sense, she's helped by the possession of the title instrument: not a compass at all but an alethiometer (Greek roots: measurer of truth) and, even more so, by Pantalaimon, her daemon. The daemon, a companion animal of a supernatural order, always the opposite sex, is Pullman's most appealing conceit. It can be theologically viewed as a visible manifestation of the soul or psychologically interpreted as a kind of Jungian *anima*—or just seen as a tangible animal version of the always loyal invisible friend you always craved. Children's daemons are shape-shifters (Pantalaimon is variously ermine, moth, lion), but after puberty a person is permanently accompanied by, say, a dog (all servants), a golden monkey (Mrs. Coulter), or a snow leopard (Lord Asriel).

Book Smart
Recommended Reading

You'll go on, of course, to the next books in the trilogy: *The Subtle Knife*, where an older Lyra meets Will Parry and feels the power of erotic attachment (there's a profound strain of sadness), and *The Amber Spyglass*.

Frankenstein

Mary Shelley

Unwed Teenaged Mother Penning Gothic Thriller! That's an imaginary and anachronistic tabloid headline about the start of the writing of this book in June 1816. Mary Wollstonecraft Godwin had fled from England to the Continent with the married poet Percy Bysshe Shelley two years earlier. (His wife was expecting their second child at the time.) Mary Godwin was sixteen and also pregnant by him. Their first child, a daughter, lived only a few days; her journal eerily—in light of the novel she soon writes—recounts her dream of the lifeless infant reviving when the parents "rubbed it before the fire." Less than a year later she gave birth to a son who was about six months old when she began this novel about the bestowing of life.

An equally dramatic, second backstory recounts the immediate stimulus for her writing. With her lover and their child, as well as her stepsister Jane (later Claire) Clairmont, Mary was staying near the Villa Diodati, where in an earlier century John Milton had visited his friend Charles Diodati. Now the villa was inhabited by the poet Lord Byron (who impregnates Claire Clairmont, but that's *another* story) and his physician John Polidori. In a "wet and ungenial" summer, these lively minded friends, tired of lolling away the days with French translations of German ghost stories, challenged each other to write a fantastic tale. Their fragmentary attempts resulted in only one completed work, that of Mary Wollstonecraft Shelley, to employ the name she used after marriage (she and Percy wed a few weeks after Shelley's first wife killed herself in early December of 1816). *Frankenstein* was published anonymously in 1818 with a dedication to the social reformer William Godwin (Mary's father), a fact that caused speculation that Godwin's disciple Percy Shelley had written the book. Five years later, the second edition bore the author's name. The public was startled to learn this "wild and hideous tale"—in the words of a contemporary—had been written by a woman.

No theatrical or cinematic version suggests the novel's depth. Subtitled "The Modern Prometheus" after Ovid's version of the myth where Prometheus creates life, the book is far from being a mere monster tale. Structurally, it's intricate: It starts (and ends) with the letters to his sister in London of one Robert Walton, captain of a ship bound on a mission to the North Pole to discover "the power that attracts the [magnetic] needle." Captain Walton tells of the ship's rescue of an icy sledge with one near-frozen man aboard. Later letters include the first-person account of this survivor, Dr. Victor Frankenstein. Dr. Frankenstein's narrative includes at its heart another layer of narrative: a touching story forced into his ears by the nameless creature whom he brought to life in his laboratory some years earlier. Although the creature later becomes a multiple murderer, his early days are marked by innocence and good will. We read sympathetically of his acquisition of language and his learning of society through his reading, including his perusal of Milton's *Paradise Lost*. And the creature's story unfolds within *it* the pilfered laboratory notes of Dr. Frankenstein written during the months of "enthusiastic frenzy" before he succeeds in infusing life into a conglomeration of anatomical parts.

The title page of the novel bears an epigraph from *Paradise Lost*, forcing readers to think whether the created being is like Milton's Adam or like Milton's Satan. It also asks the reader to weigh individualism against society's welfare and to question the possible dark side of what's called progress.

The Songs of the Kings

Barry Unsworth

Before Odysseus could struggle his slow way home, there had to be the Trojan War. Before Achilles could fight for the Greeks, he had to get to Troy. The matter of Troy—the *Iliad* and the *Odyssey*—exists because of the sacrifice of Iphigenia, the daughter of the general Agamemnon, in exchange for winds to propel the ships from the Greek port of Aulis to Troy. Classical playwrights Aeschylus and Euripides dealt with this theme in the fifth century BCE; early in the twenty-first century Barry Unsworth took up this tale of troops forestalled by a northeast wind of unprecedented duration.

Unsworth's novel is a hybrid. When he's working in a purely ancient mode, his evocative and vivid details work wonderfully to build up a sense of his two locales, Aulis and Mycenae. Aulis is a camp full of men of action forced to endure delay. It's a world where Patroclus draws red sunbursts on the cheeks of Achilles, where Menelaus rapes a peasant girl, a virgin, and tells her protesting father that she was honored in receiving his royal sperm, a world where Ajax the Great and Ajax the Lesser collaborate on plans for a Day of Games and devise the concept of a coronet of laurel leaves to the winners. There's no real Hellas—Greece—yet, and we get a strong sense of Locrians, Molossians, Boetians, Archadians, Achaians, each with their own dialect, customs, and loyalties. Calchas, the diviner, is much on the scene, sometimes butting heads with Croton, a hard-core priest of the thunder-god, Zeus. A native of a refined city on the banks of the Maeander, Calchas worships the female divinity known as the Great Mother, somewhat identified with the Greek Artemis. Both Calchas and Croton must attend on Agamemnon, seated in his incised and bejeweled throne of African ebony, to offer interpretations of dreams to explain the divine anger behind the becalmed winds.

Meanwhile, back in Mycenae, Iphigenia, nubile daughter of fourteen years, leads a life of assured entitlement in the House of Atreus. She's pleased but not surprised to be summoned to Aulis to marry Achilles—or so she's told—before he ships out for the war. She's attended by the utterly loyal Sispyla (Unsworth's intriguing addition to the myth)— same age, same shape, but a slave ripped from her home city, Miletus, in Asia Minor at so young an age that she knows only her early name, Amandralettes, and a memory of egrets.

Into this re-creation of an ancient world, Unsworth weaves a strand of comedy. At first I resented Unsworth's jarring of his elegant re-creation of the past but came to appreciate the winking parallels with modern warmongers. The chief butt of humor is Odysseus. His classic "never being at a loss" is downsized here to versatility; he diminishes everything he touches: he's glad, for example, to have Calchas "on the team." Not content with clichés, he loves crude coinages such as *incentivize*. (We all know someone like this.) The jokey banter of Odysseus and the other masters of war (big bellicose Ajax wants to be known as a "unifier") serves partly as comic relief and partly as barely veiled protest at the continuing sacrifice of the innocent under the banner of patriotism.

Behind everything at Aulis sits the Singer, lyre on lap, observing. Odysseus might call him a spinmeister. He lives partly on largesse, partly on promise. There is always another story, says Unsworth, but in the end we believe "the songs of the kings."

The Loved One

Evelyn Waugh

A prefatory note to this 1948 novel warns "the squeamish" to leave the volume unread. Perhaps some readers are too delicate to stomach the thought of a mortuary embalmer's macabre flirtation with a cosmetician by placing special smiles on corpses heading for her ministrations. It's more likely, however, that the note is merely the harbinger of the fiendishly arch tone of the novel.

Waugh, ardent English convert to Catholicism, made a brief trip to Hollywood in the mid-1940s to discuss the adaptation of his novel *Brideshead Revisited* for the screen. That project came to nothing, and *Brideshead* had to await its wonderful eleven-episode serialization on Granada television in 1981. The wellspring of bile that southern California provoked in Waugh transformed itself into the "little nightmare" of *The Loved One*. What was not to like? Hollywood, for starters. The theme-park style of handling death and burial. People who believe the lush rhetoric of advertisements. Euphemisms. Monolithic definition of female beauty. Shallow homage to Eastern religions. Nut burgers. Man's inhumanity to man—not that southern California has a monopoly on that.

The subtitle of the book is "An Anglo-American Tragedy." As the pages flip by, you see Waugh as an equal opportunity skewerer: the English expatriates are no better than the locals. Sir Ambrose Abercrombie, doyen of the ex-pat community, roams sunny Bel Air in Inverness cape and deerstalker hat. It's his job to make sure standards of English dignity are held high; he could hardly be expected to approve when the young Englishman Dennis Barlow goes temporarily native and takes a job at the Happier Hunting Ground, a pet cemetery that apes the airs of Whispering Glades. The suicide of Dennis's housemate, Sir Francis

Hinsley, leads him to Whispering Glades and to a courtship conducted by means of plagiarized poems.

Waugh's satirical arrows find many targets, but the quiver that holds them all is a hatred of inauthenticity, or, put it in good old American, "phoniness." Hollywood metamorphoses "Baby Aronson" into flamenco dancer Juanita del Pablo, who must, when trends change, be retransformed into an Irish colleen with teeth suitable for "roguish laughter." Similarly, Whispering Glades turns dead people into "loved ones," and Mr. Joyboy, legendary embalmer, and Aimee Thanatogenos, necro-makeup artist, work Hollywood-style magic on their corpses. Their souls? Shhhh. That's an obscenity. Only reminders of earthly life are permitted on the premises. Crossed cricket bats? Yes. A cross? No.

The plot is slender and characterization mostly two-dimensional, as the many humorous "ticket names" suggest ("Aimee" is also "the loved one," and her last name is Greek for "of the death kind"). There's an embedded elitism in the book: the English who never left England are the implicit heroes. So it's appropriate that Waugh rewards readers with a liberal education: a number of poems are partially quoted or alluded to. (Watch out for the "nine rows of haricots" and the machine that replicates the loudness of bees in a glade.) If you know the original, you feel you've caught a glimpse of a well-hidden Easter egg. Ultrademocratic Waugh isn't, but his pitiless satire and absolute mastery of tone can't be matched.

 Book Smart
Recommended Reading

For more jabs at Hollywood, don't neglect Nathanael West's fierce novel *The Day of the Locust* (1939), which has a character named Homer Simpson. Or try the light but hilarious treatment of Peter Lefcourt in *The Deal* (1991). Jane Smiley's Hollywood novel, *Ten Days in the Hills* (2007), was inspired, she asserts, by her reading of Boccaccio's *Decameron*.

Lighten Up:
Smiles at the Human Condition

Lucky Jim
Kingsley Amis

Headlong
Michael Frayn

The Satires
Juvenal

Foreign Affairs
Alison Lurie

Birds of America
Lorrie Moore

Pale Fire
Vladimir Nabokov

Gargantua and Pantagruel
François Rabelais

Me Talk Pretty One Day
David Sedaris

Fables for Our Time and Famous Poems Illustrated
James Thurber

The Importance of Being Earnest
Oscar Wilde

> *People say life is the thing, but I prefer reading.*
> —Logan Pearsall Smith

IT'S AUGUST, traditionally a laid-back month for many readers. The array of titles loosely linked here by the word "comedy" is varied: four twentieth-century novels, one book of translations of first-century poetry, one late nineteenth-century play, one book of short stories, two books of essays, and one utterly unclassifiable sixteenth-century offering from France.

Let's start with the novels, two from England, two from the United States, all of which have some denizen of academia as a character. Though none comes under the heading of escape reading, three are pleasantly easy reads. Kingsley Amis's *Lucky Jim* from England in the 1950s, my all-time favorite, concerns the fortunes of a hapless history professor. Alison Lurie's *Foreign Affairs* punningly takes on the fortunes of two American professors on leave in England. Michael Frayn's *Headlong* hilariously details events in the life of an art scholar who contemplates turning swindler. The fourth novel, Nabokov's *Pale Fire*, is infinitely complex and brilliant in its witty playing with life and language.

Juvenal's poetry, Wilde's play *The Importance of Being Earnest*, and Lorrie Moore's book of short stories, *Birds of America*, all offer satirical riffs on life. Juvenal is by far the most bitter, but have not most of us had moods or days of complaint or criticism at this imperfect world? Juvenal's speaker feels he could "fill up a whole notebook at the street crossings." Oscar Wilde twits society but always in a jaunty, lighthearted mode (the hair of a recent widow has "turned quite gold with grief"). The stories of Lorrie Moore, once a student of Alison Lurie, range from the raffish joke to the deepest darkest kind of humor about topics usually considered laughter-proof.

James Thurber and David Sedaris are our essayists. They're writing almost half a century apart in time, but they both see keenly the follies of mankind. Thurber, parodying the time-honored format of a fable, offers brief, easy reads ideal for, say, time on the beach. Sedaris's stock-in-trade is to poke fun at himself (or at some comically literary version of himself), but the French language also comes in for a number of jabs in this collection.

The work that defies classification is Rabelais's *Gargantua and Pantagruel*. Novel? Quasi-epic? World's longest joke? Whatever it is, it's a madcap feast for lovers of language.

Other writings that have made me laugh: anything by Evelyn Waugh (see the July lineup) or P. G. Wodehouse or S. J. Perelman or Dorothy Parker; the novels of Muriel Spark, Brigid Brophy, and Christopher Buckley; the essays of Calvin Trillin, David Foster Wallace, and Joe Queenan, self-designated "sneering churl"; Michael Malone's *Foolscap*; and Martin Clarke's *The Many Aspects of Mobile Home Living* and *Plain Heathen Mischief.*

Lucky Jim

Kingsley Amis

O f course we can be friends if you don't like this book—the world needs all sorts of people—but our chances of being soul mates go up exponentially if you do like it. I'm happy to go for the superlative and declare this the funniest novel I've ever read. I reread it when I have the flu and when my heart has been broken.

Okay, other than funny, what kind of book is it? For starters, it's British, set in the world of the red-brick university. Some see it as a part of the "Angry Young Men" movement in postwar England, but for me any hint of *ressentiment* is smothered by the welter of hilarity. Jim Dixon, recently an R.A.F. corporal in western Scotland, has a provisional appointment as a lecturer in history and labors to please his department head, the eccentric Professor Welch. We've all had Welches in our lives—quirky, demanding, maddening bosses. Welch idealizes what he calls "Merrie England" and insists that underlings participate in weekend house parties full of the execution of sword dance steps and amateur madrigal singing ("infantile fa-la-la-la-la stuff"). Those, like Jim, who endure hospitality in the form of "the smallest drink he'd ever been seriously offered" and who attempt to fake the role of first tenor by enthusiastically moving their mute mouths, get their comeuppance. Jim must also contend with a student who, unlike the island-bound Corporal Dixon, commanded a tank troop in Anzio, and with the suicide-faking Margaret, a more senior lecturer at the university, the kind of woman who wears paisley frocks and quasi-velvet shoes and who works hard at a laugh like "the tinkle of tiny silver bells."

Other villains include an editor of a scholarly periodical who for months imprisons Jim's manuscript on shipbuilding techniques in the later fifteenth century (Jim knows it "throws pseudo-light on non-problems," but its publication might solidify his hold on his job) and then plagiarizes it in another language. But if this novel has the kind of villains that populate fairy tales, it also has a fairy-tale-like rescuer and a fair maiden. Julius Gore-Urquhart and his toothsome niece, Christine, allow Jim to achieve a satisfying happy ending in the realms of both work and love, but only after he has skewered his way through many difficulties including an attempt at an important academic lecture while royally drunk. He finds himself, against his will, imitating the loathed Prof. Welch's affected pattern of speech and, worst of all, abandoning his written text to say what he really thinks.

Thirty-two when this novel was published, Amis by most accounts aged badly, becoming ultraconservative and dyspeptic. (He managed, in his last years of ill health, to become a permanent paying guest in the home of his first wife—whose father had been the unwitting model for Prof. Welch—and her third husband.) Some may find this book's attitudes toward women and relationships dated and depressing, but there is something timeless about Amis's account of Jim's monumental hangover: "His mouth had been used as a latrine by some small creature of the night, and then as its mausoleum."

 Book Smart
Recommended Reading

While *Lucky Jim* is of its era with its references to pub closing hours and boarding houses, it's a piece of history mainly in its spawning of progeny: it's the forebear of novels like David Lodge's *Changing Places* or *Small World*, Richard Russo's *Straight Man*, and Jane Smiley's *Moo*, and in the entertainment world for humor of the Beyond the Fringe variety.

Headlong

Michael Frayn

He's not a particularly admirable character, this Martin Clay, our narrator, but he's certainly an interesting fellow. He's English, married to Kate, an art historian, and the father of a baby. A scholarly type, a philosopher, he's an expert in things like nominalism, which, he tells us, is the philosophical belief that there are no universals. Everything clear now? To make matters more complex, he considers himself an *art* philosopher, much concerned with, say, the difference between iconography and iconology. You can head for the dictionary if you like, but the point is that he's not the sort of bloke you expect to find in any kind of art world heist, caper, or romp. Erudite he may be, but he's seriously self-deluded and in way over his head.

Michael Frayn, the author, unlike Martin, is someone you'd like to have in your circle of friends. He's been a journalist and a Russian translator and is now an accomplished playwright (*Noises Off* and *Copenhagen* are the best known) and novelist. This witty novel was on the short list for the Booker Prize, losing to the weighty *Disgrace* by J. M. Coetzee. Once you read him, you'll understand Anthony Burgess's assertion that Frayn is "the master of what is seriously funny."

It all starts when Martin and Kate head up to their house in the country with baby Tilda, planning an extended focus on their separate scholarly projects, free of London distractions. But neighbors exist everywhere, and they're almost immediately asked to dinner by Tony Churt, a man described as possessing both "an effortlessly landowning kind of voice" and "the grip of a man who's used to wringing the necks of wounded game birds." (Martin should be wary of *his* neck.)

The plot gets suitably tangled when Martin, casually inspecting his host's artworks while Kate tends to the baby, sees what he's positive (*positive!*) is an unidentified Brueghel, a painting long missing from a series. Selfishness and avarice gallop into his mind. How to get this painting at low cost from Churt? Will Churt's attractive young wife, Laura, serve as his unwitting accomplice? Can he conceal all this from Kate, who won't approve of the necessary borrowing of money? He's a man caught in the coils of an obsession. Like Icarus or Lucifer, he's impetuous, headlong, heading for a big, big fall.

The working out of this knotty plot is delightful. There's plenty of farce (Who's that in the bedroom? What's that in the grocery bag?) and plenty of charming psychological nuance as husband and wife, loving even when furious, divine each other's thoughts from slight variations in timing or tone. (Does the author, married to the brilliant biographer Claire Tomalin, practice this in real life?)

Book Smart
Recommended Reading

For another good novel dealing with a purloined painting, go to Katharine Weber's *The Music Lesson*. In the manner of Henry James's *The Aspern Papers*, Frayn shows us the grotesque results of monomania gone awry; in the style of A. S. Byatt's *Possession*, he lets the cerebral detective work of his character lead us through a specialized educational program.

The Satires

Juvenal (translated by Rolfe Humphries)

Someone—wish it had been me—has said that Juvenal is so pagan that he's modern. This first-century Roman poet tells us that indignation makes satire, and he should know. Fiercely, savagely angry, he's a good hater. Jonathan Swift, his disciple centuries later, wrote his own Latin epitaph saying that the grave was the only place where "saeva indignatio" (fierce indignation) didn't lacerate his heart. Swift, like Juvenal, who said it first, knew that "it's difficult *not* to write satire" if you're a person with a keen eye for mankind's innate follies and for the embellishments added by organized society. If you live in the reigns of Nero and Domitian, it's definitely not hard to find material. This translation, done in the relatively mild year of 1958, isn't quite as vicious as Juvenal in Latin, but it gives you the idea. Be warned: the concept of political correctness is no part of Juvenal's world.

Try a sampling of his sixteen satirical poems, the third and the tenth. Satire 3 is his rant against the city of Rome. Samuel Johnson, another eighteenth-century fan of Juvenal's, did an imitation transferring to the London of his day Juvenal's gibes at his Rome, and the time is ripe for someone's twenty-first-century onslaught on, say, New York. "Against the City of Rome" is framed by the scene of a farewell to his friend Umbricius, who's mad as hell and just can't take it anymore. His little store of possessions piled on a wagon, he's heading for the ghost town of Cumae. As his friend Juvenal sees him off, he evokes the Rome of the good old days, and Umbricius responds with flying vitriol: Rome is for liars, for flatterers, for suck-ups. A poor, honest working stiff doesn't have a chance, can't get no respect. And it's filled these days with upstart Greeks, pushy men who'll say anything, *anything*, if it's

what the boss wants to hear: "if you say 'I'm hot,' he starts sweating."
And it's noisy, the traffic can drive you crazy!

A country dweller, a property owner, is described as "lord of a single lizard," a detail that doesn't sound all that wonderful, so this may be exuberant linguistic venting about the city you love to hate, and we don't see the poet himself putting his goods on any cart. (Johnson, the consummate Londoner, exploits this ambivalence further.)

Satire 10—titled in this translation by the name of Johnson's imitation, "The Vanity of Human Wishes"—takes a bleaker, proto-existentialist view of life. Be careful what you long for: you may get it and then, oh boy, are you in for trouble. If you gain power, that situation can reverse itself: look at the molten statue of the once-almighty Sejanus: "few tyrants die a dry death." You could be as eloquent as Cicero—and have your head and your hands, like his, cut off. If your prayer for long life is granted, you'll begin to resemble a mother baboon, just one more look-alike Old Person. Pray for beauty? For a good-looking son? Oh man, you'll be sorry. So can't we ask for anything? (And here come his most famous lines)—yes, ask for *mens sana in corpore sano*—a sane mind in a sound body—if you've got that, you've got everything.

Foreign Affairs

Alison Lurie

Vinnie and Chuck. Fred and Rosemary. Those are the two couples carrying on affairs in London.

Fred Turner, a handsome junior academic in his late twenties, is there to work at the British Museum on the eighteenth-century playwright and poet John Gay. He's there alone because he and his wife, Roo March, a photographer, have separated over a disagreement about her public display of a photograph of his tumescent male organ—paired with her photograph of a mushroom. Lady Rosemary Radley, some years his senior, is an English actress, best known for her portrayal of highborn women on television shows such as *Tallyho Castle*. Vinnie Miner, plain, small, fifty-four, is a reasonably distinguished professor of children's literature who knows London well, indeed, thinks of it as her spiritual home. Chuck Mumpson, her chance seatmate on the plane flight to London, is also American, but as a sanitary engineer from Tulsa given to corny slang and foldable plastic rainwear, he has had so little in common with Vinnie's world that he might as well be from Saturn. A recent casualty of downsizing, he's flush with "buyout" money thrown at him on his departure but concomitantly low on ego. His wife, Sheila, a successful real estate agent back in Oklahoma, has, as Lurie's English characters might say, gone off him.

The two couples' stories are told in alternating chapters, but, since Vinnie and Fred know each other as colleagues in the English Department at Corinth University back in the States (think Cornell, where Lurie was for many years a professor), their tales frequently intersect. Indeed, Fred met Rosemary when Vinnie, as hostess, befriended her junior colleague with an invitation to tea. Fred's chapters are all prefaced with a quotation from the work of John Gay, while Vinnie's chapters have epigraphs from children's rhymes.

Lurie overtly evokes the themes of Henry James, an American who took on English citizenship and whose novels frequently offer a nineteenth-century version of the culture clash when America bumps up against Europe. Her style is highly readable, even addictive: each time I've begun reading or rereading a Lurie novel, I set it down unwillingly, eager to return to it. In this novel the doings of Fred and Rosemary (and, at a distance, Roo) hook you and amuse, but you're harpooned by Vinnie and her changing attitudes toward the increasingly admirable Chuck. (When she presumptuously throws his offending raingear in the dustbin, you cheer when he stands up for himself, even if you yourself would rather get drenched than be shielded by a transparent polyethylene garment.)

Another of Lurie's memorable characters plays a large part in both the opening and the conclusion of the novel. This is Fido, an invisible embodiment (a dogification?) of Vinnie's intermittent self-pity who longs to trip her up and smother her with kisses. With a wit typical of her style, Lurie terms him Vinnie's "familiar demon or demon familiar." Occasionally, he thinks of deserting her for Chuck, and the power of Lurie's imagery is so strong that you may find the image of Fido wagging his dirty white tail as a new pop-up on your own private screen of emotions.

Book Smart
Recommended Reading

My second favorite Alison Lurie novel is *The War Between the Tates*, which deals with the breakdown of the marriage of a foreign policy professor and his wife against the macrocosmic background of the Vietnam War. All those who, like the Tates, have watched their cherubic children transform themselves into alien adolescents almost overnight will especially enjoy it. The topic may sound gloomy, but the writing sparkles.

Birds of America

Lorrie Moore

In *The Catcher in the Rye*, Holden Caulfield asks if we've ever read something and liked it so much we wanted to just call up the author and talk. I've been wondering if I could get Lorrie Moore's number. Her stories—twelve of them in this volume—contain that piercing combination of hilarity and pathos that Holden himself inspires. While I haven't compiled a tangible notebook of Lorrie Moore quotations, I have fragments of material for it lodged in my brain lobes: "He was thinking, but she could tell he wasn't good at it." A story from an earlier collection puns on the sound-alike phonemes of "VCR" and the *Tosca* aria "Vissi d'arte" in a way that made me almost fall off my seat on the bus.

But it isn't her one-liners that make you wonder if you could convince her to let you audition for soul mate. It's her eye for details, her deft nabbing of the right word or image for those details, her sense that tragedy isn't cured by wit but that even those knocked flat on their backs feel stronger if they wriggle their legs in defiance. A wife undergoing chemo professes to laugh at her husband's philandering and fills two full pages with multiplying repetitions of "Ha!" Raccoons that fall down chimneys and run about the room aflame evoke the comparison "Love affairs are like that." A young woman in the passenger's seat in a car in left-driving Ireland notes that sitting in a seeming driver's seat without a steering wheel is emblematic. Moore paints her specimens of humanity in colors as vividly accurate as Audubon's in his *Birds of North America*.

Many people think her best story is the long (thirty-eight pages) and enigmatically titled "People Like That Are the Only People Here:

Canonical Babbling in Peed Onk." (Originally published in *The New Yorker*, the story, which has autobiographical roots, won the O. Henry Award. It was the only story she wrote for one of the eight years she worked on the collection.) "Peed Onk" turns out to be the division of the hospital for children with cancer—pediatric oncology. With such a setting, could anyone get the tone right? Except for having witnessed Moore's success at evoking simultaneous sobbing and cackling, I would have thought not. Characters are generically named the Mother, the Baby, the Husband, the Surgeon. The loving Mother is constitutionally unable to close out the part of her brain that's the Writer. (Against her will she wants to know if Wilms's tumor has an apostrophe in it, and yet she's vigorously repelled by the suggestion she earn needed money by taking notes on, say, the Tiny Tim Lounge or the Oncologist's saying "I know chemo. I like chemo. But this is for you to decide.")

Moore knew success early. On the recommendation of Alison Lurie, one of her teachers in the M.F.A. program at Cornell, she sent many of the stories written for her thesis off to an agent. The agent passed them on to Knopf, and—voilà—her first book, *Self-Help*. But published interviews with her reveal a person who feels that a sense of "inadequacy" never goes away and sees her life as teacher at the University of Wisconsin and writer (and mother of a small child) as giving her "short jarring bursts of community" juxtaposed to the "capacity for solitude" that is essential to her calling. How could you not like a writer who says of a writer's career, "Keeping your fingers crossed makes it difficult to hold a pen, but I must say it's worth it."

Pale Fire

Vladimir Nabokov

A poem of 999 lines written in rhyming couplets. A foreword to that poem. An epigraph from Boswell about Samuel Johnson's cat. Extended footnotes on the poem. An index. These are the components of this brilliant, one-of-a-kind novel. Yes, it's all a novel, including that index.

The poem, as read by your average reader, is a partly autobiographical meditation on life and speculation on an afterlife, if any. It's written by one John Shade, professor of English at Wordsmith University in New Wye, Appalachia. The opening two lines are a striking evocation of a bird killed by the semblance of itself: "I was the shadow of the waxwing slain / By the false azure in the windowpane." The poet tells of domestic routines and pleasures and of his paternal tragedy: his homely daughter Hazel drowns herself in response to the barrage of everyday social cruelties from a world that judges young women by their beauty. Prof. Shade, like Nabokov himself, is fascinated by butterflies and contemptuous of Freudian literary interpretation. An expert on the poetry of Alexander Pope, Shade has a head full of literary echoes, and readers who can detect these will gain a special measure of learned delight. One of these is the title of the poem itself—"Pale Fire"—obliquely acknowledged in lines of the poem—"Help me, Will!"—as a borrowing from Shakespeare. (Pursuing the reference, you'll find the beautiful lines in *Timon of Athens*: "the moon's an arrant thief / And her pale fire she snatches from the sun.")

Those opening lines of poetry with their imagery of resemblance and reflection and that allusive title with its theme of usurpation lay the foundation for the bizarre and lengthy footnotes to the poem. The annotator, Charles Kinbote, is a visiting professor and neighbor to Prof. Shade in a house sublet from a Judge Goldsworth who's sent away many a criminal; keep your eye on this fact to understand the murder to come. Even a mildly observant reader soon comes to realize Kinbote, proud driver of a "powerful Kramler," is an annotator whose belfry is not lacking for bats. He reads the poem as a disguised version of the tale he's been feeding to Shade, hoping he'll give it immortality in a poem. The tale involves Kinbote's delusional belief that he is the exiled king of a land called Zembla (hear the echo of *semblance*?) and now being pursued by an assassin named Gradus, aka Jack Grey. Or it can be read as a baroque spoof on literary apparatus where a scholar's recondite interpretation may bear little relationship to the surface of the original text. Alternately, see it as a brilliant writer's elaborate playroom, a setup for the most elaborate possible linguistic play. Just as Humbert Humbert, another disturbed protagonist of an earlier and even more famous Nabokov novel—*Lolita*—announces that he has only words to play with, in this novel author Nabokov engages in wordplay with a vengeance. Look up "word golf" in the index, note the in-joke about hurricanes in line 680 of the poem, build your vocabulary with delightfully useless words like *nenuphar* and *sumpsimus* and *versipel*. And reflect that much madness may conceal divinest sense, for all our lives are dogged by, in the words of the last sentence, "a bigger, more respectable, more competent Gradus."

Gargantua and Pantagruel

François Rabelais (translated by Thomas Urquhart and Peter Motteux)

Not many people, not even many famous writers, get their own adjective. But *Rabelaisian*, derived from this sixteenth-century French author, is firmly ensconced in the English language. It's always associated with humor and variously defined as earthy, bold, uproarious, and scatological. Dip into this exuberant book at almost any point for an illustration. But be warned. Rabelais is not for the faint of heart: an early chapter (I. 13) contains a lively catalogue of all the many objects the five-year-old Gargantua experiments with as what we effete moderns call "toilet paper" before awarding the top prize to the neck of a downy goose.

Does it surprise you now to learn that Rabelais was a monk? First in the Franciscan order and later in the more scholarly Benedictine order. Perhaps it's more readily comprehensible that he was also a physician— one of the very first to dissect a human body. His five-book work (some think the last may not be his) is shapeless and sprawling. Clown and philosopher overlap in whimsy that transcends buffoonery.

Whatever else it is, it's intoxicated with language ("word-mad," as one scholar puts it), rollicking with synonym after synonym, building up an incremental roar of audacious phraseology. He was not only a logophile (a lover of words) but a true logodaedalist (an inventor of words), reputed to have added five hundred new words to the French language. Needless to say, he's a challenge to translators, but Urquhart, a Scotsman translating in the seventeenth century, has achieved, in the words of critic Wyndham Lewis, not a translation but a "transmutation." (After Urquhart's death, Motteux finished the job.)

Gargantua is a giant whose very name is a pun, a compression of the French *qúe grand tu as*—how big you are. (Swift's Brobdingnagians in Book 2 of *Gulliver's Travels* are direct descendents.) One of his best-known deeds is the founding of the abbey of Thélème, where the motto is *"Fay ce que vouldras"* (Do what you want)—an embodiment of the Renaissance celebration of humanity, the antithesis of medieval orders constricted by rules and regulations. It welcomes women as well as men, forbidding entrance only to "vile bigots, hypocrites, externally devoted apes, dissembling varlets, out-strouting clusterfists, pelf-lickers" and their ilk.

Pantagruel, a worthy son to his father, appears in Book II, which Rabelais offers as "solace and recreation." He acquires a lifelong buddy named Panurge ("do all"), escaped from the hands of the Turks. While some see Panurge as a kind of devil figure, he can more benignly be interpreted as the embodiment of *joie de vivre*. Loyal to nothing else, he's always loyal to Pantagruel. He's the prime "Pantagruelist," a person whose quality of spirit is "a certain jollity of mind, pickled in the scorn of fortune." A Pantagruelist never abandons the "divine mansion of reason" and is always able to maintain a kind of merry stoicism, no matter what the external situation.

Find a fellow word-lover and read parts of this aloud to each other. You'll enjoy the various adventures (such as the incident of the "frozen words" where all the sounds of a wintry battle thaw into renewed auditory existence), but above all you'll enjoy the cataract of language.

Me Talk Pretty One Day

David Sedaris

David Sedaris's personal essays work some delightful idiosyncratic magic that transcends easy niches of readers. Nonreaders enjoy him as do hardened readers.

What are his techniques? Self-deflation, for one. Juxtaposing odd combinations of things. He also has the knack at choosing just the offbeatly right word. Take "Go Carolina," the first essay in this collection. Technique 2: He sets up a comparison between the film staple of a mysterious "agent" showing up to haul a malefactor off for some deserved but unnamed comeuppance and the situation of a speech therapist coming to get him, fifth-grader David, out of class for some special work. Technique 1: Then we see this lisping child, embarrassed at not being a sports fan, struggling to give the "right" answer to the "agent's" question about whether he prefers the team of "State" (red school color) or "Carolina" (blue school color) by scrutinizing her clothes for clues. And throughout the piece we see Technique 3: "the gentlemanly application of handcuffs," "David Thedarith," his substitution of the phrase "marine life" for "seafood" in order to avoid "the hissy *s*."

Similarly "Smart Guy"—an account of his lifelong avoidance of the IQ test so that he could maintain his certain suspicion that he was indeed a philosophical genius, that his father's scornful use in his childhood of the term "Smart Guy" might turn out to be amazingly literal. Finally, at forty-two, he succumbs to the lure of certainty, plans paying up his Mensa dues (IQ 132 and above), and takes the test. Result? "There are cats that weigh more than my IQ score." His partner, Hugh, assures him he's good at other things and, pressed, specifies the naming of stuffed animals.

The title essay, surprisingly, does not refer to his childhood problem with the hissy *s*. Instead, it deals with his move to Paris in hopes of learning French. A writer whose stock-in-trade is self-deflation thus opens up a rich new subdivision of potential humiliation! This title essay, "Jesus Shaves," "The Tapeworm Is In," and "Make That a Double" deal with his attempts to speak better French. The first two of the quartet focus on the classroom. He terms his teacher a "saucebox" but presents her as asexual dominatrix. An exercise offering practice for use of the pronoun *one*—"And what does one do on Easter?"—leads not only to the memories of his family's Greek Orthodox Easters, so peculiarly late by standards of most in Raleigh, North Carolina, but also to the multicultural exchange of rudimentary Easter facts in rudimentary French. The Son of God dies "on two morsels of lumber"? In the third and fourth of these essays he listens to a gift from his sister Amy (a noted comic actress), a tape of *Pocket Medical French*, and fantasizes his sparkling conversation onboard a yacht involving "discharges" and "stool samples" or finds unforeseen humor in the gender roles of French nouns, especially items of food. Why can't a hot dog be permitted "to swing both ways"?

Book Smart
Recommended Reading

Move on to any of Sedaris's other collections, being careful not to miss his LOL essay about working as a seasonal elf at Macy's. Also terrific is a volume he edited: comic pieces by other writers collected under the title *Children Playing Before a Statue of Hercules*.

Fables for Our Time and Famous Poems Illustrated

James Thurber

This is a light and easy read but a rewarding one. Some of the fables are shorter than half a page, and the longest consumes a page and a half. The book can be carried to the beach or toted around for those odd moments in the dentist's waiting room.

Thurber has taken the classic fable format that originated no later than Aesop in the sixth century BCE, a very short tale with a moral overtly spelled out. Thurber's particular spin is a very dark moral or a near non sequitur. It's often alliterative, sometimes allusive, sometimes punning, as in the turkey fable that ends "Youth will be served, frequently stuffed with chestnuts." Both the tale itself and the didactic one-liner have qualities that produce a wry smile or a chuckle. You'll find yourself quoting some phrases or lines, possibly to others and certainly to yourself.

Take "The Bear Who Let It Alone." The concept of a bear addicted to the honey-based wine called mead is funny in itself. Although he's generous with cronies—"See what the bears in the back room will have"—his at-home, mead-sotted reelings and snoozings frighten his wife and children. When said bear hits bottom, he goes teetotal with a vengeance. To demonstrate his radical sobriety, he turns cartwheels at home, "ramming his elbows through the windows." Result: a frightened wife and children. The moral implies the necessity of the golden mean but not in such prissy terms.

"The Unicorn in the Garden" is unusual in that, except for the eponymous unicorn, the characters are Homo sapiens, husband and wife. The tale and the moral play on Thurber's frequent theme of dominant-women-can-be-scary.

Other fables have beavers who wear their teeth down to the gum line, a philandering stork who's found a good obstetrical lie to use on his wife, a gander who gets mistaken for propaganda, and an eagle who sports his stolen lion's mane so convincingly that he gets shot by his wife. All are accompanied by Thurber's appealingly childlike drawings. These simple line illustrations also accompany the "famous poems" that, mostly, aren't famous these days. (You probably haven't read Longfellow's "Excelsior" lately or Thomas Dunn English's "Ben Bolt.") The poetry section might serve as a pleasant introduction to these poems for children, but the fables are definitely for adults.

Thurber was one of many young men who made their way from the provinces (Columbus, Ohio, in his case) to more sophisticated purlieus in the East. Thurber worked for years at the *New Yorker* (thanks to his friendship with E. B. White) and remained a contributor of copy and cartoons after he left the staff. We appreciate the dark strain of his humor all the more when we learn that he was partially blind from a childhood accident (a game of William Tell with his brother went awry) and later in adulthood became almost totally blind.

Book Smart
Recommended Reading

You can go on to the sequel *Further Fables*, but be sure not to miss the short story "The Secret Life of Walter Mitty" (with another domineering wife). Keep in mind the delightful portmanteau of *The Thurber Carnival*, a Broadway revue that won Thurber a Tony award. If you want a lot of Thurber, you can't go wrong with the Thurber volume in the Library of America series. The selections were made by Garrison Keillor, a midwesterner who knows a thing or two about humor.

The Importance of Being Earnest

Oscar Wilde

Y ou could call it a play about nothing. Or you could call it a play about language. To adopt a line from the text, "It is perfectly phrased and quite as true as observations in civilized society ought to be." It's a cream puff, a soufflé, champagne.

As a play, it's meant to be seen, so get yourself a copy of the definitive 1952 film and delight in Michael Redgrave, Margaret Rutherford, and the divine Edith Evans. The performers are all, as the British say, "spot on," including the two butlers, whose "Yes, sir's" are impeccably charming. After your first viewing, sit back with the text and savor the phrases.

Here's the setup. Two eminently eligible bachelors seek wives. Jack is eager to propose to Gwendolyn, a smart London lady. Algernon Moncrieff, Gwendolyn's cousin, has lively fantasies about Cecily, Jack's ward, who lives on Jack's country estate in a location carefully undisclosed to Algernon. First complication: Jack has let Gwendolyn believe his name is "Ernest," and she has fallen in love with him on that premise. Second complication: Algernon, that slyboots, learns where Cecily is rusticated and drops in. Presenting himself, naturally, as Ernest, scapegrace brother of Jack, he swiftly wins Cecily's heart. Both women become engaged to a nonexistent Ernest Worthing. "It is not a situation a young girl likes to find herself in," Gwendolyn muses.

Supply the backdrop of Jack as a foundling, left in a handbag in the cloakroom at Victoria Station (you'll soon be saying, "the Brighton line?") and rescued by a philanthropic gentleman worth megapounds. (The play was written in 1895, when orphans, wards, and fortunes were staples of literature.) Now Wilde is ready for spoofing use of all the conventions of comedies of manners—witty repartee about the relative merits of country and city and broad exploitation of the disguise motif (Algernon appears, as Ernest, just as Jack has announced the death of the fictional Ernest: "It is perfectly ridiculous to be in mourning for someone who has come to stay with you for a week"). Wilde supplies witty inversions of clichés—"Divorces are made in heaven"—and hurls anodyne barbs at the wealthy, "If the lower classes don't set us a good example, what on earth use are they?"

The play comes to a climax with a parody of the tragic close of *Oedipus Rex*, where intense interrogation reveals the hideous net of coincidences leading to Oedipus's unwitting patricide and incestuous marriage. Jack's discoveries are equally fortuitous but highly felicitous. Let's say here only that Cecily's governess, Miss Prism, subject to moments of "mental abstraction," was employed a quarter of a century back as nanny for a family named Moncrieff.

You can, if you wish, get yourself interested in the biographical details of the tragic fall of Oscar Wilde, husband, father, society lion, when the veil of secrecy was ripped off his homosexual practices (at the time, a literal crime), and you can use your hindsight to discern telltale delight in secrets in this play. But the mortal Wilde rests in peace in an elaborate tomb in Père Lachaise Cemetery in Paris; the immortal Wilde lives forever in the verbal pyrotechnics of this play.

Back in the Day:
Some Great Eighteenth-Century Works

The Life of Johnson
James Boswell

Letters from an American Farmer
J. Hector St. John de Crèvecoeur

Tom Jones
Henry Fielding

Selections from *A Dictionary of the
English Language*
Samuel Johnson

The Female Quixote
Charlotte Lennox

The School for Scandal
Richard Brinsley Sheridan

Tristram Shandy
Laurence Sterne

Gulliver's Travels
Jonathan Swift

Thraliana
Hester Thrale

Candide
Voltaire

If you want to know the overall health of a society, look at the quality of the books it is currently consuming.
—John Sutherland

SCHOOL BELLS are ringing, and students are taking on subjects that are new to them. Why not use this traditional month of academic return for a look at writing of the eighteenth century?

Eight of these books are by English writers, but let's start with a look at the two Frenchmen. Voltaire's *Candide* is a sparkling satire, a poke in the ribs at the belief that this world is as perfect as any world could be. Crèvecoeur's *Letters from an American Farmer* offers a mingling of fact and fiction as it reports on the early days of the American nation through the eyes of a man from France who purports to be writing from his farm in Pennsylvania.

Of the English writers, the earliest is Jonathan Swift, whose fake travel book, *Gulliver's Travels*, has earned him immortality. You've seen the cartoons involving a supine Gulliver tied up with many tiny ropes, but if you haven't actually read the book, you have a treat awaiting you. The novels of two other writers, Henry Fielding and Laurence Sterne, offer readers a great many laughs with less of Swift's underlying bitterness. Fielding's *Tom Jones* has rollicked its way into the hearts of many, and Sterne's *Tristram Shandy* uncannily anticipates a modern sensibility.

Samuel Johnson was acquainted with the other four writers on the list. Johnson, who was dubbed "the great Cham [Khan] of literature" by novelist Tobias Smollett (whose novel *The Expedition of Humphry Clinker* deserves a place here), did indeed command many areas of literature. He is represented by a selection of entries from his famous *Dictionary*. James Boswell and Hester Thrale both knew Johnson extremely well. Boswell's wonderful biography has made Johnson known to succeeding generations as "a personality." Johnson virtually lived with Hester Thrale and her husband, Henry, for many years, and she knew him in a way Boswell did not. While her Johnson anecdotes are fascinating, she's earned her place on this list mostly as a writer about herself and her household.

Charlotte Lennox and her *Female Quixote* deserve to be even better known. Johnson himself celebrated her entry into the literary world by sponsoring an all-night party at the Devil Tavern, featuring "a magnificent hot apple pie" and a crown of laurel for her. Richard Brinsley Sheridan, the only playwright on our list, was forty-two years younger than Johnson and the son of his sometime friend Thomas Sheridan (the playwright's grandfather had been a confidant of Jonathan Swift). Johnson, in 1777, proposed the young Sheridan for membership in his prestigious Literary Club as the man who had written "the two best comedies of his age."

A *New Yorker* cartoon of several years past depicts an angry long-gowned woman about to hurl a piece of crockery at her cowering, periwigged husband. He protests, "Please, dear. It's the Age of Reason." To help expunge old labels or platitudes about this century of great wit and intellectual ferment, keep in mind the perceptive title of scholar Donald Greene's delightful book *The Age of Exuberance.*

The Life of Johnson

James Boswell

On May 16, 1763, in a London bookshop a young man met his literary idol, a man old enough to be his father. They enjoyed each other's company from time to time over the years, once traveling together—to the Hebrides Islands—for ninety-four days, but their contact was limited. The young man lived in Scotland while the older man had been a passionate Londoner for many years. Twenty-eight years later (1791) their names became forever linked by the publication of the young man's biography of the older: "Boswell's Johnson" has become a household phrase and "Boswell" a synonym for a biographer. Boswell ensured Johnson's immortality and vice versa. (Ironically, Boswell's writing has proved more enduringly appealing to a general readership than has Johnson's.) Literary historians credit Boswell with redefining life-writing forever, rejecting the "great man" approach for the "warts-and-all" approach. *The Life of Johnson* is frequently termed "the best biography ever written," largely because it captures the man entire: we see the superlative intelligence and the tenderheartedness of Johnson, but we also see a gesticulating man, wig askew, slurping his soup, and we witness him "tossing and goring" others in conversation.

This book, like many great masterpieces, was highly improbable, as was, perhaps, the relationship. Johnson was eccentric, cranky, and never one to suffer fools. Boswell was a bumptious young man, who by his own admission had "an excess of self-esteem." Early in their acquaintance, Johnson, skilled in seeing through veneers, said to Boswell, "Give me your hand; I have taken a liking to you." The fact that both men suffered from depression may have been a bond, and the friendship may have been bolstered by its father-son surrogacy: Johnson was childless, and Boswell and his crusty father, the Laird of Auchinleck, were lifelong antagonists.

We now know that Boswell, even before his meeting with Johnson, was a compulsive diarist. This diary-keeping was the perfect workshop for honing his biographical skills. Unlike the occasional cartoon version of himself, Boswell did not scribble as he followed Johnson around. Instead, he used his excellent memory after every social occasion to make a kind of "bouillon cube" of succinct notes, expanding them when time permitted.

Boswell conceived of the biography as a life "in scenes," and this dramatic quality continues to intrigue. For a fine sampling, go to May 1776, when Boswell paints on a wide canvas the scene of a dinner where Johnson is seated by John Wilkes, whom he loathes. Or try a verbal miniature of May 1773 where Boswell describes Johnson breaking into laughter, where he "sent forth peals so loud, that in the silence of the night his voice seemed to resound from Temple-bar to Fleet-ditch."

Unsurprisingly, the best scenes are those where Boswell directly observes Johnson in action, but he did painstaking research for the other periods of Johnson's life, noting that he had "run over half of London in order to fix a date correctly."

 Book Smart
Recommended Reading

Do immerse yourself further in these fascinating people of this exuberant era. My top five recommendations: Boswell's *London Journal*, Mary Hyde's *The Impossible Friendship* (about the rivalry between Boswell and Hester Thrale, who knew Johnson even better), Walter Jackson Bate's wonderful twentieth-century biography of Johnson, Bruce Redford's brilliant *Designing the Life of Johnson*, and David Buchanan's *The Treasures of Auchinleck*, the mesmerizing account of how containers such as an ebony cabinet and a croquet box yielded up reams of Boswell manuscripts in the twentieth century.

Letters from an American Farmer

J. Hector St. John de Crèvecoeur

It reached the eyes of readers in 1782, with the author listed simply as Hector St. John—no pesky French name. Taken at face value, it's a series of twelve letters depicting life in the colonies shortly before the Revolution. Calling himself James, a man who inherited his farm from his father, the letter writer sends Mr. F. B. a series of epistles about life in America. Many describe doings on his farm, but to give his recipient a sense of the country as a whole, he includes a lengthy report from his travels to Nantucket and a briefer account of "Charles Town" in South Carolina.

The letter writer is the first to raise the question: "What, then, is the American, this new man?" He's the first to present the ideas now termed "the American dream." And he's the first to show that America wouldn't be America without ethnic groups living cheek by jowl. All these show the author ahead of his time, a man grappling with the metamorphosis into an identity that "extinguishes European prejudice . . . that mechanism of subordination, that servility of disposition which poverty had taught him." This book was immediately popular in England and Ireland, giving two generations of Europeans their dominant impression of the American colonies.

So why does Hector St. John call himself James in these letters? Is he really in "Carlisle, in Pennsylvania"? Well might you ask, for things are not what they seem. It's not a hoax by a complete "travel liar," not the tale of a Prester John, a medieval European purported to have traveled to Ethiopia. But it's not literally true. Read these fascinating letters with ambivalent eyes. They're fiction, but a fiction based on truth—well, up to a point. Scholars continue to debate what is literally true, what is well-intentioned hearsay (Nantucket women take opium every day), and what falls in the realm of wishful thinking.

This fascinating author was born in Normandy to a well-off French family and partly educated in England. As a French lieutenant, he fought on the losing side in the Battle of Quebec, switching his name and his language as he wended south. He buys a farm, "Pine Hill," near Goshen, New York, and marries a young woman from Westchester. For a time he lives the idyll of farmer, husband, and father, somewhat like that fictional farmer in a neighboring state.

But James is much more innocent than Crèvecoeur, whose life was exotically varied and cosmopolitan (he was to serve as French trade consul in New York and, many years later, spent time in Munich, where his son-in-law, Count Otto, was Napoleon's ambassador to Bavaria). James, a swell fellow, has nothing like that in his future. He consults his wife about everything, and he's pleased as punch to have been called "a farmer of feelings." (D. H. Lawrence terms him the "emotional proto-type of the American," as contrasted with that "dollar fiend" Benjamin Franklin.) And if he didn't seem such an openhearted provincial, you might occasionally wonder if he's pulling your leg. Take his tale about splitting open a bird that has eaten 171 bees. James lays them on a blanket and 54—count 'em—revive! Doesn't this seem like what Huck Finn calls "a stretcher"?

If Crèvecoeur's letters foreshadow the American tall tale, they also anticipate *Walden* (James teaches a new immigrant to produce a meticulous ledger of expenses, printed here), and the Nantucket section prints a catalogue of twelve types of whales—just the ticket for that nineteenth-century whalemeister Herman Melville. All pretty American after all!

The History of Tom Jones, a Foundling

Henry Fielding

enry Fielding had a thriving career as a writer of plays that satirized the government and also filled theaters. His *Tom Thumb* is still worth a look. But in 1737 the passing of a Licensing Act for theaters effectively closed down his career as a playwright and his work as manager of the New Theatre. The penurious but enterprising Fielding soon seized on the new literary kid on the block—the novel. In 1740 Samuel Richardson achieved literary popularity with his epistolary work *Pamela, or Virtue Rewarded* about a chambermaid who catapulted herself into the marital bed of her master by refusing to yield to his unlicensed advances. Fielding sensed the falsity in this kind of virtue and soon produced the wonderfully titled *Shamela*, following it with the longer *Joseph Andrews*, which featured a sexually reluctant male protagonist. But in 1749 Fielding came most fully into his own with this novel. A century later Samuel Taylor Coleridge pronounced its intricate story line one of three perfect plots.

That plot holds charms for the first-time reader that I'll not spoil. (Those who are rereading will enjoy the new charm of recognizing the red herrings that misled them before.) The start of a long interlocking chain of events comes the night that the benevolent Squire Allworthy, a childless widower, finds a sleeping baby boy nestled among his sheets. Questioning of his domestic staff makes reasonably clear that the mother must be the schoolmaster's servant Jenny Jones; Allworthy's servants are quick to label her "an impudent slut, a wanton hussy, an audacious harlot."

That baby grows up under the care of Allworthy's sister, Bridget, who soon marries and gives birth to Master Blifil, a constant foil for the rowdy Tom. Blifil has a pious exterior but is a loathsome sneak underneath; Tom is a roisterer lacking "prudence and religion" but with a good heart. (He's the archetypal attractive "bad boy" that women hope will be good only for them.) As you watch him grow through childhood, studying with the delightfully contrasting tutors Mr. Thwackum and Mr. Slouch, and move on into early manhood, he becomes a friend. You wink at his many amorous liaisons, including the scary moment of seeming to have bedded his biological mother; you wish him well in his virtuous love for Sophia Western (a character modeled on Fielding's beloved first wife); and you're optimistic when he's jailed and sentenced to hang.

Along with gaining Tom Jones as a jolly companion, the reader also gains Fielding as a friend. Each of the eighteen books is prefaced by a chat from the author. Some readers skip these, eager to get on with the action, but I commend them to you for their tone and for the deep background they supply about life in eighteenth-century England. They are charming—from the first preface where he compares an author to the keeper of a tavern and offers "Human Nature" as the specialty of his menu to the touching farewell where Fielding predicts these pages will outlive both him and the "abusive writings" of those who have treated him with "scurrility." A character in Kingsley Amis's novel *I Like It Here* (1958) affirms that prediction, calling Fielding "the only noncontemporary novelist who could be read with unaffected interest."

Be sure to see a young Albert Finney as Tom in Tony Richardson's delightful 1964 film (screenplay by John Osborne). A witty use of the camera replaces the arch tone of the narrator, and Hugh Griffith as Squire Western walks right out of the pages of the novel.

Selections from *A Dictionary of the English Language*

Samuel Johnson (edited by Jack Lynch)

I n that delightful eighteenth-century fashion of nicknaming, Samuel Johnson became known for a time as "Dictionary" Johnson, so famous was his work and so closely connected the personality of the maker. If you've never considered the extended perusal of a dictionary, this is the time to start and this is the book. You may discover that you, like me, have a full-blown case of that happy disease *lexicographilia* (love of dictionaries).

Published in 1755, it's sometimes called the first English dictionary, which of course it wasn't. But it was the first dictionary in English to go beyond hard words, to take into account both difficult ("inkhorn") words and the everyday language. It's also compelling as an incidental dictionary of quotations, for the full-length work contains more than 110,000 quotations, mostly taken from English literature from the Elizabethan era up until the Restoration, years that Johnson regarded as "the wells of English undefiled." Happy exceptions occur for words from Chaucer, at one end, and words chosen "in the tenderness of friendship" at the other. Shakespeare, not surprisingly, makes many entrances; lines from all thirty-six of his plays are quoted. So, if you choose to look up so common a noun as, say, *trumpet,* you will find two quotations from Shakespeare, one from Milton, one from Dryden, one from Pope, three from less famous writers, and one from the eighteenth-century newspaper *The Tatler.*

Should you or I set out on so mountainous a chore today, our task would still be stupendous. But if compelled to find, say, ten different sources for the adjective *green,* we'd sensibly head for the nearest search engine. Johnson had only his gargantuan memory and his prodigious reading. No search engine . . . and no public library: he ransacked his own ragged stock of books and borrowed widely from uncomplaining friends who welcomed home volumes liberally marked up in Johnson's heavy lead pencil. Occasionally he quotes himself (see, for example, "luxurious" or "pimp"), but his lack of ostentation compels him to name the work, not the author or, in deeper obscurity, attribute the lines to "Anonymous."

Some people have the idea that Johnson's dictionary is a collection of idiosyncratic definitions, but perhaps it's the very rarity of these that makes them frequently quoted. You can check out "oats" or "Whig" or see "lich" for an interpolated salute in Virgilian Latin to his hometown of Lichfield. But what *is* truly personal is Johnson's Preface. If this is your introduction to Johnson, know that you're in the hands of a very great writer. Adopting a posture of extreme modesty, he stresses the painful enduring of the erosion of his linguistic ideals during nine years of work. But even as he's expressing disillusionment, the beauty of his phrasing demands our cheers. The sadness of the last paragraph is particularly noble: he dismisses the work "with frigid tranquility, having little to fear or hope from censure or from praise."

Book Smart
Recommended Reading

If your *lexicographilia* becomes severe, you may have to buy the CD-ROM of the complete text of Johnson's *Dictionary*. (If money is no object, buy the two folio volumes themselves.) Meanwhile, Lynch's selection, with its own helpful introduction, index, and bibliography, will serve you admirably. Beware of the related affliction of *Johnsonmania*. If it strikes, start with Henry Hitching's pleasant *Defining the World: The Extraordinary Story of Dr. Johnson's Dictionary* and move on to Allen Reddick's scholarly and compelling *The Making of Johnson's Dictionary*.

The Female Quixote, or the Adventures of Arabella

Charlotte Lennox

Jane Austen loved it and thought her second reading of it as good as the first. Samuel Johnson wrote the dedication and may have written the chapter entitled "Being in the Author's Opinion, the best Chapter in this History." (And he seems, in general, quite taken with "Mrs. Lennox," the wife of an employee of his printer.) And yet most humanely educated people I've talked to have never heard of this 1752 novel nor of its intriguing author.

The novel has a very literary premise: how do "romances" differ from "novels"? "Romance" is notoriously difficult to define, but it's generally associated with excess of imagination, fantastic occurrences, and two-dimensional characterization, while the "novel" makes stronger attempts at mimicking or mirroring the world. Lennox's book manages to be rather like a romance while also satirizing romances. The title implies the premise: just as Cervantes' Don Quixote had his head turned by the reading of romances of knights of old and set out to tilt at windmills, so has *The Female Quixote*'s heroine Arabella (motherless daughter of "The Marquis of _____") delved too deeply in her mother's cache of frivolous French romances, and bad translations of these to boot. Lacking proper guidance in her perusal and her interpretation of these flimsy volumes, she's mistaken them for guides to how the real world works. (Imagine a modern reader who took the stereotyped Harlequin Romance as a guide to conduct of her personal life! She might wait forever for a clone of Fabio to appear.)

The hapless Arabella, whom one scholar calls "Snow White's daughter," sees all men as either potential ravishers, protectors, or ideal mates. Believing that a woman must be initially haughty to a suitor, she instructs her maid Lucy to return unopened a letter she's quite curious to peruse. She scorns the fine Mr. Glanville because he ignores the rules of romance. And when she believes imaginary ravishers are at her heels, she throws herself into the Thames. Once she is providentially rescued and restored to bodily health, a "good Divine," a "Doctor," engages in Socratic/therapeutic dialogue with her, demonstrating that "the likeness of a picture can only be determined by a knowledge of the original." She is cured of romances and the book must end. Don Quixote had to die when his illusion was removed, but Arabella can now wed Mr. Glanville and live happily ever after or, as Congreve put it half a century earlier, "dwindle into wife."

Charlotte Ramsay Lennox is a historical being, yet her life reads almost like that of a fictional character. Born in Gibraltar, she came to England at fifteen to be a lady's companion. She labored in many parts of the literary vineyard—magazine editor, poet, essayist, translator, actress, and novelist. Her acquaintance with Johnson helped vault her into prominence, and Henry Fielding, like Johnson himself, published favorable reviews of her work (failing to win friendship with the London bluestocking circle, she seems to have been what used to be called "a man's woman"). You can see her likeness in the National Portrait Gallery in London as one of the "Nine Living Muses." How sad to learn that this intelligent, witty, hardworking woman who briefly escaped the jaws of oblivion died—in 1804—in poverty and lies in an unmarked grave.

The School for Scandal

Richard Brinsley Sheridan

In 1777, when at least some of the English were fretting about the war with those upstarts across the Atlantic, others were laughing their heads off at the new play at the Drury Lane Theatre. Richard Sheridan, native of Dublin and thus pro-liberty for the colonists, had made his name known in 1775 with his popular comedy of manners *The Rivals* (featuring the famous Mrs. Malaprop, who deranges the language so well); now, he had done it again. This new play can today seem a delightful period piece, but it also has a timeless concern with the public enjoyment of scandal, whether real or manufactured, and with the contrast between illusion and truth. In the first of two major plotlines, two brothers compete for the love of a young woman; in the second, a young wife, essentially virtuous, becomes caught up in scandalmongering and the titillation of tittle-tattle.

In the first plotline the two brothers, Charles and Joseph Surface, contrast wildly. Charles is sowing a prodigal crop of wild oats, uttering sentiments such as "I'm never so successful as when I am a little merry: let me throw [the dice] on a bottle of champagne, and I never lose." Joseph (whose first name is a tip-off to students of the eighteenth century who remember the oh-so-chaste title character of Fielding's novel *Joseph Andrews*) has no heart beneath his proper exterior. Both brothers are attracted to Maria (ma-RYE-uh), the wealthy ward of Sir Peter Teazle—Charles, to Maria herself, Joseph, to her money.

Sir Peter is that classic figure of farce, the elderly man who takes a young bride—a crime, according to this play, that carries its own punishment with it. Lady Teazle has fallen in with a pack of gossips and, in an effort to seem au courant, now pretends to carry on a surreptitious fling (with Joseph Surface). These gossips are the "faculty" of the school for scandal, and they bear such "ticket names" as Lady Sneerwell and Sir Benjamin Backbite. (They are the more literate progenitors of modern writers of gossip columns.)

High points of the play include the scene of an auction where scapegrace Charles refuses, out of sentiment, to sell a portrait of his uncle Oliver, long resident in the East Indies (but the audience knows he's present in disguise). But the most famous scene elevates a mere stage prop, a folding screen, to fame; its collapse produces a marvelous moment of farce uniting the two plotlines.

All, of course, comes out well: the good end happily and the bad unhappily, the very definition of fiction, as Oscar Wilde, Sheridan's spiritual descendent as a writer of brilliant dramatic repartee, said some 120 years later.

Sheridan's life is the essence of drama. He ran off to the Continent, making a secret marriage with a young singer, later fighting two duels over her. He chose to end his comet-like success as comic playwright at the age of twenty-nine, becoming manager of the Drury Lane Theatre, and then member of Parliament, where he brought down the House with a brilliant speech, collapsing after four hours into the arms of Edmund Burke. Despite dying in debt, he continued to amaze, receiving a bodacious funeral and burial in Westminster Abbey.

Tristram Shandy

Laurence Sterne

There are two well-known negative remarks about this novel originally published in nine volumes between 1759 and 1767. In one of Samuel Johnson's few errors, he noted in a 1776 conversation with James Boswell, "Nothing odd will do long. *Tristram Shandy* did not last." Johnson managed to wrongly damn the book not only for the future but for the present. In the 1950s, F. R. Leavis, English literary scholar whose prestige was then lofty, dismissed it humorlessly in his judgmental book *The Great Tradition* as "irresponsible (and nasty) trifling." These remarks would not perturb Sterne, for he firmly believed, "De gustibus non est disputandum" (a line quoted early in the novel)— there's no arguing about taste. On the plus side of the opinion ledger, Virginia Woolf deemed it "the greatest of all novels," Thomas Jefferson and his wife read it aloud to each other, and Salman Rushdie thinks it's nifty.

What kind of book is this? It's part comic novel, part ruminative essay, part satire. Someone has called it "the biggest shaggy dog story of all time." Hundreds of dashes help to suggest the conversational tone, and progression moves by digression. While it draws on a long tradition of learned wit, it's self-reflexive and postmodern—before there was modern. I'll explain. The title character narrates for us the story of his life. Sterne appears as a character named Yorick, after Hamlet's "fellow of infinite jest," but dies early on, getting two pages of solid black in mourning tribute. There are also a textual marbled page and intermittent lines of asterisks and various typographical oddities. Dave Eggers's drawing of the stapler on his desk early in his book *A Heartbreaking Work of Staggering Genius* is right in the Sterne tradition.

So, Tristram narrates the story of his life, as I was saying—I've been attempting Sterne's technique here—and we also get to know his father and his Uncle Toby, who's currently courting the Widow Wadman, and whose hobbyhorse is the siege of Namur, where he received a soldierly wound.

That's about it for plot. The uniqueness appears early with Tristram's telling us about the night he was . . . *conceived.* At a primal moment, Mrs. Shandy asks her husband if he remembered to wind the clock. Tristram thinks all his lackings as a rational being may have started at this moment when Mr. Shandy, whose "animal spirits" were thus "dispersed," was not able to concentrate on launching the "homunculus" safely to his destination. (Contemporary beliefs about conception saw the sperm as carrying "the little man" toward his nurturing receptacle in the female.) So we're off and running with all ensuing aspects of plot being whatever goes through the mind of Tristram or another character.

Perhaps Tristram's sullied begetting influenced his difficult delivery, for Dr. Slop's use of forceps rendered his nose flatter than a pancake. And it's with this mention of the "nose" that the irrational association of ideas may cause even the pre-Freudian reader to make downward associations. By Volume III, Tristram has spoken so much of noses that he's constrained to assert that "where the word *Nose* occurs,— I declare, by that word I mean a Nose." The author doth protest too much?

As you can deduce, the element of bawdy is mild by modern standards, but perhaps it gained an eighteenth-century piquancy because it came from the pen of a clergyman. Yes, Sterne, born in Tipperary, Ireland, was an Anglican priest near York and includes one of his sermons in its entirety in this delightful book. As Sterne notes in a letter, the book has "more handles than one."

Gulliver's Travels

Jonathan Swift

"Travels into Several Remote Nations of the World in Four Parts by one Lemuel Gulliver, First a Surgeon, and then a Captain of several Ships"—its formal title—appeared before the public in 1726. When it first emerged from Benjamin Motte's print shop in London, it was likely to have been viewed as one more specimen in the popular genre of factual travel accounts. An engraved portrait of Capt. Gulliver, the neatly drawn map accompanying each of the quartet of voyages, and an elaborate array of prefatory material reinforce this sense of verisimilitude. We now know it by its more mouthable title, and we know the true identity of the author. Similarly, we're under no danger of shelving it under nonfiction. Today's delusion, held by many not familiar with the book, is that it is a story about little people and big people written for children. Not so.

The little people, the Lilliputians (about six inches high), exist, as do their really big counterparts, the Brobdingnagians (about seventy-two feet high), whose court ladies employ Gulliver as a sex toy. Any child who comprehends the bitter satire in these first two sections would indeed be a prodigy. As Swift says of the book, "I wrote it not to divert mankind but to vex it." These first two voyages, the best known, are succeeded by a voyage to a medley of invented nations where Gulliver has his eyes opened to the falsity of history, the folly of longing for earthly immortality, and the fatuousness of technology for the sake of technology (sheep that can't grow fleece—how marvelous!). He briefly visits Japan, a country so little known in England of the early eighteenth century that it could well have been fictional. The final voyage transports him to an island where horses—the Houyhnhnms—reign supreme, and the loathed, all-too-humanlike Yahoos slouch about, hurling feces and gnawing on ass's flesh.

Swift, born in Ireland of English parents, earned his daily bread as dean of Saint Patrick's Cathedral in Dublin. He cloaks his attacks on humanity's madness and badness with a great deal of charm (the fallacy of this book as children's literature didn't come from nowhere). He knows the lesson every satirist must learn: those offered vitriol in a honey-rimmed cup are more likely to imbibe. Gulliver meets with a varied array of irrationality and cruelty. Sometimes, particularly in the odd-numbered voyages, he's able to identify these qualities. In Books II and IV, however, Gulliver is more likely to transform into Capt. Gullible, a silly creature who strives vainly to impress his hosts with the excellence of his countrymen ("Look, we created gunpowder and now we can kill lots of people simultaneously!"—I paraphrase). Alternatively, he may "go native" in his adulation of the Other: he becomes so besotted with the horse sense of the Houyhnhnms that, arrived home, he chooses chatting up the creatures in his stables over talking with his loving wife and children.

 Book Smart
Recommended Reading

Introduce yourself to Swift's satiric mode by reading his near-perfect essay, "A Modest Proposal," written two years after *Gulliver*. Or start by perusing the English translation of the Latin epitaph he wrote for his tomb in Saint Patrick's: (He has gone) "where savage indignation can no longer lacerate his heart."

Thraliana, the Diary of Mrs. Hester Lynch Thrale (Later Mrs. Piozzi) 1776–1809

Hester Lynch Thrale (edited by Katharine C. Balderston)

What a fascinating woman was this Hester Lynch Salusbury Thrale Piozzi! Living in Wales and England from 1741 to 1821, she made her strongest hold on fame by her friendship with Samuel Johnson. He was a frequent partaker of the domestic comfort of both her country home, Streatham Park, and her townhouse in Southwark, the site, a century earlier, of the Globe Theatre. Johnson's time at Streatham with Hester and Henry Thrale and their children "soothed a life radically wretched," as Johnson put it. She knew a side of him not accessible to his best-known biographer, James Boswell. Two years after Johnson's death she published *Anecdotes of the Late Samuel Johnson*, composed mostly of memories she extracted from her journal of family history, which she called *Thraliana*. Her *Thraliana* began when her husband presented her with six calf-bound volumes with the word *Thraliana* embossed on each. It was a tribute to her declared interest in the French tradition of collections of material that reflect the character of a person or place: "These Anas have seized me so," she had said.

She began her writing in these six volumes, now in the Huntington Library in California, in 1776. She noted the sad irony of the fact that the last entry in this gift from her first husband, who had died in 1781, was the record of the death of her second husband, Gabriel Piozzi, an Italian music master, who passed away in 1809. These two marriages in themselves make an enthralling study in mores of the time. Her essentially loveless union with Henry Thrale, a wealthy owner of a brewery, was solid in material terms. She bore him twelve children, only four of whom lived to maturity (yet this quartet of daughters lived a combined total of 312 years). She had met Piozzi at the home of the great music historian Charles Burney and soon engaged him as harpsichord teacher and singing master to her daughters. Contemporary standards judged their 1784 marriage as scandalous; it caused a rupture with the soon-to-die Johnson and with her daughters, aged twenty, thirteen, twelve, and seven at the time—An Italian! A Catholic! A singing master! It's gratifying to report their happiness in their marriage and their adoption of Piozzi's nephew.

Although she called this collection a "farrago" and once uttered, "Let it never be printed, oh never never never," the reader feels her spirit would have been pleased with the 1942 publication that detailed "ev'ry thing which struck me at the Time." This intelligent, witty, and enormously energetic woman threw herself a ball in the city of Bath for her eightieth birthday. Doffing the black she had worn for twelve years since Piozzi's death, she—and around seven hundred guests—followed up a concert and a supper with dancing until 5 A.M.

 Book Smart
Recommended Reading

Mary Hyde's *The Thrales of Streatham Park* is a fascinating study that draws on *Thraliana* and on the *Commonplace Book* that succeeded it. But a unique source for her volume is *The Children's Book*, later called *The Family Book*, which Hester Thrale compiled for thirteen years. A superb researcher, Mary Hyde also followed the family through the next two generations with delightful small details such as the fact that the godfathers to Queeney's only child were two future kings of England. Want even more? Read either (or both) of the two biographies by James Clifford (1941) and William McCarthy (1985). And for something different, try Beryl Bainbridge's novel *According to Queeney*.

Candide; or, The Optimist

Voltaire (translated by Tobias Smollett)

The complete works, including the letters, of this eighteenth-century Frenchman will fill about 150 volumes, but the proverbial *l'homme de la rue* (man in the street) would be hard pressed to name any title other than *Candide*. In his lifetime Jean François Arouet, l.j. (the younger) was frequently on the run from authorities: at least twice he was imprisoned in the Bastille, where he devised his pen name, an anagrammatized version of his last name and the French initials for "junior."

His continuing fear of the authorities made "location" his guiding principle in selecting his estate: Ferney was just over the border in the more liberal Switzerland. Thirteen years after his 1778 death, however, the changed climate of post-Revolution France permitted him near apotheosis. His body was removed from its obscure country burial and reburied in the church building newly renamed the Pantheon (all gods). One longs for truth to the tale of his corpse later being disinterred by religious fanatics and thrown in a lime pit along with the body of his lifetime rival, the equally undevout Rousseau, but, alas, it is apocryphal. (They've checked, and he's right where he was planted.) Also untrue is the attribution to Voltaire of the statement of longing for the last king to be strangled with the entrails of the last priest (that was a more obscure writer, Jean Meslier). The fact that Voltaire's image as sardonic rationalist tilting at injustice, oppression, and superstition still attracts stories like these conveys the lingering power of his iconoclasm.

Candide appeared anonymously under the guise of a translation from the German by a "Doctor Ralph." It takes on a fairly specific target—the optimistic concept formulated by Gottfried Leibniz that this is the best of all possible worlds, that, in Alexander Pope's phrasing, all partial evil [is] universal good. God, so the reasoning goes, is a perfect being and, given the choice of an infinite number of worlds to create, would of course select the world mirroring his perfection.

Into this atmosphere of "Isn't it pretty to think so?" Voltaire sends his naive protagonist, a youth of sweet disposition, the illegitimate nephew of a German baron, a student of the tutor Pangloss (all tongue), who perpetuates a doctrine of "metaphysico-theologo-cosmolo-nigology." What follows is an extended romp, what one commentator neatly calls "a comic book adventure." Expelled from the paradise of his Westphalian castle because of amorous activity with Cunegund, the baron's daughter, he's off to the army of the Bulgars, Holland, Lisbon, South America (including the mythical land of El Dorado), Surinam, Paris, and Constantinople. He experiences or attests to, among other unpleasant phenomena, auto-da-fé, buttock-amputation, cannibalism, chain gang, earthquake, imprisonment, major-scale thievery, malaise, public flagellation, rape, slavery, storm at sea, strangulation, and syphilis.

Candide tries hard to keep the faith, to believe that whatever happens is for the best, but comes to replace this grand theory with the simpler wisdom of love and work. And so Candide and his few trusted companions (including Cunegund, miraculously restored to him) settle down, commune style, to take short views and to cultivate their garden.

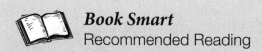

Book Smart
Recommended Reading

Move on to Samuel Johnson's *Rasselas*, an English tale of a wide-eyed young man, published by bizarre coincidence the same week as *Candide*. And don't neglect the musical/opera version of *Candide*, a brilliant tribute to Voltaire's legacy by a number of fellow, but twentieth-century, geniuses—Leonard Bernstein, Stephen Sondheim, Richard Wilbur, Lillian Hellman, and Dorothy Parker.

Growing Up:
The Pains and the Pleasures

OCTOBER

Little Women
Louisa May Alcott

My Ántonia
Willa Cather

The Curious Incident of the Dog in the Night-Time
Mark Haddon

The Go-Between
L. P. Hartley

A Portrait of the Artist as a Young Man
James Joyce

To Kill a Mockingbird
Harper Lee

The Emperor's Children
Claire Messud

The Chosen
Chaim Potok

The Yearling
Marjorie Kinnan Rawlings

A Tree Grows in Brooklyn
Betty Smith

My education was the liberty I had to read indiscriminately and all of the time, with my eyes hanging out.

—Dylan Thomas

IF GROWING up is a move from innocence to experience, the ten novels here scatter themselves all along the spectrum. Four of the ten are staunchly rooted in American childhood: *Little Women*, set in Massachusetts during the 1860s, is the only one aimed at a young audience. *The Yearling* is set in Florida during the last years of the nineteenth century. *A Tree Grows in Brooklyn* focuses on a girl growing up in that borough of New York from around 1912 to the outbreak of World War I. *To Kill a Mockingbird* takes on the lives of a brother and sister in Alabama during the Depression years. All the children of these books may be called somewhat innocent compared to most children growing up today, but they are exposed to trials as various as poverty, the harshness of nature, disruption of family life by war or by alcoholism, and increasing awareness of racial prejudice. Two of the novels, *The Go-Between* and *The Curious Incident of the Dog in the Night-Time*, focus on boys in England: the first in 1900 and the second in the contemporary era. Both Leo Colston and Christopher John Francis Boone must adjust their view of the world to encompass their jolting awareness of the complicated private lives of adults.

My Ántonia involves a male narrator looking back at the life of the title character whom he knew in her girlhood and adolescence in Nebraska and extends into their reacquaintance in adulthood. *The Chosen* is the only book of these ten to center on teenagers: two young men in the World War II years are both observant Jews, but one of them, Danny Saunders, faces the torturing decision of whether to break with the demanding expectations his father, a Hasidic rabbi, has for him.

The final two books are definitely written for adults. The most recent novel listed here, *The Emperor's Children*, features both a college freshman dropout and a trio of graduates from an Ivy League university who are about to turn thirty, but measurement by many yardsticks of maturity would pronounce them all very old adolescents. The final book, James Joyce's *A Portrait of the Artist as a Young Man*, is by far the most ambitious in literary terms. It takes its hero, Stephen Dedalus, from babyhood through early boyhood at a harsh boarding school into adolescence and a milestone coming-of-age moment as he prepares to leave his native Ireland for the Continent.

Other great books on this theme abound: for three classics, try Mark Twain's *Adventures of Huckleberry Finn*, J. D. Salinger's *The Catcher in the Rye*, or Carson McCullers's *The Heart Is a Lonely Hunter*. T. H. White's *The Once and Future King* is also terrific.

Little Women

Louisa May Alcott

Alcott once stated, "Though I do not enjoy writing 'moral tales' for the young, I do it because it pays well." While I continue to love *Little Women* and to love the memory of my first reading of it, Alcott's observation on the realities of the publishing market adds a tonic touch of reality. This 1868 novel about one year in the life of Meg, Jo, Beth, and Amy March includes many autobiographical touches from the life of Louisa May Alcott. (Knowing that May was her mother's maiden name gives a different connotation.) She was the second daughter of Abigail ("Abba") and Bronson Alcott, a Transcendentalist noted for innovative teaching methods as radical as aiming for student enjoyment of learning. Despite Alcott's benevolence toward his students, he and his "difficult" daughter often had a clash of wills. (He once called her "demonic.") Perhaps he envied her writing talent: James Russell Lowell in his *Fable for Critics* caricatured Bronson Alcott as a talker whose brilliance was snuffed out "like a taper / When he's shut up in a chamber with ink, pen and paper."

Louisa May Alcott, after a stint as a Civil War nurse, was editing a magazine for girls called *Merry's Museum* when the perceptive publisher suggested she write a book for children. Twelve weeks of work brought forth this novel. Its immediate popularity demanded a second part in the following year. Alcott proceeded to write related titles such as *Little Men* and *Jo's Boys*. The original book, never out of print, has been translated, filmed, abridged, and adapted. Gertrude Stein and Adrienne Rich, as well as many a non-famous woman, have testified to Jo's power as role model—an eagle amid the usual parade of fluffy chicks.

What qualities make this book so appealing to girls? The quartet of sisters, aged eleven to sixteen at the start of the book, offers infinite appeal: They are close and loving, each with a distinct personality. Meg, like oldest sister Jane Bennet in *Pride and Prejudice*, is nice, pretty. The rebellious Jo is already writing. You can imagine her saying, as Alcott herself did, "I will make a battering ram of my head and make my way through this rough and tumble world." Beth is so adorable a little musician that a neighbor gives her a piano. Amy is a little stuck on herself and her blonde curls, her turquoise ring, but she's so open about it all that you only occasionally want to kick her. The mother ("Marmee"), though saintly, acknowledges her struggles with her temper. The wealthy neighbors, Mr. Laurence and his grandson "Laurie," add a bracing whiff of the masculine world.

The book's original edition bore an epigraph from *The Pilgrim's Progress*, Bronson Alcott's favorite book, and the text has many allusions to the John Bunyan classic. The mother and four daughters are much concerned with goodness and duty while Mr. March is away, voluntarily serving as chaplain to Union troops, but Alcott's robust writing style bans the mawkish and the maudlin. The sleuthing of Madeleine B. Stern in the 1970s uncovered Alcott's use of her talents (under the pseudonym A. M. Barnard) in gruesome Gothic tales with titles such as "A Modern Mephistopheles" and "Pauline's Passion and Punishment." No "niminy-piminy chit" she!

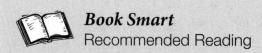

Book Smart
Recommended Reading

For more on the March family, check out Katharine Weber's *The Little Women* and Geraldine Brooks's *March*.

My Ántonia

Willa Cather

A lthough this novel contains attempted rape, suicide, and a tale of howling wolves attacking a sledge carrying a bride and groom, it's no action novel. The title implies it's a character study. It's also an homage to a time and place, the vast Nebraska prairie in the years before and after the turn of the twentieth century. Additionally, it's a fascinating study of a writer's selection of a way to unscroll the story.

The last of these, the point of view, is unusual. The novel starts with a purported "introduction" by the author. She meets up on a train with Jim Burden, a childhood friend from her hometown in Nebraska. He's a successful lawyer in New York, a man who made "a brilliant marriage," only to find himself now in the shell of a union. They discuss their memories of Ántonia Shimerda, daughter of a Bohemian immigrant family back in Black Hawk. They agree to write their memories of her, but it's Burden, months later, who presents her with a bulging portfolio. She notes that she's publishing it "substantially as he brought it to me." All this is, of course, fanciful. Jim Burden is only as real as Black Hawk, Nebraska, that is, a fiction. If Black Hawk is a stand-in for Cather's hometown of Red Cloud, then Jim Burden is a projection of Cather's masculine persona. It was a bold conceit for the writing of the novel, but Cather had blurred gender lines earlier in her life as well, sporting men's shirts and short hair (in 1890!).

The epigraph for the novel "Optima dies ... prima fugit" (the best days flee first) comes from Virgil's *Georgics*, a poem celebrating the rhythms of the year as punctuated by the arduous work of the plowman, the beekeeper, and their like. Jim studies this "perfect utterance" of Virgil as a college sophomore, and "his" own text paints the Nebraska landscape in all its bleak particularity—the wind-lashed snow, the wheel-ruts in the road "like gashes torn by a grizzly's claws," and the iconic image of the sinking sun irradiating a plow that now looks like "picture writing on the sun."

Now to Ántonia (pronounced AN-ton-ee-ah) herself. She and her family arrive in Black Hawk on the very train that brings the orphaned Jim Burden, aged ten, from Virginia to his grandparents'. (Cather is so associated with Nebraska that few people know that her family left for verdant Virginia when she was nine.) Ántonia's image darts in and out of the years covered by the text, always a vigorous, nurturing figure, always working for others' comfort whether in the house or harvesting or driving cattle in the fields. The last of the novel's five books—"Cuzak's Boys"—is set twenty years later. Jim visits Ántonia, now the wife of a kind farmer, presiding over a houseful of children. A genuine earth mother, she makes Jim "feel the goodness of planting and tending and harvesting." The novel ends with his plans to continue to know "Tony" and her family, this woman with whom he shares "the precious, the incommunicable past."

The novel is a paean to Ántonia, to all her hardy pioneer sisters, to all who live to serve others. Rooted in one perpetual place, she perhaps represents for "Jim" (and Cather) a destiny antithetical to their paths of education, city life, worldly success. Cather's skill as a writer keeps the novel from toppling into sentimentality, but you may prefer Lena Lingard, central figure in Book III, who, in one critic's words, "almost runs away with the show."

The Curious Incident of the Dog in the Night-Time

Mark Haddon

How often does a truly fresh storytelling voice come along? My answer is a vague "not often," but here's guessing that fifteen-year-old Christopher John Francis Boone, narrator of this novel, could come up with something more precise. After all, he's able to take two to the twenty-fifth power in his head. The jacket copy of some editions will tell you that he's a high-functioning autistic, but no clinical terms are used in the novel itself unless you count that the brother of a schoolmate calls him a "spazzer." He studies at a special school in Swindon, a midsized town in southwest England, where he (a) practices understanding what facial expressions mean and (b) achieves the highest possible score on a challenging national math test.

Christopher's mind receives information as a flood of data: a big orange leaf stuck to a policeman's shoe weighs equally with the fact that he's arresting Christopher. (As Christopher might tell it: "He's arresting me for hitting him. I hit him because he touched me. I don't like to be touched.") His straightforward approach to the world means that he cannot tell a lie and that he doesn't "get" metaphors. He's fine with similes and analogies though, comparing his own frequent mental overload with, once, a bread slicing machine that has too much bread coming at it and, another time, with a crashing computer: covering his ears and groaning works the equivalent rebooting magic of CTRL+ALT+DEL.

Christopher needs patterns to help him make sense of his world. In this way he's like his hero Sherlock Holmes, who seeks for schemes that allow him to fit together "disconnected episodes." (And you Baker Street Irregulars out there have already identified the book's title as a clue in a Holmes story.) Christopher is both Holmes and Dr. Watson, for he writes up his solving of the puzzle of the death of Wellington, a neighbor's poodle. Christopher found Wellington pinioned to the ground with a garden fork. Since he likes dogs—they don't lie and you can always tell which of their four moods they're in—he sets out to find the killer. As in the best of detective novels, prying the covering off an enigma jolts forth a number of slimy, squirming dark truths.

Christopher's extended sleuthing (Wellington's killer? No problem!) compels him to leave the comparative safety of his neighborhood. With only his pet rat, Toby, in his pocket—and quadratic equations in his head—for comfort, he confronts the perilous unknown of cash machines, train stations, and a labyrinth of unknown streets (all this with cops in hot pursuit) to sort out the new mysteries of his existence.

We feel the frustration of those who need to interact with Christopher (when stymied, he often screams). But we admire his resiliency as he undergoes a fast-forwarded growing up and come to love him. Besides, who can resist a storyteller who designates his chapters by prime numbers only (2, 3, 5, 7, 11, etc.)?

Book Smart
Recommended Reading

Haddon's second novel, *A Spot of Bother*, is very different but worth your time. For other novels from unusual points of view, try Gabriel García Márquez's *Chronicle of a Death Foretold* or look for Philip Wylie's *The Disappearance*—half of this 1951 novel deals with a world disaster where men must learn to cope with a womanless world; the other half shows the same world as experienced by women without men.

The Go-Between

L. P. Hartley

J uly of 1900 and only a few months left for the Victorian Age. An
English boy is on the verge of his thirteenth birthday in that hot
summer at Brandham Hall. Transformations of all sorts shim-
mer in the summer air as Lionel ("Leo") Colston, innocent in a way
soon to be obsolete forever, has adulthood thrust on him in the form of
a concentrated dose of heightened awareness of social class, knowledge
about sexual passion, and an introduction to the ways adults can wield
affection as a tool.

Hartley's 1953 novel beautifully conveys Leo's Edenic view of the
world. The son of the widow of a bank clerk, Leo is visiting his boarding
school classmate Marcus Maudesley. The wealthy Maudesleys, whose
footsteps, in Marcus's eyes, leave a "trail of gold" behind them, lease
the Hall from Lord Trimingham. The 9th Viscount himself is visiting, a "guest in his own house," as Leo phrases it. Facially disfigured
from an injury in the Boer War, Lord Trimingham is a true gentleman. He's kind to Leo, urging that he call him "Hugh," and when Leo's
aunt sends him a birthday gift of a "made" tie (one requiring no tying),
Hugh insists on donning it and soliciting compliments from the guests.
Marcus, though a year younger than Leo, helps him understand the
social horror of such an accessory, almost as gauche a phenomenon as
Leo's habit of bundling up his clothing rather than flinging it on the
floor for servants to retrieve. It's rumored that Marian, Marcus's beautiful older sister, aided by pressure from her mother, is about to enter
into an engagement with the Viscount, that time-honored, pragmatic,
English union of gentry wealth and ancient aristocracy. Hugh occasionally asks Leo to give a spoken message to Marian and thus dubs

him "Mercury," the messenger of the gods. The phrase is apt, for Leo, himself nicknamed for his zodiac sign, views these privileged adults as breathing an Olympian ether.

Leo's talents as the go-between of the title are more extensively employed by Marian and a neighboring farmer, Ted Burgess. Ted is of the School of Mellors, the gamekeeper for Lord Chatterley, in that earlier novel of a virile peasant who trumps a damaged lord. Young Leo, in his androgynous innocence, finds Ted's "powerful body" compelling, but Leo is also in amorously chivalric thrall to Maid Marian, who emphasizes the Robin Hood parallel by buying him an expensive green suit. ("Is green a color for a man?" gently asks his loving though conventional mother when informed by post of the gift.) Both Ted and Marian extend the hand of friendship, some small portion of their motive possibly sincere, in exchange for his confidential carrying of "business letters" between them. Leo inadvertently sees "Darling darling darling" written in one of Marian's epistles, and his nascent understanding of "the system" of the human heart is sent spinning like a hyperactive slot machine.

Hartley opens this sensuous novel with the Colston of sixty-odd years mentally revisiting his damaged past, and closes it with Colston's literal pilgrimage back to Brandham. But the glorious part of the book is the lyrical evocation of those straw-stacks, cricket matches, village "sings," bathing machines in the river, and, especially, of the fatherless boy who, as he later puts it, prefers the life of facts to the facts of life. You know you're in the hands of a superb writer when you read the one-sentence opening (note the elegant colon) of the novel: "The past is a foreign country: they do things differently there."

A Portrait of the Artist as a Young Man

James Joyce

"There's nothing in the literature of the world today and not much in the literature of the past that is up to it." Thus spoke Ezra Pound, the fine poet and great promoter of young writers, as he encouraged a French translation of this book. This work of fiction is heavily autobiographical: Joyce, "the artist," casts a fond, if somewhat ironical, glance back at his younger, more callow self. The material began life as an essay, turned into a longer manuscript called *Stephen Hero*, and after Joyce spent a decade of intermittent work (1904–1914), settled down as this novel. It was published, serially, in *The Egoist* and achieved its first book-length publication in the United States.

The main character is Stephen Dedalus, whose name is an amalgam of Christian and pagan elements. "Stephen" evokes the first Christian martyr—as the character walks across St. Stephen's Green in Dublin, he thinks of it as "my green." "Dedalus" calls up Ovid's myth of the father-son pair of Daedalus (the original spelling for Joyce's character) and Icarus. The great inventor Daedalus crafts waxen wings that enable the two of them to fly. As the imprudent adolescent Icarus mounts periously near the sun, the wax attaching the wings melts, and he is hurled into the sea below. The father, though desperately saddened by his loss, achieves safe landing in Sicily where he devises the intricate labyrinth that imprisons the Minotaur. Joyce's character Stephen Dedalus is part the rebellious son who, like Lucifer, declares "Non serviam" (I will not serve) and part the father, who sets his mind onto "unknown arts."

The first sentence of the novel plunges us into infantine language and the world of Stephen's babyhood. The opening sentence: "Once upon a time and a very good time it was there was a moocow coming down

228

along the road and this moocow that was coming down along the road met a nicens little boy named baby tuckoo." Soon he's a little boy sent off cruelly early to his Jesuit boarding school where he encounters bullying both from fellow pupils and from the priests. No reader forgets the "pandybats" with which priests blister the hands of idlers or Father Arnall's sermon about the physical and mental punishments in hellfire, which Joyce modeled on a sermon first given in 1688.

As Stephen moves into adolescence, the book's language becomes more complex, more romantic. The alluring world of sex opens to him (in, alas, the well-worn madonna-whore dichotomy). He comes to know the guilty world of prostitutes but remains capable of dreamy fantasies about Emma, whose slightest finger-touch can send over him "an invisible warm wave."

With the third stage of Stephen's development, the language becomes more dramatic, as Stephen finds himself unable to tolerate living among the Irish, "a race of clodhoppers." In Stephen's view they have passively absorbed their subjugation by England. Simultaneously rejecting his Roman Catholic faith, he readies himself with his "new secondhand clothes" to head for the Continent and the beginning of his vocation as an innovative writer.

 Book Smart
Recommended Reading

By the novel's end the earlier third-person narration has changed into Stephen's "I," as his journal entries give us a kind of ancestor of the interior monologue so familiar to readers of *Ulysses*, Joyce's later and more complex novel. Move on to it, or prepare further for that major undertaking by sampling Joyce's earlier *Dubliners* ("Araby" is my favorite) and by dipping into Richard Ellmann's masterly biography.

To Kill a Mockingbird

Harper Lee

The title has become so familiar that we forget how strange it is (though less strange than the originally planned "To Set a Watchman"). On the literal level it's the advice Atticus Finch received along with his first air rifle: in rural south Alabama the killing of birds like blue jays won approval, for these birds destroyed farmers' crops. The *Mimus polyglottus* did not; and its array of songs sent beauty through the air. It's an easy allegorical leap to figurative mockingbirds, benign human beings whose lives are threatened or taken.

Atticus Finch is lawyer, widower, and father of the six-year-old Jean-Louise ("Scout") and her older brother, Jem. The household is enriched with the presence of Calpurnia, black family retainer who comes to the household every day to labor as housekeeper, cook, and teacher of manners and values to the children. It's 1933. We're in Maycomb, Alabama, a thinly disguised version of Harper Lee's Monroeville, a "tired old town" that, remarkably, gave rise not only to Lee but to her lifelong friend Truman Capote, sent there for summers with his aunt. (He's the inspiration for the novel's precociously eccentric Dill Harris, who proclaims, "I'm little but I'm old.")

The first third of this novel, which spans slightly more than two years, replaces plot with immersion in the feel of growing up in this time, in this town. The Finch siblings and, seasonally, Dill have free run of the streets, with neighbors like Miss Maudie to offer cake and kindness. Deprived by time of videos and computer games, the children read and make up skits. It's close enough to Eden (if you're white and middle-class) that the children enjoy conjuring up villains: the elderly neighbor Mrs. Dubose is rumored to keep a Confederate pistol under her afghan and Arthur ("Boo") Radley, emotionally damaged earlier by parents with a misguided sense of family honor, is metamorphosed from recluse to eater of live squirrels.

The action starts after Atticus agrees to defend Tom Robinson, a black man accused of raping Mayella Ewell, offspring of a family in the lowest socioeconomic echelon of whites. The songs of innocence end: Atticus's assignment plunges the children into knowledge of race, class, and evil. Aunt Alexandra arrives in the household, ready to indoctrinate the hoydenish Scout about gender roles and to instruct both children in the limits of noblesse oblige: they should be "friendly and polite . . . gracious to everybody" but never dream of inviting into their home Walter Cunningham, schoolmate from a poor but proud white family, or—heaven forfend!—visiting Calpurnia in her neighborhood.

The trial is the centerpiece of the novel. Its inherent drama maintains a crescendo: you hiss at Bob Ewell's racist assertions, you find pity in your heart, up to a point, for Mayella, who interprets as mockery Atticus's everyday courtesy, you feel tears well up at Tom Robinson's testimony (see Brock Peters's moving film interpretation), and you admire Atticus's eloquent charge to the all-white, all-male jury.

The novel is not without flaws: The narration wobbles between those of a looking-backward adult Scout and the child. Some images and phrases, well past their shelf life, make me cringe, as does the ending. But with more than fifteen million copies in print and translations into forty languages, the book has clearly won its place in readers' hearts. Just keep in your mind, as a possible corrective, Flannery O'Connor's acerbic judgment that it is, at heart, "a children's novel."

The Emperor's Children

Claire Messud

T o be almost thirty is not always to be an adult. This novel's three main characters, once friends at Brown University, have prolonged their struggle with those major concepts of love and of work. Danielle longs to make serious television documentaries but is stalled in her current project about liposuction. She embarks on an affair with a married man old enough to be her father. Julius, gay and half-Vietnamese, reviews books for a pittance but escapes his Lower East Side hovel when he is copasetic with an upwardly mobile lover to whom he feigns fidelity. Marina, daughter of acclaimed writer and cultural critic Murray Thwaite, snagged a contract years ago for a book about children's clothing but can't seem to pull it all together.

Into their privileged but not very happy lives come two additional and very different people who claim a hold on the reader's attention, though not the reader's admiration. Ludovic Seeley, whose "hooded eyes" alert us to a serpentine streak in him, comes from Australia, hoping to take New York by storm with his plans for *The Monitor*, a magazine of cultural exposé. (You can't stop thinking of pictures you've seen of the monitor lizard.) Frederick "Bootie" Tubb, nephew of Murray Thwaite, but exiled by circumstance and penury in Watertown, New York, wins our sympathy with his circumstances (and his unfortunate name), but he loses that sympathy with his overzealous idealism. His sophomoric sense of self-righteousness clashes with Everyreader's common sense. Your uncle may hire you to do some clerical work for him and give you a bed in his posh apartment, but that does not make it okay for you to read his private e-mail messages. Nor is it okay for you to rifle his locked desk drawer and riffle his private papers, his maundering drafts for a new book on How to Live. (What part of "duh" does Bootie not understand?) A corollary to these self-evident truths: it's also not okay for you to plan to publish your findings in a new magazine of cultural exposé being started by an Australian who's dating your first cousin Marina.

Letting us into the consciousnesses of Murray Thwaite and each of these five young people produces a fascinating tableau of modern city life. The fact that Messud wields not only the keen scalpel of psychological observation but also the acid-tinged pen of satire makes for a wonderful read. Now add in the fact that the action of the book takes place between March and November of 2001. You know that the day of infamy in early September will not exempt these city dwellers from its terrible shadow. There will be one funeral—but not necessarily a body.

Writer and critic Norman Rush has a superb phrase for this novel: a "comedy of mores." You enjoy the family dramas, the small guilty rivalries of close friends, the glimpse into tony settings in the city. You loathe some characters and pity others. And if you keep looking hard enough, you'll find a character—not mentioned here—whom you can like. Clue: it's the only character who doesn't make a full-time job out of maintaining her personal myth.

 Book Smart
Recommended Reading

Join the company of other ardent readers who recommend reading this fourth novel by Messud—widely acclaimed as her best—after her earlier books: *When the World Was Steady*, *The Last Life*, and *The Hunters* (two novellas).

The Chosen

Chaim Potok

S et in Brooklyn during World War II, this novel tells the story of two teenagers, Danny Saunders and Reuven Malter. Both young men are Jewish, but they belong to very different subgroups. Reuven attends a yeshiva (Jewish school) where his father teaches the Talmud, using modern textual scholarship as a guide to interpretation. Other comparatively liberal practices of this school: not considering Hebrew as too sacred for the study of secular subjects and even offering more than the minimum of English subjects. Danny, however, attends a yeshiva that reserves Hebrew for the sacred and uses Yiddish for most other subjects. It was founded by his father, the rabbi of a Russian Hasidic sect whose members are deeply loyal to him. Danny wears the traditional Hasidic accessories of side curls and prayer shawl fringes outside his trousers.

Danny and Reuven meet as softball players on the teams of their respective schools. This is no mere sports rivalry. Danny, poised as a runner on Reuven's second base, finds enough time to mutter, "I told my team we're going to kill you apikorsim this afternoon." (*Apikorsim* is the Hasidim's contemptuous term for comparatively secular Jews.) Later, in the last inning when Reuven has been asked to pitch, Danny, hitting hard, sends the ball streaking toward Reuven's face. Spectacles broken, nauseated, and dizzy, Reuven is sent off to the hospital, where broken glass is removed from near his pupil. Will scar tissue form there, damaging his sight?

It's not a promising start for a friendship, but friendship ensues. Reuven absorbs a great deal of information about the history of the Hasidim, and any reader without the rudiments of Jewish learning also gets a fascinating exposure to, for example, the difference between the Sephardic and the Ashkenazi, or of the varying attitudes within Judaism toward the Holocaust or toward the founding of Israel. Danny ponders his own nature and his relationship to his father. Reb (Rabbi) Saunders is rearing his son to succeed him as *tzaddik*, the charismatic and formidably learned leader of his people. His harsh methods of training his son include treating him with silence when he is not formally instructing him and exposing him to intense questioning, including *gematriya* (intricate numerological puzzles) in front of the family or the synagogue. Reuven, himself put to a test as an occasional visitor, feels that a look from Reb Saunders can peel away his skin and photograph his insides.

The end, becoming a *tzaddik*, may justify the stringent means, but—big problem—Danny doesn't want to follow in his father's footsteps. He wants to become a psychologist and—even worse—he's begun a clandestine reading of Freud, who offers a view of man that, Danny knows, is "anything but religious." The walls start closing in as his family begins to choose a wife for him; he knows he must find a way to lead his own life without dishonoring his father.

 Book Smart
Recommended Reading

This is a novel that nourishes your brain as it warms your heart. You're happy that Potok, who died in 2002, wrote a sequel, *The Promise*, and many other wonderful books such as the novel *My Name Is Asher Lev* and the nonfiction work *Wanderings: Chaim Potok's History of the Jews*.

The Yearling

Marjorie Kinnan Rawlings

A sk anyone to name a writer who worked under famed Scribner's editor Maxwell Perkins. You might hear "Fitzgerald" or "Hemingway" or "Thomas Wolfe," and all those answers would be correct. But broaden your perspective by adding Marjorie Kinnan Rawlings to the list of writers who knew Perkins as editor and mentor. He suggested to Rawlings that she consider writing "a boy's book," and she emended his suggestion to say she'd write a book "about a boy." *The Yearling*, like some other fine books now linked with children's literature, was always aimed at adults, and indeed the view of life in the novel is simultaneously affirming and bleakly harsh. And some younger readers may stumble over passages in the rural southern dialect. (Ivan Doig's 2002 introduction to this novel calls it "Cracker dialect," which, I'm told, is correct in esoteric linguistic terms, but it strikes the common reader's eye offensively.)

The novel follows twelve-year-old Jody Baxter from one April to the next. The title character is the orphaned fawn that Jody, an only child in the scrub country of north central Florida, makes his pet (the animal gets the name Flag from the way the tail is just "a leetle white merry flag"). It's the late 1800s, and Jody is barely literate from just one season with an itinerant teacher, but he's no child left behind. He has a rich education in the ways of the woods: in the course of the book he goes on a bear hunt, experiences a flood, sees his father almost die from a rattlesnake bite, and on one night of marvel he witnesses the "slow frenzy" of the mating dance of the whooping crane.

Jody also has an early initiation to the harsh mystery of life and death. His one friend, improbably known as Fodder-wing, is a misshapen cripple, youngest child of the otherwise robustly crude For-rester family, who are given to all-night "frolics" of music-making and drinking in the altogether. Fodder-wing dies just before Jody comes to display the fawn to this gentle boy who is a young master of the animal kingdom. As Jody's father, Penny Baxter, largely a pagan despite his "Christian raising," eulogizes Fodder-wing in his prayer over the dead boy's body, "he could o'takened a she wild-cat right in his pore twisted hands."

The book contains many interesting side incidents such as Jody's vis-its to Grandma Hutto and her son Oliver, Jody's hero, and romantic rivalries Jody can barely comprehend. (Nonetheless, he hopes that the yellow-haired Twink Weatherby will eat wolfbane and die because she's hurt Oliver and caused him to sail away to Boston.) But what every reader will remember is the scene near the end when Flag goes in a few weeks from the equivalent of cute toddler to obnoxious adolescent. With the Baxter family's very existence imperiled by Flag's antics (eat-ing seedlings, kicking over fences), Jody is compelled to finish off the job Ma Baxter, a poor shot, began and pull the trigger while staring at those "great liquid eyes." Fodder-wing's death was an ache, but kill-ing the thing you love is a wound. Jody runs away from home, largely planless, and returns. Pa gives the eulogy for the boy Jody, now a man. "I knowed the lonesomeness he [Flag] eased for you. But ever' man's lonesome. What's he to do then? What's he to do when he gits knocked down? Why, take it for his share and go on." Samuel Beckett couldn't have said it better.

A Tree Grows in Brooklyn

Betty Smith

George Orwell's birth name? Sylvia Plath's married name? Voltaire's "real last name" from which he anagrammized his pseudonym? Sure, I can toss these off: Eric Blair, Hughes, Arouet, l. j. But if you'd thrown at me "Elizabeth Wehner's name as author?" I wouldn't have known the wonderfully plain "Betty Smith." (Her first husband was a Smith; her second, a Jones.) The simple name suits her tale of a precocious and optimistic young girl, Francie Nolan, growing up in the harsh poverty of her immigrant family's home in the slums of the Williamsburg section of Brooklyn. The original title *They Lived in Brooklyn* was altered to the symbolic: Francie thrives amid adversity as robustly as the tree of the title, the ailanthus tree, the Tree of Heaven.

The novel opens when Francie is eleven. She and her brother Neely are hauling rags and metal and rubber, earning a few coins by selling junk. Francie earns an extra penny for not flinching when the "junkie" pinches her cheek. It's 1912, but it's no nostalgic Eden in Brooklyn, and a serious child molester appears later in the novel. Francie and Neely's mother, Katie Rommely, made of "thin invisible steel," is empress of the art of making-do without a jot of self-pity. What do you do when the larder is nearly empty? You play the game of North Pole: you're an Arctic explorer waiting for more supplies to arrive. Katie is fierce—she shoots the child molester—and fiercely committed to delayed gratification and education. Her children read a page of the Bible and a page of Shakespeare every day; a tin can nailed to the floor holds spare coins dedicated to the eventual purchase of land.

If Katie, born to an Austrian immigrant family, embodies the yin of the immigrant stereotype, her husband, Johnny, of the "shanty Nolans," is the complementary yang. Johnny, a singing waiter, is charming, passionate—and a feckless drunk. We're unsurprised, but sad, when his early grave is the "piece of land" bought with the savings in the tin can.

Francie absorbs the Brooklyn sights, sounds, and sensations (including the extramarital doings of her Aunt Sissy) and withstands unsympathetic teachers. She graduates from eighth grade and enters the world of work. She grapples with the question of passion versus stability in early romances. We catch our last glimpse of Francie at seventeen, triumphantly headed for the University of Michigan. Francie fares educationally better than her creator: Betty Smith, who moved to Michigan with her husband, attended Ann Arbor High School as a married woman before gaining permission to enroll as a "special student" at the university. (She never gained academic certification beyond a junior high diploma.) Two daughters, one divorce, and a move to Chapel Hill, North Carolina, later, Smith transcended renewed bouts of poverty with the instant success of this novel. Her annual income in 1942 was $300; in 1943, more than $95,000 (and climbing). The book, which went on to further enormous success as a Broadway musical and as a film (Elia Kazan's debut), blooms heartily today, earning its place as one of the New York Public Library's "books of the century."

Book Smart
Recommended Reading

A good companion read to this novel is Anzia Yezierska's autobiographical novel *Bread Givers*, first published in 1925. Born in Poland, Yezierska treats the experience of a Jewish immigrant family in New York from a female perspective. Learn more in Mary V. Dearborn's biography *Love in the Promised Land: The Story of Anzia Yezierska and John Dewey.*

War and Peace:
On the Battlefield and Back Home

My early and invincible love of reading I would
not exchange for all the riches of India.
—Edward Gibbon

YOU SHOULD read Tolstoy's *War and Peace*. And of course you should read Kurt Vonnegut's *Slaughterhouse-Five*. And Ha Jin's *War Trash*. Not to mention Norman Mailer's *The Naked and the Dead* and James Jones's *From Here to Eternity* and Erich Maria Remarque's *All Quiet on the Western Front* and Guy Sajer's *The Forgotten Soldier* and all the other favorite war books, fiction and nonfiction, that friends have recommended to me. The ten representative books here offer a variety of angles of vision.

The oldest work here is, of course, also the most famous: Homer's epic poem the *Iliad*. Homer, if there was a Homer, is writing in the seventh or eighth century BCE about the Trojan War, if there was a Trojan War, which took place in the thirteenth or fourteenth century BCE. The one thing that is certain about the *Iliad* is that it is a poem of enormous force, savagery, and humanity. If I could select an epigraph for the *Iliad*, I'd pick the last stanza of a poem written by the Englishman Patrick Shaw-Stewart, killed in France in World War I: "I will go back this morning / From Imbros over the sea; / Stand in the trench, Achilles, / Flame-capped and shout for me."

The American Civil War has given rise to an enormous number of books. Stephen Crane's 1895 novel *The Red Badge of Courage*, certainly one of the best, amazes because at the time Crane wrote this book with its vivid depictions of battle and of a soldier's emotions, he had never witnessed war firsthand. Geraldine Brooks's *March* was written 110 years after Crane's book and with a very literary impetus: to describe what was going on with Mr. March, chaplain for the Union Army, when his wife and four daughters (of Louisa May Alcott's *Little Women*) were living life without him. (Don't confuse this book with another excellent Civil War novel also published in 2005: E. L. Doctorow's *The March*, which takes on General Sherman's ravaging sweep through the South.) The third Civil War selection is Edmund Wilson's *Patriotic Gore*, his excellent series of sixteen essays about the painful internecine strife.

We have two novels about World War I. Ernest Hemingway, in his touching and influential *A Farewell to Arms*, deals with the lives of a defecting soldier and of the woman he loves in prose that forever changed the way writers deal with war. Pat Barker's *Regeneration*, written in 1991, gives a powerful sense of the anguish soldiers suffered while attempting to recover from the assaults of war.

Joseph Heller's *Catch-22* deals with the agonies of World War II through the entirely innovative means of bitter satire. In Heller's view the brutality of the bureaucracy vied with the horrors of the field. William Styron's *The Long March* focuses not on action in Korea itself, but on the miseries experienced by reservists unexpectedly thrust back into active service.

The final two books take on the Vietnam conflict, the war that rived the United States in the late 1960s. Tim O'Brien, himself a veteran, piercingly shows what it was like to be there in *The Things They Carried*. Bobbie Ann Mason's literary canvas, *In Country*, shows the long-lasting effects of the war through the life of a seventeen-year-old girl, whose father was killed in Vietnam, and through the life of Emmett, her uncle who was there.

War books will be written as long as there are wars. John Milton, who lived through the English Civil War, deserves the final line (taken from his sonnet "On the Lord General Fairfax"): "For what can war, but endless war, still breed?"

Regeneration

Pat Barker

This is a war novel with no direct scenes of battle. That fact does not ensure the absence of disturbing or violent images: the men seen in a World War I mental hospital in Craiglockhart, Scotland, have haunting memories to spare, and the reader must trace such grisly images as that of a human eye blown into the wall of a trench and the respiratory tract of a living man that has inhaled the exploding fragments of a German soldier.

Barker's note at the end of this novel makes clear that the book is a blend of fact and fiction. The facts: In 1917 the poet Siegfried Sassoon, whose bravery in action as a lieutenant earned him the sobriquet "Mad Jack," published a statement that he himself termed a "willful defiance of military authority." In this "soldier's declaration" he denounced not the conduct of the war itself but the fact that the soldiers were deceived about the fact that the war of "defence and liberation" which they thought they were fighting had become a war of "aggression and conquest." He was promptly shipped off for rehabilitation at Craiglockhart. There he encounters Dr. W. H. R. Rivers, a distinguished anthropologist and neurologist, a man of innovative thinking about how to treat soldiers whose minds are traumatized by the experience of war. Two other real-life poets, Robert Graves and Wilfred Owen, also put in appearances.

In the novel Dr. Rivers's earlier experimental work on regenerating nerves that have been destroyed becomes the metaphor for his attempts to regenerate the minds of soldiers who are suffering from hallucinations, nightmares, mutism, paralysis, anorexia, and other hellish torments. His official goal is to cure them from the injuries of war so that they may return to it. (His methods look quite humane compared with those of his colleague Dr. Yealland—also based on a real medical man—who tortures a mute solider into speech and forces him to utter thanks for the cure.)

Barker, whose earlier novel *Union Street* established her as a social-realist writer concerned with the problems of impoverished women, takes us away from the hellish hospital scenes to show us working-class women dealing with a different set of problems. Many of them are employed in the local munitions factory, turning themselves into machines in order to turn out machines of war. You care about street-smart Sarah, who's involved with the patient Billy Prior. Her conversations with her mates and with her mother, who brought up two girls on her own, make clear the problems of economic survival and the delicate balance of attempts to satisfy desire and to avoid pregnancy; nicely fixed widowhood is a career goal for some.

When Sassoon is "discharged for duty," at the close of the book, he makes a jaunty reference to "the sausage machine," and when he's urged not to take "unnecessary risks," reserves the private thought that he just might. The real-life Sassoon survived the war, living on till 1967. The less lucky Wilfred Owen was killed in 1918.

 Book Smart
Recommended Reading

If you like this book, you may want to go on to the other two books in what's called "the *Regeneration* trilogy": *The Eye in the Door* and *The Ghost Road*. Even better: supplement your reading of the novels with some of Sassoon's and Owens's poetry.

March

Geraldine Brooks

Readers of Louisa May Alcott's *Little Women* remember lovingly the March family: that quartet of daughters—Meg, Jo, Beth, and Amy—and the saintly mother, called Marmee. The father of the family is known chiefly by his absence and, later, his illness. A chaplain for the Union Army in the Civil War, he becomes ill and spends a period of time recuperating in a hospital in Washington and returns home in time to witness his oldest daughter's engagement. We last see him as he and his wife sit together ruminating on how all the current scene came from their own union some twenty years earlier. And though she follows Alcott's practice of depriving March of a first name, Geraldine Brooks not only supplies the details of March's romantic union with Marmee (pond, moonlight, flute music) but also gives him a busy independent existence. She re-creates many brutal tableaux from the Civil War—the battle scene at Ball's Bluff in Virginia, a commandeered plantation in Mississippi under the protection of Union soldiers, the chaotic military hospital in Washington.

The fortyish Mr. March writes home ultrapoetic letters in ink made of blackberries, letters that spare his family of females any of the gross details of his existence. In between these letters we readers learn his real experiences as well as his memories of his pre–Civil War days as an itinerant salesman in Virginia, a peddler of books and geegaws, and of his days in Concord, Massachusetts, as friend of Emerson and Thoreau and as ardent abolitionist (his investments in John Brown's schemes cause the loss of his fortune) and stationmaster of a hiding place on the Underground Railroad. Most successful, perhaps, are the scenes on the Mississippi plantation where March attempts to set up a school for formerly enslaved children and adults. They continue to lead a largely slavelike existence under the supervision of Ethan Canning, a Northerner, attempting with small success to transform this cotton plantation into a commercially successful farm.

Just as Alcott used the personal history of her own family as raw material for her novel, so Brooks draws on journals and letters of Louisa May Alcott's father, Bronson Alcott, an idealistic pioneer in the world of education (he's said to have created the concept of "recess"). She also makes a novelist's free use of historical records of the Civil War (her husband, Tony Horwitz, is a Civil War historian) and, more amply, her own imagination.

One warning about the invented character of Grace Clement. She is first a house slave on a Virginia plantation visited by March as young salesman and later as an army chaplain who preaches not damnation but love. By further coincidence she is later a nurse at the hospital where he is a patient. She is beautiful, intelligent, cultured, self-accepting, kind, and proud of the potential and burgeoning achievements of Black people. Perhaps, the choice of the words *grace* and *clement* is meant to signal Brooks's unabashed awareness of the paragon called into unrealistic existence by her pen. Brooks's notes recall her childhood memory of being warned that Alcott's Marmee was just too good to be true; in Grace Clement, a woman more out of the realm of Lifetime television than that of prizewinning novels, Brooks has created a character that renders Alcott's Marmee almost, by comparison, tarnished. Otherwise, the novel is a good read, a pleasing complement to Alcott's book and addition to the slightly artificial realm of historical novels where a shawl may be rutilant and a character may wear a rigolette and pour from a jorum.

The Red Badge of Courage

Stephen Crane

tephen Crane died of tuberculosis in 1900 at age twenty-eight, but he lived his abbreviated life well. The last of fourteen children of a Methodist minister and his wife and no stranger to hardship, Crane left a literary legacy that includes poetry of startling originality and bleak beauty as well as short stories and novels that helped to shape twentieth-century American literature. Noted scholar Andrew Delbanco cites his prose as a major influence on Ernest Hemingway and the early Norman Mailer. Crane, born seven years after the close of the Civil War, wrote this convincing account of the experience of Henry Fleming, Union soldier, out of his reading and his rich imagination. A few years after the novel's publication, Crane served under fire as a journalist in the Greek war for independence and the Spanish-American War and happily verified that his earlier novel was "all right."

The novel makes a strong impact through its credible and sympathetic rendering of young Fleming's emotions before and during battle. A farm boy, he had "burned" to enlist and does so with a head full of thoughts of glory and of "large pictures extravagant in color, lurid with breathless deeds." His widowed mother, a sympathetic figure who needs her boy on the farm, dilutes his Homeric fantasies by stalwartly sending him off with comments about the eight pairs of socks she has knit for him and the importance of sending them back for darning.

Henry's strutting stance weakens as real fighting draws near. His survival instinct clicks in and he bolts in battle, running pell-mell through the woods of the fray. He very humanly draws up facile justifications for his action: if that squirrel runs from a tossed pine cone, well then,

Nature means for men to run from danger. Still he knows down deep he's done wrong and longs for a battle wound, a "red badge of courage." A blow to his head from a fellow soldier's rifle butt gives him his second chance. When comrades interpret the bloody results of that accidental thump as a grazing by a cannonball, he lets that interpretation stand. His heroism is rooted in his resolve to earn, ex post facto, honorable status. Fighting beside his lieutenant, Fleming now achieves a bold belligerence, plunging "like a mad horse," springing at the falling flag "as a panther in prey." No longer a dreamy boy or a scurrying coward but the new color bearer for his regiment, he feels his hard-won success in battle has brought him into "a quiet manhood."

The novel's success in its perceptive depictions of the soldier's emotions is matched by the brilliance of the style. Scholars have noted the influence of visual representations of Civil War battles on Crane's wording, and his simple sentences and complex images do indeed make the reader *see*. Every few pages your attention is caught by the force and interest of the phrasing, the most famous example being this chapter-ending sentence: "The red sun was pasted in the sky like a wafer."

In the waning months of his life Crane, along with his common-law wife, Cora, lived in England, where he was accepted as fellow author and friend by writers of the stature of H. G. Wells, Joseph Conrad, and Henry James. No one wants to leave this earth at twenty-eight, but the horror of the blow might be slightly softened if you knew that James would make the remark he made about Crane's death, "What a brutal, needless extinction—what an unmitigated unredeemed catastrophe."

Catch-22

Joseph Heller

If you've ever fantasized about writing a novel, your first, and giving up your day job, you'll enjoy identifying with the reception of this novel featuring the madcap main character Yossarian. Joseph Heller at thirty-four had taught a little English and written advertising copy while working for years, hopefully and doggedly, on his novel. He received a $750 advance with promise of that much more on completion. The book received some highly admiring notices ("a giant roller coaster of a book") but also some that called it disorganized, "not a novel." It failed to make the bestseller list. Then John Chancellor became head of the "Today" show and interviewed Heller. Chancellor reported that he'd privately had "YOSSARIAN LIVES" stickers printed up and was pasting them all over the NBC building. Huge numbers of paperbacks were printed, and the novel zoomed to the top of bestseller lists. Oh, and while you're fantasizing, how about having the title of your novel become a household phrase? (By the way, we'd all be saying "Catch-18" if the publisher hadn't changed Heller's original to avoid confusion with Leon Uris's *Mila 18*, now largely forgotten.)

The title, of course, refers to the "double bind" situation where one part cancels out the other: The company won't hire you if you don't have experience, but you can't get experience if you haven't had a job. A pilot who sees the dangers of a mission and requests dismissal on the grounds of insanity has just proved his sanity and therefore must fly.

This is a new kind of war novel. Set near the end of World War II on a fictional island off the coast of Italy, this book is far from the usual harshly realistic account of war's brutality. Instead, it contains zany and loony satire, very dark humor that attacks not only the grisly horrors of war but also the killing power of bureaucracy. And you have to keep reminding yourself it was published in 1961; it's pre-Vietnam. These characters who see so fully the spirit-killing force they're up against are part of the much-touted "greatest generation." The perplexed protagonist, Yossarian, struggles to escape death while maintaining his integrity. When he's eventually offered a deal that he will be sent home if he praises his commanding officers, he refuses and, inspired by a comrade's escape, plans to row his way to Sweden. (The 1970 movie version actually puts him in his little yellow raft, paddling away.) As Huck Finn, lighting out for the territory, knew, the only sane response to an insane "civilization" is getting out of there.

Equally memorable is the satire involving others stationed on the island. Milo Minderbinder sees the war as a giant private "profit potential," willing to sell mission plans to the enemy for capitalistic gain. Dunbar seeks out boredom in hopes of prolonging his life. A clerical ruse makes the living Doc Daneeka appear dead, and no quantity of his human breath can change the record. Major Major picks up Yossarian's habit of signing Washington Irving's name to documents. Lieutenant Scheisskopf (ask a German speaker to translate) is fanatical about parades. Intravenous liquids designed for a wounded soldier go straight into a bucket, thus efficiently "eliminating the middle man."

How do we know Yossarian survived his frantic row? Because there's a sequel, *Closing Time*, where he's achieved the age of sixty-eight. It's not as good, but then few books are.

A Farewell to Arms

Ernest Hemingway

He took the lovely name of the book, he says, from the title of a poem by George Peele, which he found in *The Oxford Book of English Verse*. The 1590 verse bids adieu to war and stresses the flight of beauty, strength, and youth, underlying themes in Hemingway's novel. But you wonder if Hemingway might also have in mind the *Aeneid*, for nothing in Peele's poem suggests Hemingway's potent emphasis on the double sense of "arms"—war and love—a meaning powerfully found in the sense of the opening words of Virgil's poem, for the great warrior-hero knows also the pain of the end of a love affair.

The novel was Hemingway's first bestseller, and a part of its power may arise from its semi-autobiographical elements. Frederic Henry (often called "Tenente," the Italian word for "lieutenant") is an American associated with the Italian Army in 1916–17. Hemingway, an ambulance driver for the Red Cross, was also at the front. Henry and Hemingway each suffered a painful leg wound, and each had an erotic liaison with a military nurse. Hemingway's experiences mellowed in his mind for ten years; then, combined with imagination, issued forth from his pen, mostly in an Arkansas town with the unromantic name of Piggott. (This was the home of relatives of Hemingway's second wife, Pauline Pfeiffer; the novel is dedicated to her Uncle Gus, who helped the couple through financial difficulties.)

The plot is simple enough. A soldier of courage but few beliefs falls deeply in love, makes "a separate peace" with the war, and enjoys a few months of bliss with his beloved. It ends badly.

At the start of the book Frederic Henry enjoys a kind of detached pleasure in banter with Rinaldi, the military surgeon with whom he shares quarters. Rinaldi, who expresses a belief in drink, sex, and work, is downright effusive compared with Lieutenant Henry. He's had enough of fine words: "I was always embarrassed by the words sacred, glorious, and sacrifice and the expression in vain. . . . There were many words that you could not stand to hear and finally only the names of places had dignity."

Once he falls in love with Catherine Barkley, the English nurse whose fiancé had been killed in the Somme, life changes. As the old Count Greffi says to Frederic of being in love, "Do not forget that is a religious feeling." He forsakes the clash of ignorant armies and rows, with the pregnant Catherine, over the lake from Italy to neutral Switzerland. (No pesky financial concerns clog the plot: Frederic has a grandfather who exists in the novel for the purpose of supplying him with money.) The mutual love with Catherine fills his hollow heart. Not that Hemingway ever uses a phrase like this! Catherine and Frederic express their feelings in the spareness that makes Hemingway Hemingway: "I'm grand now" or "I want you to have a fine life." They consider themselves married.

The ending of this heart-wrenching five-part novel touches the reader as powerfully as the end of a classic five-act tragedy. Some of Frederic's most famous lines have forewarned us: "The world breaks everyone and afterward many are strong at the broken places. But those that will not break it kills. It kills the very good and the very gentle and the very brave impartially. If you are none of these you can be sure it will kill you too but there will be no special hurry."

The Iliad

Homer (translated by Robert Fagles)

n the eighteenth century the titled but not overly bright Philip Dormer Stanhope, Earl of Chesterfield, called this work the story of a bully and a whore. Lord Chesterfield is in the minority, for the world has for centuries given this long epic poem about the Trojan War the greatest of praise. (The name derives from *Ilium*, the Greek name for Troy.) The brutally graphic descriptions of the battles between the Greeks and the Trojans in the tenth and final year of the war are the standard by which all subsequent descriptions of war are judged. It's telling that one of our stock phrases for dying—"to bite the dust"—originates with Homer.

The poem begins with the word "rage" and a commandment to the Muse to sing of the rage of Achilles. This greatest of the Greek warriors is angry because the beautiful young woman Briseis, who he had reason to assume was one of his personal trophies of war, is being reassigned to Agamemnon, leader of the Greek army. Achilles feels "dissed" by this action and goes into a major sulk, refusing to fight. He decides to teach the Greeks a lesson in how much they need him. It helps that his mother is a goddess (the sea nymph Thetis), who winsomely persuades Zeus to send the Greeks into a major losing streak. War injuries dog Agamemnon and his brother-leader Menelaus as well as Diomedes and Odysseus, but Achilles persists in his pout.

His lone contribution to the war effort is the loan of his armor to his closest friend, the "greathearted" Patroclus. Bad idea: helped by Apollo, Hector, the greatest of the Trojan fighters, kills Patroclus and takes the great armor, "blazoned with stars," for himself. Now Achilles reconciles with Agamemnon—what a petty snit, after all—and sets out for the real enemy, Hector. Outfitted with new armor by Mom (who gets the Olympian blacksmith to craft it for him), Achilles comes out roaring; after fighting with Xanthus, a river of fire, he, moving like a champion stallion, a lion, a hound in the mountains, seeks single combat with Hector, achieves it, taunts the dead body—"Die, die!"—and drags it, headfirst, behind his chariot around the walls of Troy. Hector's mother and father and then his wife, Andromache, watch helplessly.

The violence can be hard to take, but the poem also contains beautiful scenes of peace and of sorrow. If you want a preview before you commit yourself to the English for all 15,693 lines of this twenty-four-book poem, dive first into Book 6, a domestic scene where Hector, heading off for battle, bids farewell to Andromache and their baby, Astyanax, "radiant as a star." When his giant-plumed helmet frightens the infant, he takes off the helmet and joins the baby's mother in an affectionate laugh; kissing his little boy, he tosses him in his arms. It's his last sight of wife and child. Or start with Book 23. Old King Priam, father of Hector, goes to Achilles to beg, successfully, for the return of the maimed body for burial: "I have endured what no one on earth has ever done before— / I put to my lips the hands of the man who killed my son."

Book Smart
Recommended Reading

Listen to the great audio version by Derek Jacobi. (That oral poet Homer would be proud.) And if you find yourself getting interested in varying versions of what Simone Weil called a "poem of force," take a look at Christopher Logue's wonderful adaptations.

In Country

Bobbie Ann Mason

"How odd it feels, as though all the names in America have been used to decorate this wall." Seventeen-year-old Samantha (Sam) Hughes, whose father died in Vietnam shortly before she was born, is standing at the Vietnam War Memorial with her maternal uncle, himself a Vietnam veteran, and her paternal grandmother. Finding her father's name—Dwayne E. Hughes—high on a panel of the east wall, they borrow a workman's ladder so they can step up high enough to touch it. On another slab she finds a name eerily like her own—Sam A. Hughes—and places her fingers on its letters as well. But her feelings at the wall surpass reverence. The monument and the flag reflected in its dark stone seem to her "arrogant," like an obscene gesture to the dead soldiers.

The short scene closes this three-part novel. The book opens as Sam's newly purchased but highly imperfect used Volkswagen jolts the three toward the nation's capital from western Kentucky (Mason herself grew up on a dairy farm there). We get to know them a little. Sam, whose mother Irene has remarried and moved to Lexington, continues to live with Emmett Smith, Irene's brother. Neither of them knows "Mamaw"/ Mrs. Hughes, the dead veteran's mother, well, but they thoughtfully help tend the pot of geraniums she carries with her. The novel then goes into a long flashback of the days immediately preceding their pilgrimage before it returns to the traveling trio as they near the Vietnam Memorial.

Much of the novel focuses on Sam's moving over that invisible line dividing child and adult. Lifelong resident of the hamlet of Hopewell, she's in many ways your average teenage girl, immersed in a world of

Springsteen songs, serial ear-piercings, boyfriend pressures (she's on the pill), part-time work at Burger Boy, and buying a pregnancy test kit for her embarrassed girlfriend. The Korean War as filtered unrealistically through *M*A*S*H* is more real to Sam, a little girl when American troops pulled out of Vietnam, than the conflict that took her father's life.

In many other ways, Sam's life is far from typical. She lives with Emmett, her not-at-all-avuncular uncle. Kind and caring to Sam and to his cat, Moon Pie, he's never been able to get his post-service life together: no job, intermittent backing off from commitment to a relationship, worrisome lumps on his face that may come from exposure to Agent Orange. (His cronies Tom and Earl, also Vietnam alums, have problems ranging from psychologically caused impotence to general belligerence.) When Sam comes into possession of the diary her nineteen-year-old father kept "in country" in the months before he was killed, her world widens—and darkens.

Book Smart
Recommended Reading

No soldier herself, Bobbie Ann Mason was eager to get her technical facts right. Mason did most of her research in oral histories—possibly Al Santoli's excellent 1981 volume *Everything We Had: An Oral History of the Vietnam War by Thirty-Three Soldiers Who Fought It*. Mason was one of the earliest writers to depict the Vietnam War Memorial, and you must also seek out Yosef Komunyakaa's beautiful poem "Facing It," written four years later. Bobbie Ann Mason is sometimes quoted as saying "Writing is my rock and roll," so you may also enjoy going to the Penguin short biographies series and trying her take on Elvis Presley.

The Things They Carried

Tim O'Brien

he seventh of these twenty-two related stories is entitled "How to Tell a True War Story." Vignettes in this story interlock with O'Brien's overt comments about trying to write about war, a challenge he faced and met superlatively in this book. Among the many wise things he says here: "You can tell a true war story by its absolute and uncompromising allegiance to obscenity and evil. . . . You can tell a true war story if it embarrasses you. If you don't care for obscenity, you don't care for the truth; if you don't care for the truth, watch how you vote. Send guys to war, they come home talking dirty." The truest war stories may be woven together from threads of memory, imagination, and the power of language. O'Brien has them all here in this forceful book in which "Tim O'Brien" features as young boy, soldier, and narrator.

The war memories derive from author O'Brien's service in Vietnam. After growing up in a Minnesota town that calls itself "the Turkey Capital of the World," he found himself holding a college diploma and a draft notice. This young man who describes himself as "someone who hated Boy Scouts and bugs and rifles" served in Vietnam in a combat infantry unit in 1969–70. He received a Purple Heart for a shrapnel wound from a hand grenade. While the title page carefully contains the words "a work of fiction," O'Brien underlines the I-was-there aspect of the book by his choice of epigraph, which comes from John Ransom's Civil War diary: "a statement of actual things by one who experienced them to the fullest."

You can read the book straight through, or you can pick and choose stories at will. If you're like me, you'll need to alternate the grimmest war sections with other pages, such as the closing tale of his memories of Linda, a girl he loved in the fourth grade. (It has its own brand of sadness.) They all coalesce in your head, a painful swirl of anger, fear, isolation, an intensified awareness of the enigmatic aspect of life. "On the Rainy River" tells of the character Tim O'Brien's six agonizing days of decision making, days he spent near the Canadian border deciding whether to slip northward or to return and put that draft notice to use. He reaches the conclusion that he would go to the war because he was a coward, he would go to the war and kill and die because he was embarrassed not to. But much of the power of the story is in the quiet account of Elroy Berdahl, owner of the Tip Top Lodge, expert fisherman, octogenarian, who gave him silence and quiet understanding while his mind hacked out its decision.

The title vignette starts the book off on the note of pathos that never leaves the pages. His list of "things" soldiers carried with them is compelling in the way that facts do compel. There are the things everyone carried—"pocket knives, dog tags, mosquito repellent, chewing gum"—and there are the items that bespeak their owner—a good luck pebble or a diary or grandfather's hunting hatchet or pictures of a girl who might love you. The catalogue gathers momentum as it slides into instruments of killing, to name only a few—"a pistol that weighed 2.9 pounds fully loaded," fragmentation grenades, "blocks of pentrite high explosives." You barely need O'Brien's move to the metaphorical, the "baggage" soldiers could not shrug off—distrust of the white man, memories, "all the ambiguities of Vietnam." It all adds up, in one more of O'Brien's stunning phrases, to "real heavy-duty hurt."

The Long March

William Styron

This beautiful short novel by a writer who spent three years in the Marine Corps begins with a scene of sick-making violence. An accident—mortar shells misfired, and eight young Marines lie dead at noon "in a cloudless Carolina summer." It's peacetime or "what passes for peacetime" in the early 1950s when the United States was waging a "police action" in Korea. Lieutenant Culver, who witnesses the scene, is a survivor of World War II fighting at Okinawa where he sustained an unamusing dose of shrapnel in the buttocks, and a reserve officer startled to have been levered out of six years of comfortable civilian life. The third-person narration seems shaped through his sympathetic eyes.

Despite this noonday tragedy and despite maneuvers that have deprived men of sleep for three days, the walk planned for that night remains on the docket. Colonel Templeton, given to decorative slaps of the thigh when issuing orders, fears that the men in the Headquarters & Supply Company of the battalion have been "doping off." Rather than returning to their home base on trucks, they will walk the thirty-six miles to build "group *esprit.*" We fall deeply under the spell of Culver's compadre Captain Mannix, a huge man, a Jew, owner of a radio store until called out of reserve status, and, like Culver, a husband and a father. Al Mannix, a Brooklyn boy, sees the night march in the comparative geography of home. Thirty-six miles? That's Grand Central Station to Stamford, Connecticut! Different moments in the novel depict Mannix as resembling the face of a mask for a Greek tragedy, a shackled slave, a "rakehell Civil War general" just before a battle, and a chain-gang convict who never whimpers during a beating in order to spite the flogger.

Mannix knows the order for the hike is brutal, but he will see himself in hell before he will give Templeton the satisfaction of faltering. He both shepherds and hectors his men. "Close it up! *Close it up*, I said." His concentrated fury may issue from the nail that protrudes into the inside of the heel of his shoe despite his efforts to subdue it with his bayonet. The Colonel first suggests and later commands the wounded Mannix, as unconquerable as that nail, to ride in on one of the trucks, a suggestion/order guaranteed to press him onward on his limping feet.

The more analytic Culver knows that he himself is more marine than free man; he will keep up the punishing walk, and he perceptively asserts that Mannix (whose name suggests "manic") is "so much a marine as to be casually demented." Mannix completes the march. He's facing, variously, immediate shipping out for Korea, court-martial, and, with an ankle the size of a grapefruit, possible tetanus. Our last glimpse of him shows him clawing his grotesque way down the hall to the shower. A black woman cleaning the barracks offers her compassionate acknowledgement of his pain: "Do it hurt? Oh, I bet it does. Deed it does." The book closes as Mannix repeats her last three words, his shared awareness of the power of agony and of enduring.

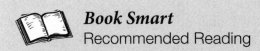

Book Smart
Recommended Reading

A native Virginian, Styron wrote a first novel, *Lie Down in Darkness*, that reflected his southern upbringing and his stylistic debt to Faulkner. He transcended that limiting label of regional writer with his own varied excellence as a novelist. He deals with his struggle with depression in his nonfiction work *Darkness Visible*.

Patriotic Gore: Studies in the Literature of the American Civil War

Edmund Wilson

The ironic and startling title of Wilson's eight-hundred-page book derives from a verse of a Confederate song urging Maryland to "avenge the patriotic gore" that stained Baltimore's streets when "the despot" invaded. Wilson's title page bears not only this lyric but also a line from John Brown about "the shedding of blood" as a necessary partner to the remission of sins.

All this makes a bloody first impression of this wonderfully erudite book that consumed fifteen years of labor by Wilson. There's nothing sensationalized about Wilson's sixteen chapters: each is a solidly fascinating investigation of its subject. Despite its heft, the book is selective. Wilson only touches on such famous writers as Melville and Whitman and completely omits Frederick Douglass. But he gives pungent and incisive treatment to the individuals he selects. Some names are well known, such as Harriet Beecher Stowe or Abraham Lincoln or Oliver Wendell Holmes; others are recondite—Charlotte Forten, Hilton R. Helper, Richard Taylor. Some individuals get chapters of their own while others cohabit with the like-minded under headings such as "Northerners in the South" or "Novelists of the Post-War South." Despite the implications of that last chapter title, Wilson stresses the fact that "belles lettres" were not the chief glory of the printed word during the war years; instead, the conflict stimulated a "remarkable literature" of speeches, pamphlets, letters, diaries, memoirs, and newspaper articles. Wilson further underlines the interest offered by different viewpoints on the same event or individual, citing how different U. S. Grant appears in the eyes of Charles Francis Adams and in the eyes of his son Henry. (He, a native of Red Bank, New Jersey, notes elsewhere that his childhood included visits to Virginia cousins who kept him in mind that the Civil War had had two sides.)

So, the book is not exhaustive—nor is it exhausting. While it's the unusual (and highly leisured) reader who will give it cover-to-cover attention, you'll find fascinating subject matter wherever you choose to dig in. And you'll delight in the clarity of Wilson's prose, nicely described by W. H. Auden as "unassertive elegance."

Some small but typical examples of trivia gained from *Patriotic Gore*: (1) Most people have gotten their ideas about *Uncle Tom's Cabin* from dramatized versions of the novel, which are considerably different. (2) The origin of Julia Ward Howe's floral imagery in this line from "The Battle Hymn of the Republic," "In the beauty of the lilies Christ was born across the sea," is not biblical. (3) Oliver Wendell Holmes's will left his money to the United States government.

Do not let those bits of provocative trivia deceive you about the nature of the thinking of this deep and original writer. Start by reading all twenty-three pages of his preface. Wilson, writing in 1962, takes a mistrustful look at the rhetoric of "war aims." Surprisingly for a man who disliked popular culture and hated the very word *movie* (it's part of his greatness that he *does* surprise)—Wilson derives his central image for any country's motivation for war to a Disney film: the "vigorous voracity" of a giant sea slug ingesting another sea slug of slightly smaller size.

The Glittering Prizes:
Winners of Major Awards

A Death in the Family
James Agee

Herzog
Saul Bellow

Absalom, Absalom!
William Faulkner

The Remains of the Day
Kazuo Ishiguro

The Leopard
Giuseppe di Lampedusa

The Moviegoer
Walker Percy

Angle of Repose
Wallace Stegner

The Lives of a Cell
Lewis Thomas

All the King's Men
Robert Penn Warren

Leaves of Grass
Walt Whitman

Everything in the world exists in order to end up as a book.

—Stephane Mallarmé

THE DARK short days of December call forth a sprinkling of lights in the religious festivals of Diwali, Hanukkah, and Christmas and in the secular halls of shopping. Time to turn to authors and books that have earned the glamorous glitter of external recognition of varying kinds. (The phrase "the glittering prizes" is from Frederic Raphael's television drama about a group of Cambridge undergraduates in the 1950s and 1960s.)

The highest international award for excellence in literature is the Nobel Prize in Literature given by the Swedish Academy with money from the estate of Alfred Nobel, who had second thoughts about the service he'd done mankind in inventing dynamite. Involving a large sum of money and enormous renown, the prize is given for an author's entire career, not for any one book. Two authors on this December list, both Americans, have had the honor of this prize. William Faulkner won in 1949, thirteen years after the publication of *Absalom, Absalom!* He had to be cajoled into attending the acceptance ceremonies in Stockholm on the grounds that his teenaged daughter would enjoy the trip. Despite his initial reluctance, he rose to the occasion with great eloquence: his short acceptance speech is often quoted, especially the line "I believe that man will not merely endure; he will prevail." Saul Bellow won the Nobel Prize in 1976. In his acceptance speech he refers to the novel as "a latterday lean-to, a hovel in which the spirit takes shelter."

Bellow's novel *Herzog* had won its own prize, the National Book Award in 1964, twelve years before Bellow took the Nobel. Another National Book Award winner was Walker Percy's *The Moviegoer*. When Percy won in 1962, many members of the literary world scrambled to find out just who *was* this forty-year-old first-time novelist.

The nonfiction work on this list, Lewis Thomas's *The Lives of a Cell*, won both the National Book Award (1974) and the Christopher Award, given to books that "affirm values of the human spirit." Furthermore, Thomas, in 1993 near the end of his life, had the double pleasure of seeing an award established in his name—the Lewis Thomas Prize for writing about science—and of being the first recipient of that prize.

Another prime American award, the Pulitzer Prize, has gone to three novels on this list: Robert Penn Warren's *All the King's Men* in 1946, James Agee's *A Death in the Family* in 1958, and Wallace Stegner's *Angle of Repose* in 1972. Overseas, the Booker Prize in Great Britain went to Ishiguro's *The Remains of the Day* in 1989, while Italy's top literary award, the Strega Prize (Premio Strega), funded by the folks who make the liqueur of the same name, went to Lampedusa's book *The Leopard*. (Alas, Lampedusa had died a little earlier, and the award was given posthumously.)

All the awards mentioned above are creations of the twentieth century. In 1855 Walt Whitman won the greatest of all unofficial accolades. The virtually unknown Whitman sent his *Leaves of Grass* to America's most renowned intellectual, Ralph Waldo Emerson. Emerson responded with a letter containing prescient words that could form the wildest of dreams of any young writer: "I greet you at the beginning of a great career."

A Death in the Family

James Agee

Agee had been working on the manuscript for this novel based on the death of his father for around a decade, when his own death came at age forty-five, in the form of a heart attack in a New York City taxi. He was on his way to a doctor's appointment. Not ironic enough? The trickster Death chose May 16, the anniversary of the senior Agee's death in a car accident some forty years earlier. (The novel was published posthumously as edited by David McDowell. Parts of Agee's manuscript that had not yet been placed in a chronological sequence appear in italic type as dream sequences at the ends of two sections.)

Despite the foreboding title, the novel plunges the reader into the vibrant life of the Follets, a middle-class family in Knoxville, Tennessee—Jay, Mary, their children Rufus (Agee's middle name), age six, and Catherine, age four, as well as members of the extended family of both Jay and Mary. He conveys the deep-rooted differences of the background of husband and wife: Jay, a self-made man (his father-in-law calls him "a lot like Lincoln"), is from a rural background. He easily reverts to country dialect when a middle-of-the-night call summons him over home to the bedside of his father: "My Paw. Took at the heart," says he to the man ferrying him across the river into deep country. He loves Charlie Chaplin, whom Mary finds "horrid" and "vulgar." Jay seems to have no religion, while Mary, despite her father whose worldview seems formed by Thomas Hardy and lines from *King Lear*, is a devout Catholic like her Aunt Hannah. But Agee knows the complexities within any relationship and reveals through small details the deep tenderness between the two as Jay prepares for his trip.

The senior Mr. Follet doesn't die, but Jay does. A freak accident (a malfunctioning "cotter pin") on his return drive makes him an instant victim of "the flat of the hand of Death." Part II of the novel: anyone who's ever helped plan a funeral or choose an epitaph will recognize the admixture of anguish, irritation, pettiness, unreality, jealousy, and absurdity that can wash over a mourning family. The grandmother's ear trumpet, the rival undertaker, the song that lodges in the brain—Agee's selection of details evokes laughing and grief.

The final section of the novel focuses on Rufus's attempts (and to a lesser extent, Catherine's) to fit death into his small scheme of things. God may have "put his father to sleep," but Rufus thinks of the attention he'll get by telling schoolmates what's happened. The novel ends with Rufus's confusion as his Uncle Andrew tells him, reverently, of the butterfly that lighted on the casket as it was lowered for burial and then savagely rails at the "priggish, mealy-mouthed" priest who refused full services for the unbaptized Jay.

Book Smart
Recommended Reading

The adult Agee, whose accomplishments include the screenplay for *The African Queen*, struggled to make sense of his turbulent life but retained an awareness of the sacred nature of every human. Read his letters to Father Flye (an Episcopal priest he met at the age of nine), or take a look at *Let Us Now Praise Famous Men*, Agee's wonderful study—a collaboration with photographer Walker Evans—of Appalachian families during the Depression.

Herzog

Saul Bellow

I n the foreword to his friend Allan Bloom's *The Closing of the American Mind*, Bellow says his aim in *Herzog* was "to make fun of my own type." If his own type is a tragicomic man who feels as deeply as he thinks, he has succeeded.

Little happens in this book in the sense of a plotline, but hellzapoppin' inside the head of Herzog. At the start Mr. Moses E. Herzog Ph.D. —he sardonically notes this form of his name on leftover invitations to his second wedding—has been cuckolded by that second wife, Madeleine. She is a beautiful, intelligent, and enormously dislikeable woman (in the reader's eye at least), who uses the blade of a dinner knife to examine her after-dinner appearance. She has the lack of originality to choose Herzog's best friend, Valentine Gersbach, as her partner in adultery. Bellow bestows ungainliness upon the "loud, flamboyant, ass-clutching brute Gersbach" by giving him only one leg, but he balances that ambulatory castration with the most agile of similes: "he walked on a wooden leg, gracefully bending and straightening like a gondolier."

The novel begins and ends in Herzog's white elephant of a house in the lushly verdant Berkshires. The middle section takes place partly in New York, where he sees his current inamorata, the Catullus-quoting florist Ramona, "no mere sensualist, but a theoretician, almost a priestess." She soothes him not only with her black lace underpants and her bustier but with shrimp remoulade and Pouilly-Fuissé, with spiky red gladiolas and Egyptian music.

Bellow captures New York's mingled privacy and community with images such as the wooden turnstiles of the subway worn shiny by the hips of passengers. Similarly, Chicago, Bellow's home for many years as both student and professor at the University of Chicago, leaps off the page when Herzog travels there. He has wildly determined, briefly but not fleetingly, to kill Madeleine and Gersbach with his father's old pistol.

However well painted these two cityscapes, the terrain of Herzog's mind is more vivid. He mentally fires off letter after letter, some to himself, some to Madeleine, some to Secretary of the Interior Udall, or to the young son of his first marriage. (Herzog is tenderly patriarchal about both Marco and June, his child with Madeleine.) When the epistolary shards ricocheting in his head permit, Herzog indulges in vivid memories of former lovers Wanda and Sono, and of Papa and Mama Herzog, immigrant parents like those of the author himself, the only member of his Russian Jewish family, originally named Belo, to be born in the New World.

The ending is unresolved but happy, for Herzog has transcended his "wild internal disorder." The angry mental letters become more kindly, then cease. Ramona is coming for dinner, and he assures his worried brother that when they next meet he'll still be unmarried, that he won't yield to the "progenitive, the lustful quacking" in his head. As readers we're less sure, perhaps because we know Bellow himself married five times, the last at age seventy-four. We are sure, though, of wishing we could read about that candlelit dinner (swordfish steaks) of Ramona and this "throb-hearted character," with whom we've fallen in love.

 Book Smart
Recommended Reading

Pick another Bellow book. You can't go wrong. Whether you choose an early novel such as *The Adventures of Augie March*, or his New York novel, *Mr. Sammler's Planet*, or *Humboldt's Gift*, a fictionalized version of his friendship with the quirky poet Delmore Schwartz, you have hours of reading pleasure in front of you.

Absalom, Absalom!

William Faulkner

onor, heritage, burdens of the past, civil war—these themes from earlier writers are all here. Race, gender, class—these themes from contemporary writers are all here. High Modernist style with multiple viewpoints and shifts of time? Here. This book is a challenge to read, and if you want to retreat right now, you have my permission. But if you take on the challenge, you'll be rewarded with a hypnotic verbal spell, the fascinating verbena-scented world of the fictional Yoknapatawpha County, Mississippi, William Faulkner, sole owner and proprietor. You know this "postage stamp of native soil" must exist, because Faulkner drew a map of it in the front of this very volume.

The biblical allusion of the title is the least of your challenges, but let's get it out of the way now. It refers to the story of Absalom, the son of King David. The young man rebels against his regal father and is killed after he's grotesquely trapped, his luxuriant hair entangled in the limbs of a tree. The father mourns plaintively for the loss of his wayward son.

This is the complicated tale of Thomas Sutpen, another man supremely unlucky in his sons. He was born early in the nineteenth century somewhere in the mountains of what was not yet West Virginia. After his family moves to the more genteel Tidewater area, this young white man of no fortune is rebuffed by a liveried slave at the door of a mansion. This seed of rejection blooms, years later, into his obsession with building a private kingdom of Sutpens, a dynasty. He's ultimately unsuccessful in a spectacular way. An initial foray to a sugar plantation of Haiti brings some wealth and the birth of a son, but his discovery that his wife's bloodline is "impure" causes racial panic and he puts them from him. He next surfaces in northern Mississippi accompanied by what the book calls "wild Negroes," men who labor, naked, to wrest out of the Mississippi clay a mansion for Sutpen, who acquired the land for a pittance from the Chickasaw chief Ikkemotubbe; a new wife, impeccable this time; and two new children, Henry and Judith. Son number one, now called Charles Bon, meets up with Henry at the fledgling University of Mississippi. Deep friendship forms, the sort of bond that leads a man to introduce his friend to his sister. The complex family tragedy about to ensue is presided over by another Sutpen daughter, a faithful family retainer casually conceived on a slave woman and bearing the ominous name Clytemnestra.

That's the essence of the complex "what." The baroque "how" involves (1) narration by Miss Rosa Coldfield, much younger sister of Sutpen's dead wife, to young Quentin Compson, grandson of Sutpen's first friend in Mississippi, (2) narration by Quentin Compson's father to young Quentin, and (3) Quentin Compson's collaborative and intensely speculative narration with his college roommate Shreve. What we've got here is an elaborate puzzle of how we know what we know and who knew what when. Amidst the intellectual workout is an underlying pathos since we know, if we've read Faulkner's *The Sound and the Fury*, published four years earlier, that Quentin will drown himself in the Charles River at the end of this freshman year at Harvard.

If you endure, you'll have an ample understanding of what is perhaps his most famous and often misquoted line: "The past is never dead; it isn't even past."

 **Book Smart**
Recommended Reading

If you're daunted by the challenge of *Absalom, Absalom!* may I suggest Faulkner's more accessible *Intruder in the Dust* with its adolescent protagonist Chick Mallison?

The Remains of the Day

Kazuo Ishiguro

shiguro was born in Nagasaki in 1954. His family moved to England when he was five. He describes himself as growing up with a "dual" perspective on the world. (He was briefly employed as "grouse beater" for the Queen Mother at Balmoral.) His first two novels are set in Japan, but this, his third, is narrated by a butler, Stevens, who couldn't be more English. You never learn his first name.

Stevens is, uncharacteristically, on a motor trip while his new, American employer is away. He's driving Mr. Farraday's "vintage Ford" from Oxfordshire to Cornwall to visit Miss Kenton, who once served as housekeeper with Stevens at Darlington Hall. Ostensibly, it's a leisurely business trip: consummate professional Stevens is pursuing a hint in her recent letter that she might be ready to return to Darlington Hall, where to Stevens's dismay he recently had to remove an ill-polished fork from Mr. Farraday's place setting. Not so in the glory days when, not four, but more than twenty servants staffed the mansion!

Although the novel is set in 1956, much of Stevens's elegiac narration of a more civil (if more hierarchical) world comprises memories, recollections of the years between the two wars when Lord Darlington hosted many a gathering of English, French, German, and the occasional uncomprehending American. These guests, mostly male, were there not only to consume fine food and wine but to discuss matters of international importance, possibly hewing out decisions that would later *seem* to be made in Parliament. Stevens maintains a dignified front of constant attendance while his aged father, also serving at Darlington, dies upstairs of a stroke. What a mercy that the doctor who arrives too late to help the elder Stevens can be shuttled right in to tend the blisters on the diplomatic feet of Monsieur Dupont!

Many of Stevens's memories recall his exchanges with the young Miss Kenton, a below-stairs version of the witty couple. She invades his butler's pantry with a vase of flowers, attempts to arouse his jealousy, tries unsuccessfully to puncture his rectitude. Even the densest reader who misses this quality in Stevens's memories can't mistake it in their charged reencounter. Once more, Miss Kenton silently yells, "I love you. Do you love me?" and once more Stevens responds, "It is a great pleasure to see you." Tears fill her eyes, and a slightly awkward postlude depicts a stranger on a seaside bench offering Stevens a handkerchief.

Is Stevens a dolt? Has Ishiguro deliberately created a laughingstock? A pathetic creature who has missed out on his whole life to serve a man who, like Neville Chamberlain, temporarily thought appeasement of Hitler was a great idea? There's some room for saying yes, and humor and pathos abound in Stevens's story. But it's reductive to think he's meant as a caricature of a moronic idealist. Ishiguro comments that the film version of this novel is about "emotional repression," whereas he wrote a book about the crucially different topic of "self-denial." Perhaps Stevens represents all that was best about a vanished (and imperfect) past, a true gentleman's gentleman, who, like Stevens, defined dignity as "not removing one's clothing in public."

Book Smart
Recommended Reading

Ishiguro's novels are all different. *Never Let Me Go* falls into the futurist subgenre: it deals with children who are cloned for the purpose of providing organ transplants for others. The earlier *An Artist of the Floating World* is set in the novelist's native Nagasaki during post–World War II reconstruction.

The Leopard

Giuseppe di Lampedusa (translated by Archibald Colquhoun)

"**N**unc et in hora mortis nostrae" (now and in the hour of our death). The opening phrase of this beautiful novel sounds the keynote of vespers, of twilight. Literally a line from the Catholic Rosary being recited by the Salina family and its servants, these words also connote the dying of a way of life for this aristocratic family headed by the beguiling and introspective Don Fabrizio. A gutted corpse of a soldier has recently appeared in the garden of the villa in Palermo; change is on the way. Each of the eight chapters bears a date, the first being that of the month Garibaldi landed at Marsala on the western coast of Sicily, gathered volunteers, and made his way across the island toward Rome in his successful attempt to unify Italy.

There's little plot. Six of the chapters are set in 1860–62, the seventh in 1888, and the last, punningly entitled "The Relics," in 1910. We observe eating, hunting, dancing on Salina's Palermo estate and at his beloved country refuge Donnafugata. We get to know family members, especially the dashing nephew Tancredi, more like Don Fabrizio than are his sons. Tancredi, whose name evokes Tasso's epic hero of the freeing of Jerusalem during the First Crusade, fights for Garibaldi—at least until his politics change. We enjoy his bewitchment by Angelica, the voluptuous, convent-educated daughter of Don Calogero, crude and wealthy parvenu. (Tancredi and Angelica's subsequent marriage embodies the old order giving place to the new.) But we especially get to know, to fall in love with, the elegant, the cynical, the brooding Don Fabrizio, a man who once controlled matters with "a wave of his paw."

A vigorous man of the flesh, he visits a favored daughter of joy in Palermo, and when subsequently chided by his resident priest for infidelity to his wife, he roars, "seven children I've had with her, seven; and never once have I seen her navel . . . she's the real sinner!" But there's an equal measure of passion in his head. During a splendid ball scene, his contemplation of golden youth in one another's arms produces only thoughts of "those bodies destined to die." (Lampedusa's narration reinforces this sense of transience, noting that even the great frescoed palazzo itself will be destroyed in 1943 "by a bomb manufactured in Pittsburgh, Penn.") The internal solitude and ironic resignation of the Don, an amateur astronomer of some repute, are soothed only by his contemplation of the heavens, "the sublime routine of the stars." E. M. Forster calls this novel "one of the great lonely books."

Lampedusa, an aristocrat of scholarly bent, had led mostly the life of a dilettante. Then his fifty-year-old cousin stirred himself to a first effort of submitting his poems to the judgment of others—and won a prize. Lampedusa wryly noted he was "no more a fool than Lucio" and began writing this novel based on his great-grandfather's life, often while sitting in a local café (now a restaurant named Charleston). His years of labor knew only rejection before death claimed him. After eventual publication, the book raced up the sales charts, as did its many translations. It posthumously won Italy's highest award for fiction, the Strega Prize.

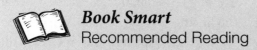

Book Smart
Recommended Reading

Lampedusa wrote little else, but do find his exquisite short story "The Siren." You might also look at David Gilmour's interesting biography *The Last Leopard* and supplement your reading with the opulent Visconti film.

The Moviegoer

Walker Percy

Walker Percy, M.D. He could have joined the clump of medical doctors like Arthur Conan Doyle or William Carlos Williams who gain literary fame while wielding by day a stethoscope or a tongue depressor. Recovering from pulmonary tuberculosis contracted during his internship gave Percy time to think. He turned his back on the practice of medicine, converted to Roman Catholicism, and became a writer of medical and philosophical essays, earning a whopping twenty-five dollars for his first work in print, an essay on stoicism in the South. He was over forty when he published *The Moviegoer.*

It's a strange and thoughtful novel, a suitable work for this author of intense integrity whose life twisted oddly even before his path-altering illness. His father committed suicide when Walker, the oldest of three boys, was thirteen. His mother died not long afterward in an ambiguous car mishap. The trio of orphans left Alabama to live with their bachelor "Uncle Will," a literal cousin and the author of *Lanterns on the Levee* (*The Moviegoer* is dedicated to him). This new life in Greenville, Mississippi, placed Percy in a literary ambience (and into high school with Shelby Foote, later the noted Civil War historian).

The title character of this novel is Jack "Binx" Bolling, a seemingly ordinary man approaching his thirtieth birthday. A veteran of the Korean War, he rents an apartment in a generic suburb of New Orleans, earns a good living as a stockbroker, keeps lusty company with a succession of his secretaries—Marcia, Linda, and Sharon. Yes, an ordinary man, perhaps carefully ordinary as he allows only the "little way" of sensuality to provide occasional intensity. He looks to movies and the larger-than-life images of the on-screen clan of William Holden, John Wayne, and Orson Welles to give meaning to his life. (Are you old enough to identify "Rory," to whom Binx makes an impassioned appeal?)

Binx also follows an elaborate philosophical system of techniques with such labels as certification, repetition, rotation, and doubling; these help disperse the noxious particles of "everydayness," the soul-numbing quality of familiarity that can block people from genuinely experiencing their lives. (Think how you can "see" your living room—and then only for a few seconds—when you reenter it after a long trip.) He's been on a search, ever since an experience in the Far East when, as he explains, "I came to myself under a chindolea bush." (Dante lovers will pick up on "came to myself" and the arboreal image as an echo of the second line of the ultimate literary search—the *Inferno*. It's an image Percy repeats in the opening of his novel *Love in the Ruins*, written ten years later.)

Binx sees himself as "a malaisian," one who quests for meaning amid the nebulous unease of life. Corporal entities in his private universe include his Aunt Emily, who sees the patrician and stoic values of the past sufficient for modern challenges; her stepdaughter Kate, whose emotional problems evoke a quasi-romantic response in Binx; his mother, who shrinks tragedy with her "election of the ordinary"; and Lonnie, his fifteen-year-old half-brother, deformed by illness, whose religious intensity contrasts with Binx's "invincible unbelief."

Late in the novel Binx's description of a "Negro" leaving a church on Ash Wednesday leaves readers with a feel of saturnine optimism: "His forehead is an ambiguous sienna color and pied: it is impossible to be sure that he received ashes." Binx can neither affirm nor deny a "dim dazzling trick of grace . . . God's own importunate bonus."

Angle of Repose

Wallace Stegner

This novel is two stories: Lyman Ward, former professor of history and scholar of the American frontier, lives out his own struggle with illness and betrayal while he tries to reconstruct in a biography the life of his paternal grandmother, Susan Burling Ward, from a copious stock of letters and papers. The fifty-eight-year-old Lyman spends his days in a motorized wheelchair. Degenerative bone disease has mandated the amputation of one leg, and in a cruel irony for a historian, looking backward is impossible for him, for his head knows only stony uprightness. His physical woes are complemented by the fact that his wife abandoned him while he was in the hospital recovering from his amputation, informing him by a note left on his bedside table. Her partner in desertion? The surgeon who performed Lyman's operation.

The story of the grandmother who brought him up is more compelling, but this daughter of a poor Quaker family in upstate New York is hard to love. The image that emerges from the combination of quoted correspondence and Lyman's recasting of Susan Ward's experiences is of a strong woman, an interesting woman, but a person you like only in spots of time. Like the grandson who's writing in 1970, she struggles in the 1870s and 1880s for autonomy—a condition then unusual for a female—and gains it through a lifetime of steady work as a writer of magazine pieces and as an illustrator.

Ahead of her time perhaps in "wanting to have it all," she looks for a husband who will not chafe at her independent career but will also be a traditional protector. More damagingly, she incessantly weighs the worth of Oliver, a pistol-toting mining engineer whose work takes him to the unfenced terrain of California, Colorado, or Mexico, against the gentilities and greater affluence of her soul mate–friend Augusta and her husband, the sophisticated Thomas Hudson. Susan, the hardy pioneer woman, can give birth to her third child in an Idaho canyon while a double rainbow brightens the sky, and she is also a wife who sends her slightly drunk husband off to sleep in the shed. (The tales Lyman's young, braless secretary, Shelly Rasmussen, tells of *her* difficult husband offer another strand of counterpoint on the theme of the woe that is in marriage.)

The most enjoyable scenes are those where the young Susan adventurously joins her husband in rude and perilous habitats. You'll remember best scenes of their baby Ollie rolling about on a rug of wildcat skins and of the gently reared Susan spending a night by her husband's side in a crowded Western boardinghouse where only a thin cloth curtain separates them from a coughing stranger. And you'll be saddened by the chain of events set in motion by Oliver's assistant Frank Sargent, ten years younger than Susan, who carries his courtly love for her like a chalice.

The memorable title is a geological term for the angle of a slope at which gravel will stop rolling downhill. But it's clear that Lyman Ward (and Stegner) also offers a more universal connotation. As W. H. Auden puts it, "Let us honor if we can / The vertical man / Though we value none / But the horizontal one."

Book Smart
Recommended Reading

When researching the character of Susan Ward, Stegner used—with permission from her two granddaughters—the correspondence of Mary Hallock Foote (1847–1938), a fact that struck up an intriguing controversy. See Foote's autobiography and a recent biography by Darlis Miller to compare the more likeable real-life woman.

The Lives of a Cell: Notes of a Biology Watcher

Lewis Thomas

A pathology researcher who wrote like an angel—what pleasure this fact would give C. P. Snow, the Englishman whose book *The Two Cultures*, published almost a half century ago, lamented the gap between the world of science and non-science. One can only hope that Snow, who lived until 1980, read these twenty-nine essays of 1971–73, which were published monthly in *The New England Journal of Medicine* and came out in book form in 1974. Rarely, there's a tiny note of aging, as in "An Earnest Proposal," which alludes with a sense of semi-wonder at an advertisement for what we'd now call computer dating; for the most part, however, the essays are timeless and deserve their frequent comparisons with his acknowledged model, the sixteenth-century French essayist Michel de Montaigne. (Thoreau is another fellow spirit.)

In an interview elsewhere Thomas asserts that he is "flabbergasted" at the wonder and variety of life, and that sense of informed amazement pervades these essays. Even as he is writing about death, his tone can put a smile on your face, and his odd anecdote can delight you.

Along with death, frequent Thomas themes include language, music, humans as social beings, and the relationships between the "micro" and the "macro." Indeed, the second noun in the title of the book bears not only the obvious biological meaning but refers also, say, to ants as "mobile cells" or to the great globe itself. Ants themselves turn up frequently, as in real life. It was news to me that a single ant (likewise, a single bee) cannot long survive: its raison d'être is to be a part of a whole. Even more fascinating is the single essay with its punning title "Antaeus in Manhattan" (Antaeus is a Greek mythological character who perished away from contact with the soil). Who knew that an art gallery once had an exhibition of two million live army ants going about their business "in crescents, crisscrosses, and long ellipses"? And that those ants all died within a few days? Since I consider myself a word maven of the first water, I was humbled—but more greatly intrigued— to learn here that *pismire* is a synonym for *ant* and that the first syllable does mean, yes, "urine," a smell human olfactory senses connect with anthills.

Thomas's enthusiasm for his topics is contagious. If the word *mitochondria* ever crossed my path, I forgot about the fact decades ago. Thomas's description of them as "stable and responsible lodgers" in our cells had me marveling and actually moving to the Internet to look up more about them. In describing these power sources for our cells, Thomas's lexical choices of words like *lodgers* or phrases like "little separate creatures, the colonial posterity of migrant prokaryocytes" (note to self: look that word up too) make these biological phenomena seem friendly while stopping short of anthropomorphizing them in an offensively cutesy fashion.

A writer who can get me interested in what happens to termites placed in a dish of fecal pellets is a writer I can love. I also venerate a writer who suggests we stream "Bach, all of Bach" into space as a form of bragging to any life-forms out there and listening.

Book Smart
Recommended Reading

Follow this book up with Thomas's *The Medusa and the Snail: More Notes of a Biology Watcher* and any of his other books. I'm partial to *Late Night Thoughts on Listening to Mahler's Ninth Symphony*.

All the King's Men

Robert Penn Warren

Two film versions have been made from this novel, the older one (1949) vigorously starring Broderick Crawford and Mercedes McCambridge and the recent version (2006) with Anthony Hopkins and Patricia Clarkson. Both versions are worth seeing; happily, the power of the novel still streams out from the inert word on the printed page.

This is the ultimate novel about politics. Willie Stark, successful demagogue, might be EveryPol, but he is directly inspired by real-life Huey Long, governor of Louisiana from 1928 until his assassination in 1935. (Long's speeches asked how many in his audience had holes in their socks; Stark calls out to anyone with holes in the knees of his pants.) Robert Penn Warren draws on Dante, that exiled victim of medieval Italian politics, for notes of both gloomy realism and optimism. Late in the book the narrator speaks of taxes: "The pocketbook is where it hurts. A man may forget the death of the father, but never the loss of the patrimony, the cold-faced Florentine, who is the founding father of our modern world, said, and he said a mouthful." The epigraph for the novel, a single line, printed only in the original Italian of Dante's *Purgatory*, alludes to a triad of lines. In Allen Mandelbaum's translation it reads. "There is no one / so lost that the eternal love cannot / return—as long as hope shows something green."

This is a wonderful novel—great plot, spellbinding style, fascinating characters. Joyce Carol Oates has stated that Willie Stark "has entered our collective literary consciousness" along with such as Captain Ahab, Gatsby, and Holden Caulfield. He's a fascinating mixture of idealism and corruption, a man who apologizes not at all for dealing with "the bad" because that's all there is as raw material for "the good." He's a demagogue in both its manipulative sense and its "man of the people" sense. When Willie talks, people listen. (Warren's original name for Stark was Willie Talos, referring to the mythological bronze figure made by Hephaestus. Although not fully human, Talos had wit and power sufficient to protect the island of Crete from its enemies.)

While Oates's assertion about Willie Stark is true, the character of Willie's henchman Jack Burden intrigues equally. Jack, who narrates the novel, has an aristocratic background that contrasts with Willie's lower origins. He grew up in elite Burden's Landing, forming, first, childhood friendships with Adam and Anne Stanton, offspring of the governor, and, later, with Anne, a lyrical romance, whose pathway toward marriage is obstructed by Jack's lack of vocational aspirations. (The adult lives of Adam and Anne continue to intertwine with Jack's life.) Jack has been a student of history—he might call it History. Forty-six pages of this book comprise the story of Jack's doctoral research, the tale of Cass Mastern, who met the bullet he set out to find, dying in a Civil War hospital. His story of the clashing claims of sexual passion and loyalty to a friend, of death over life without honor, of attempts at restitution for harm done the innocent form leitmotifs that subtly thread through the novel.

I haven't mentioned Judge Irwin, Jack's childhood mentor, or Jack's mother with her "famished cheeks," or her first husband, the Scholarly Attorney turned religious fanatic, or pock-faced Sadie Burke, or Sugar Boy, or Tiny Duffy. And I haven't mentioned The Great Sleep or The Great Twitch. But you'll enjoy making the acquaintance of all of them.

Leaves of Grass

Walt Whitman

Whitman is the last and the greatest of the Americans. At least, that's what D. H. Lawrence thought in 1922 when he wrote an essay on Whitman for his *Studies in Classic American Literature*. Similarly, Allen Ginsberg, fellow poet, added his homage when, in his poem "A Supermarket in California," he dubbed Whitman "lonely old courage-teacher."

Leaves of Grass is the title Whitman gave to his body of poetry; every edition contained a larger collection of poems. Start wherever you like in reading the poetry of this supreme champion of individualism and optimism. The first edition appeared in 1855 when Whitman was thirty-six. It was published by Fowler and Wells, a company specializing in booklets on phrenology. To say it contained only twelve poems is both true and misleading, for the opening poem, "Song of Myself," is more than fifty pages long.

You're surprised this volume of intensely personal poetry (Song of *Myself*, after all) bears no author's name on the title page. There's the oddly formal "Walter Whitman" in the copyright information and "Walt Whitman" embedded in the first poem, but otherwise you're greeted not by the author's name but by his image—an engraving of an appealing guy in working-class clothes, hat on head. His right arm is akimbo, his left in his pocket. He regards you with confidence, lures you further. This volume, roughly the length of a man's hand, foreshadows the words Whitman wrote five years later: "Camerado! This is no book; / Who touches this, touches a man."

Any attempt to treat Whitman's uniqueness concisely must mention how American he is. As the last line of Whitman's preface to the 1855 edition puts it, "The proof of a poet is that his country absorbs him as affectionately as he has absorbed it." Whitman's near-obsession with Abraham Lincoln was at least partially reflected in Lincoln's early reading of Whitman; Daniel Mark Epstein's fascinating book *Lincoln and Whitman: Parallel Lives in Civil War Washington* argues strongly that Lincoln's later style of writing was directly influenced by his reading of Whitman. (But forget the popular "O Captain! My Captain!"—it's one of Whitman's least typical (worst?) poems; go instead for the consummately beautiful elegy "When Lilacs Last in the Dooryard Bloomed.")

Whitman is also unique in his embodiment of several paradoxes: He's a poet of nature but also the quintessential poet of the city (he had a niece named Manahatta). He blurs any firm distinction between poetry and prose. And he's the master of indirection: his vibrant catalogue of specific details, many of them intensely earthy and sexual—"Unscrew the locks from the doors! / Unscrew the doors themselves from their jambs!"—leads us to a strong sense of the abstract, the idealized. Ralph Waldo Emerson put it well when he described the poetry as "a remarkable mixture of the Bhagavad-Gita and the New York *Herald Tribune*."

More than anything else, an attempt to explain Whitman must treat him as an onomatomaniac, a man in love with the sound of words. Listen to what he wrote elsewhere, "Monongehela—it rolls with venison richness upon the palate." For Whitman, to be absorbed with language, with "the blab of the pave," was to be absorbed in the surging of life. His later comment, "I sometimes think the *Leaves* is only a language experiment" is by no means a disparagement of this work that forever changed the nature of poetry. It's a boast, as is his memorable line "I sound my barbaric yawp over the roofs of the world."

Index